UP CLOSE
AND ALL IN

UP CLOSE AND ALL IN

LIFE LESSONS FROM
a WALL STREET WARRIOR

JOHN MACK

with Linda Kulman

SIMON ELEMENT

New York   London   Toronto   Sydney   New Delhi

SIMON
ELEMENT

An Imprint of Simon & Schuster, Inc.
1230 Avenue of the Americas
New York, NY 10020

First Simon Element hardcover edition October 2022

SIMON ELEMENT is a trademark of Simon & Schuster, Inc.

For information about special discounts for bulk purchases, please contact Simon & Schuster Special Sales at 1-866-506-1949 or business@simonandschuster.com.

The Simon & Schuster Speakers Bureau can bring authors to your live event. For more information or to book an event, contact the Simon & Schuster Speakers Bureau at 1-866-248-3049 or visit our website at www.simonspeakers.com.

Interior design by Jaime Putorti

Manufactured in the United States of America

1 3 5 7 9 10 8 6 4 2

Library of Congress Cataloging-in-Publication Data has been applied for.

ISBN 978-1-9821-7427-9
ISBN 978-1-9821-7428-6 (ebook)

Names and identifying characteristics of some individuals have been changed. Some dialogue has been re-created.

To the immigrants

CONTENTS

CONTENTS

UP CLOSE
AND ALL IN

INTRODUCTION

I want to tell you about two career-defining conversations during my forty-three years on Wall Street. One took place in 1992 with a Morgan Stanley senior trader. It was about his breakfast sandwich. The other was in 2008 with the three most powerful people in the US economy. *That* was about my refusal as the CEO of Morgan Stanley to sell the firm for two dollars a share.

Each reveals different facets of my personality. I am compelled to stand up for people who don't have power. I also tell people the truth, no matter the consequences.

The breakfast sandwich story has passed into Wall Street lore. On my way to an 8:00 a.m. meeting, I saw a deliveryman standing at the elevator bank. When the meeting was over, he was still there, holding a paper bag. "Weren't you here thirty minutes ago?" I asked him.

"Yeah," he said.

"Have you called the guy?"

"Twice," he told me.

"Give me his number."

I snatched the slip of paper he was holding, walked over to the phone, and dialed the guy's extension. "This is John Mack. Get out here and pick up your breakfast." I was head of the Operating Committee at the time and a few months away from being president. When the employee appeared, I tore into him. "Who do you think you are? This guy is trying to do exactly what you do: make a living. When you keep him waiting, you're taking money out of his pocket. Do this again and I'll fire you."

This story is about how you treat people. To me, we all have equal value, no matter what our job or how much money we have in the bank. I demanded that my employees do the right thing whether they were dealing with a CEO, a colleague, or somebody from the deli around the corner. Confronting the senior trader was not me losing my temper at a subordinate several rungs below me. It was a calibrated decision to send a message about the kind of behavior I wouldn't tolerate. Sometimes I had to be tough to get my message across.

Wall Street attracts a certain type—hypercompetitive, super-aggressive people who want to make a lot of money; people who are 100 percent convinced they're smarter than everyone else in the room and are hell-bent on proving it. As a general rule, if you're the sort of person who wants to help others, you become a doctor or a teacher, not a trader or an investment banker. I was determined to convince them that the best way to go about their work every day was to consider the collective benefits of their actions before they thought of their personal benefits.

In other words, I wanted to build a culture where these driven Wall Streeters pulled together as a team, and calling out an inconsiderate trader was one of the ways I did it.

Another career-defining moment occurred when I hung up the phone on Henry "Hank" Paulson, Ben Bernanke, and Timothy Geithner—respectively, the US Treasury secretary, the Federal Reserve chairman, and the New York Federal Reserve Bank president. It was a reckless act during a period when Wall Street and Main Street were engulfed in the worst financial crisis since the Great Depression. Morgan Stanley was on the brink of collapse. But I refused to sell out the firm's forty-five thousand employees and its shareholders. It was those ten minutes on the phone that convinced me I have something valuable to teach others.

You may not have to defy the US Treasury secretary. But at some point in your life, you will have to make difficult decisions when all eyes are on you. The essence of leadership is making decisions under pressure, whether you're running a business, raising a family, or simply living your life. Making the hard calls when you have no idea of the outcome—taking the risk, putting yourself out there—*that's* when you prove your mettle.

During more than four decades on Wall Street, I learned a lot about managing—and mismanaging—people, both in times of crisis and the ordinary day-to-day. I see too many people call themselves leaders without truly leading. They shy away from confrontation and put off making hard decisions. They believe they have all the answers and surround themselves with people who tell them only what they want to hear. They demand that employees do things they won't do themselves. They don't learn to praise as easily as they learn to criticize, and they believe that money is the only motivator. These faux leaders take themselves too seriously, overreact to bad news, and expect others to do things exactly the way they would do them, failing to appreciate that sometimes a fresh approach can yield better results.

On one level, this is a book about how a talker became a listener, a listener became a better person, and a better person became a better leader. My self-confidence came naturally, but I had to learn how to foster confidence and collaboration in others, and to get groups of people to produce substantially more than they would as individuals. I saw firsthand that leaders are made, not born. Leadership is a discipline, something you practice. Like salesmanship, some learn it more easily than others, but it can be learned.

Over thirty-four years at Morgan Stanley, my goal was to build the strongest and most productive team on Wall Street, and I'm proud to say I believe I succeeded. We anticipated trends before other firms, achieved record profits, and survived daunting crises. Morgan Stanley also transformed into a global juggernaut during this time, opening offices in forty-three countries and growing from three hundred employees in 1972 to more than fifty thousand employees today.

I'll share the strategies and philosophies that drove my success within the larger story of my journey from a small North Carolina mill town to a fortieth-floor corner office on Wall Street—a quintessentially American arc. At the turn of the last century, my grandfather and father came to this country from a tiny village in southern Lebanon and settled in Mooresville, North Carolina, a one-stoplight town where almost everyone was Baptist. We were different. Both my parents were devout Catholics and spoke Arabic at home. There was no talk about the financial services industry around the dinner table, and the only securities in town were shares of the local bank. My dream was to open a menswear shop in North Carolina with my cousin.

In college, everything I thought I knew about myself turned out to be wrong. I arrived at Duke University on a full athletic scholarship as an all-state football player. I was a standout in a high school senior class of ninety students. Not at Duke. I almost flunked out. My time on the football field was worse. I went from being a star to riding the bench. Then my father passed away, and, needing to pay my own way through my senior year, I took an entry-level job in the back office at a local securities firm.

It wasn't long until I realized my future was in New York. I arrived in Manhattan in 1968. It was a transformational time. The role of preeminent banks like Morgan Stanley had always been to advise blue-chip clients like IBM and AT&T. They didn't participate in what they considered to be the grubby world of trading stocks and bonds. But in the early 1970s, as deregulation and new technology changed the playing field, scrappy trading houses like Salomon Brothers and Merrill Lynch disrupted the long-standing business model by aggressively poaching clients. Overnight, sedate Wall Street became fiercely competitive—and I had a front-row seat. In the coming years, I developed a titanium-strength stomach for risk, pressure, and big personalities. The raucous, smoke-filled bullpen where I started immediately felt like home. In the pages ahead, you'll learn not only how Wall Street transformed in the past five decades but how to stay ahead of the curve in a continually evolving industry.

Up Close and All In is a labor of love that reflects input from more than ninety interviews with people from every sphere of my life. It is a story of grit, survival, and triumph—and a deeply personal guide to living and leading well.

CHAPTER ONE

————————————————

I couldn't stop staring.

The offices of F. S. Smithers & Co., a pedigreed investment bank, overlooked the Statue of Liberty in New York Harbor, at the very tip of lower Manhattan. It was 1970, and I was on a job interview. I knew the corporate bond business, and I had aced my soon-to-be boss's questions. Lady Liberty, holding her torch high, filled the floor-to-ceiling glass window in front of me. As her green oxidized copper caught the late-afternoon sun, I kept thinking, *That lady is where it all began for my family.*

Sixty-seven years earlier—three days before Christmas—on December 22, 1903, my grandfather Hanna Makhoul Fakoury steamed past the Statue of Liberty, wreathed in snow flurries, as the SS *Belgravia* made her way into New York Harbor. Wealthy passengers simply stepped onto the dock and into a new life without stopping. But passengers in steerage class, like my grandfather, were transported by barge to Ellis Island to be inspected and processed. Uniformed officials eyed these new arrivals as they lined up to mount the staircase leading into the massive, echoing two-story Registry Room. The inspectors and white-gowned doctors were looking for any medical reason—a hacking cough, watery red eyes, a limp—to send passengers back to the country they'd just left. About 120,000 would-be immigrants were denied entry during Ellis Island's sixty-plus years as an immigration inspection station.

My sturdy grandfather passed muster, no problem. When he stepped up to the clerk keeping the immigration ledger, Hanna Makhoul had already dropped his last name, Fakoury. But now his name underwent additional alteration. Because Hanna was a girl's name in the United States, the clerk wrote down John, the most popular boy's name in America that year. Makhoul became McCall, which my grandfather shortened to Mack.

The first John Mack had arrived in America.

MY GRANDFATHER HAD been a farmer in Roum, a mountain village in southern Lebanon, then part of the Ottoman Empire. He probably grew wheat and olives. But economic times were hard and getting harder. He had traded letters with a Lebanese friend living in Marion, South Carolina, who encouraged my grandfather to join him there. The new John Mack had upended his life at age thirty-five to go where there was money to be made. Without knowing a syllable of English, my grandfather said a temporary good-bye to his wife, Naceem, and their children. The family couldn't have been destitute; otherwise, he couldn't have afforded the sixty-five-dollar transatlantic passage. Naceem might have given him her gold bracelets—her dowry—to pay for the trip. Wives often did.

From Roum, he traveled twenty-five miles by donkey on a dirt road to Beirut. Then he sailed to Alexandria, Egypt, and on to Marseilles,

France. There he spent weeks in a medically required quarantine to check for contagious diseases like smallpox, cholera, and typhus. With a clean bill of health, he boarded a train north to catch the steamship *Belgravia*. Leaving from the French port city of Boulogne-sur-Mer, it crossed the Atlantic Ocean in about fifteen days.

Having cleared Ellis Island, John Mack headed south. But the railroad clerk in New York City sold him a ticket to the wrong Marion—Marion, North Carolina, 227 miles north of my grandfather's intended destination. Obviously, no one was there to meet him, and he couldn't ask for help. He had no idea he was in the wrong state. He sat on a bench outside the redbrick train station all day, presumably hungry, confused, alone. Finally, when the stationmaster locked up for the night, he realized he couldn't leave the man out in the cold on Christmas Eve. He took my grandfather home, fed him, and gave him a bed.

The stationmaster telegraphed two Lebanese brothers he knew who ran a diner next to the Charlotte, North Carolina, railroad station. He put John Mack on the train to Charlotte, a hundred miles to the southeast. The brothers gave him a room and a job in their restaurant. My grandfather saved up his earnings and eventually became his own boss. Buying pots and pans, tablecloths, bed linens, women's and men's clothing—even ladies' lingerie—from wholesalers, he began peddling his wares on foot, carrying about two hundred pounds at a time, selling to farmers and their wives. His territory was a roughly fifty-mile radius outside Charlotte in the center of North Carolina—the hilly, pine-scented region known as the Piedmont. It included towns like Cooleemee, Salisbury, China Grove, and Kannapolis. I can't imagine the guts that got my grandfather to this country—or how terrified he must have been, walking up to strangers' houses and knocking on doors, trying to make sales.

Some immigrants abandoned their wives and children in the old country. My grandfather was not one of them. He returned to

Lebanon in 1907 to bring his family to North Carolina. Unable to convince Naceem to come with him, he left her with some of their children in Roum. Two children, Nora and Tsharlz—Charles in English—did accompany my grandfather back through Ellis Island and on to North Carolina in 1908. Charles, fourteen years old when he arrived in the United States, was my father. My uncle Side, my father's older brother, came a year later.

In 1912, my grandmother Naceem relented. She asked her husband to send money for tickets to the United States for her and the three remaining children. But she died before they were able to leave. My grandfather sent Charles, eighteen, to Roum one last time to retrieve his other sisters.

Charles and Side joined their father as peddlers. They made enough money to buy a wagon they pulled by hand, and then a horse. Once I ran into an acquaintance of my father at the annual Coddle Creek Presbyterian Church barbecue in North Carolina. Setting down his plate of peach cobbler, the old man told me about a night in 1914 when he put my exhausted grandfather, Side, and my dad up in his barn to give them a place to sleep for the night. "Your grandpa, uncle, and your daddy— they were good people. I could just tell." Farmers like this man became my grandfather's customers after he established John Mack & Son, a dry goods store in Mooresville—thirty miles north of Charlotte—in 1912.

My father went his own way. He opened a shoe store, manufactured candy, and invested in an ice cream company. Eventually, he settled on the wholesale grocery business. He operated as the middleman between manufacturers like Campbell Soup Company, Hershey, and Kellogg's Corn Flakes and retailers—grocery stores, drugstores, hospitals, restaurants, pool halls. He named his new business Charles Mack & Sons Wholesale. The "sons" referred to my dad's four boys from his first marriage.

It may surprise people that there was a thriving Lebanese community in North Carolina. More than 360,000 people left Lebanon between

1880 and 1914, and some settled in the American South. At one point, there was a Lebanese peddler in every county of the United States, including in Alaska. The next generation of these Lebanese immigrants ran small businesses like appliance stores, cafés, and bowling alleys.

The men my grandfather sailed with on the *Belgravia* became close friends, almost brothers, their families becoming second families to our family. At least a couple of times a month, my grandfather—and later my father, mother, aunts, and uncles—traveled an hour or two to visit with this extended Lebanese community in North and South Carolina. Speaking in Arabic, everyone gossiped about the old country and the new. They ate Sunday lunch at various families' houses. This was not just tossing a few burgers and hot dogs on the grill. The women woke up before dawn to start chopping the onions, browning the meat, and letting the dough rise to make traditional Lebanese dishes like *kibbeh*, *shawarma*, and *manakish*.

This is the warm, close-knit world I was born into on November 17, 1944: Johnnie Joseph Mack. I joined four half brothers and my full brother, Franklin, who was three years older than me. I grew up surrounded by family and Lebanese traditions. It was my core identity. If you took the basketball hoop out, our backyard could have been in rural Lebanon. My parents kept goats, rabbits, and chickens and planted grapes whose vines wrapped around poles twenty feet long and so high you could walk under them. When we were little, Frank and I helped our mother pick the tender leaves and then stuff them with meat and rice to make *warak enab*.

I was proud of being a Mack, and I loved Mooresville. But it was a small world. My grandfather and father had arrived in New York Harbor and headed south. I reversed their journey and moved to New York City right out of Duke University in 1968.

I wanted a career in the financial industry, and Wall Street was the place to start.

CHAPTER TWO

I showed up in Manhattan on the third Sunday of August with eight dollars in my bank account, a distant South Carolina cousin's offer to let me sleep on his couch, and a spot in the Smith Barney training program. I had been to New York City before, back when I was a little kid traveling with my parents. This time I was on my own.

I was accustomed to the suffocatingly humid summers of North Carolina. But I wasn't expecting Manhattan sidewalks shimmering with heat during the day or sweltering summer nights when the temperature barely dropped. The smog made the sunsets, which I could catch only in glimpses between skyscrapers, fiery and dramatic. The uncollected garbage stank, and I got used to seeing rats as I walked home to Thirty-Third Street between First and Second Avenues. The noise never stopped. Trucks roared down Second Avenue in the middle of the night. Times Square was seedy, filled with peep shows, prostitutes, and pimps. Crime was out of control. No one looked anyone in the eye. The city gave off a hostile vibe.

None of this bothered me. I loved the place. Sure, I crossed the street at night if I saw someone walking on my side, and I never entered Central Park after dark. I wasn't stupid, but I felt no angst. I was energized.

My focus was on two things. First, when could I move off my cousin Ray Frances's couch? I had been there for more than a month. Ray had the soft-spoken manners of the South but had begun to inquire daily how my hunt for an apartment was going. Second, and more important, I wanted to make sure I stood out at Smith Barney.

My path to Smith Barney had not been clear-cut. My football scholarship paid for four years, but I needed one last class to graduate. So I got a full-time job at First Securities of North Carolina, a brokerage firm in downtown Durham, and squeezed in the class—Russian history—during my lunch break. A tobacco town, Durham was rough back then, with high unemployment. It was a real culture shock to go from the groomed Gothic splendor of the Duke campus to the grimy back office of First Securities. They paid me $60 a week—about $476 in today's dollars. This was more money than I had ever made in my life.

Whenever a broker at First Securities bought or sold a stock for a client, the transaction was recorded by hand. This ticket then came to me, and I calculated the commission. Next the ticket was passed along to the person who operated the IBM mainframe computer, which spit out the data on a punch card. A single computer in those days took up an entire room.

I couldn't wait to get to work every morning. My coworkers were ten middle-aged women, and I loved the camaraderie we shared. I saw how they cared about one another and me. I put on seven pounds from all the home baking they brought in. I was also learning about how investing worked, and I was hooked. My family had founded businesses, run them successfully, and taken out loans from banks.

But like most middle-class people in those days, we kept our money in a savings account.

The world of stocks and bonds was a mystery at first. One day, a First Securities client bought ten thousand shares of Toyota stock. We howled about this. Who would be crazy enough to invest in a Japanese company called Toyota Motor Corporation? Toyota stock was then selling for around fifty cents a share. Little did I know what would happen to that stock, which sells today at around $152 a share.

I got to know the salesmen in the front office. These guys were smart and confident and seemed to like their jobs. They were the kind of people I wanted to work with. I saw how these salesmen were helping clients increase their personal wealth. The idea of researching companies and investing in them seemed exciting. It dawned on me that these corporations were part of a bigger economic world.

The First Securities job changed how I saw my future. Until then, I had always expected to open a men's shop in Charlotte or Greensboro with a cousin, Mitchell Mack. Mitchell, who was more than twenty years older than me, was one of the smartest guys I knew. He had graduated from Davidson College and then had gotten an MBA at Harvard Business School after serving in the navy during World War II. Our plan was for Mitchell to supply the money and for me to manage the operation. Running a menswear store was a natural for me. Every summer, every school vacation, there I was at John Mack & Son, which had grown into a department store. I worked as a salesman in the men's and boys' departments, sorted inventory and returns in the stockroom, and was a fast-fingered regular at the Christmas present wrapping station.

I decided the financial services business was a better fit for me than selling high-end suits, shirts, ties, and shoes. I thought it would be a difficult conversation to have with Mitchell. Despite earning an MBA from the top business school in the country, which would have opened corporate doors everywhere, he had returned to Mooresville to help his father, Uncle Side, run the store. Mitchell felt he had no choice because his older brother had moved to Greensboro, where he had become a top executive at Burlington Industries. In the end, life had worked out for Mitchell. He was happy. But he didn't see his path as one-size-fits-all. "Do what you want, Johnnie," he told me. "Don't let me hold you back."

Another factor influenced my decision: a woman whom I became very close to at Duke.

No, not in that way.

Fannie Mitchell, who had a big heart and a smile to match, never appeared on campus without her pearl necklace and tortoiseshell cat-eye glasses. She did not look the part of a shrewd corporate talent spotter. But as the director of the university placement center, she was responsible for jump-starting a lot of people's careers. When Miss Mitchell was appointed acting director in 1942, just twenty-one recruiters came to interview Duke students. By the time she retired twenty-six years later, in 1968, that number had swelled to six hundred recruiters from around the world, plus a hundred schools looking to fill their postgraduate and professional programs. Fannie Mitchell believed deeply in her mission of helping soon-to-be graduates get placed with the right company and in the right job. Unusual for the time, she also believed women could pursue a career beyond becoming a "Mrs." She was a business matchmaker with unerring insight into who belonged where. You—or more probably your parents—might have thought you were destined for insurance underwriting, but she saw you as a career diplomat at the United Nations. She never let students sell themselves short. Recruiters valued her judgment and took her recommendations.

In the 1960s, if you saw an older woman on the Duke campus, you assumed she was a student's mom or a secretary. Most kids paid no attention to Fannie Mitchell until the last weeks before graduation, when they realized they needed a job, STAT.

That wasn't me. Yes, I needed a job, but I also really liked her. Miss Mitchell and I would sit in her cramped office next to the university cafeteria and have long, lively talks that ranged far beyond my prospects. She knew she could count on me to hold my own in a conversation with anyone. When recruiters came to campus from Coca-Cola, Procter & Gamble, Mobil Oil—all the major corporations—she told them, "You've got to talk to John Mack." I was like the prize hog at a 4-H competition.

This led to a few unusual interviews. The Central Intelligence Agency showed a real interest in me because I had taken Russian language classes and my parents spoke Arabic. But when the recruiter handed me an application thicker than the Mooresville phone book, I was like, *Are you kidding me? I have to fill all that out?* So much for a career as a spy.

I seriously considered a job at American Hospital Supply in Chicago. They flew me out, bought me a big steak dinner, put me up at the Palmer House, and offered me a starting salary of $12,000 a year, worth almost $90,000 today. They wanted me to handle personnel at their subsidiary V. Mueller, which made surgical instruments: scalpels, forceps, clamps. "We're looking to shake things up," they said, "and you seem like the guy to do it." The pay was amazing. But I wasn't focused just on the money. Looking at the bigger picture, I feared that I'd be stuck in a corporate backwater. "There's not enough excitement in it for me," I said to Miss Mitchell before turning them down.

Bache & Co. and Merrill Lynch, both big, respected investment firms, offered me positions in their New York back offices similar to what I was doing at First Securities. I would log transactions as well as issue purchase and sales tickets. Bache told me they would start me at

$8,000 a year. I asked the three Bache managers who interviewed me if I could, in two or three years, expect to make $12,000.

"I think we can make that happen," one said.

I also interviewed at Smith Barney. Originally based in Philadelphia, Smith Barney was now an aggressive New York operation eager to expand. After my initial Duke interview went well, they flew me up to their office. They didn't guarantee a set salary like Bache or Merrill Lynch. But Smith Barney offered to train me as a retail broker. Selling stocks promised more independence than working in a back office, and I liked the idea of being rewarded for any sales I generated.

I told Smith Barney yes. I am so happy that I didn't settle for the safety of a guaranteed salary.

You have to do what you like. I think too many people hear about investment banking, consulting, and hedge funds and get enamored with the idea of making a lot of money. They go into things that they're not satisfied with five years later.

Don't be pulled in just because a job or an industry seems glamorous. Investment banking is *not* a glamorous business. The compensation can be out of this world, but you have to have a massive appetite for risk, stress, and competition. And the higher up you go, the greater the intensity. When you're handling other people's money, you are expected to make it grow. There is no forgiveness if you lose it.

THE FIRST THING I had to do was learn the ropes at 20 Broad Street, Smith Barney's headquarters in the heart of the financial district—Wall Street. It was a ten-cent subway ride down from my cousin Ray's Kips Bay apartment. I kept myself alive by consuming tuna fish sandwiches on toasted white bread that I bought for $1.85

at the Clover Deli on my way home from work. I lost eight pounds in my first four months in New York. But I couldn't afford anything else.

The twenty people in my training group were a lot like me—white guys in dark suits and skinny, striped ties. No sixties-era Nehru jackets, bell bottoms, or love beads. No women. No people of color. Most of my fellow trainees were right out of college. There were a few older men who wanted to change careers and get into the securities business. Married with families, they really didn't associate with us.

We were exposed to all the departments and all the businesses. Everyone felt like rookies—freshman year again. We were friendly, but we were competing. We all wanted to make a good impression so the managers would recruit us into their departments. Some of the men in the class would go into investment banking, some into asset management, some into administration, and some into the retail business.

I wasn't nervous, but I was fine-tuned; focused; never slouching. When you're an adult and someone is paying you, you have to be on your A-game. I certainly was.

My original plan was to complete my training in New York and then move to Atlanta, a booming, progressive, probusiness city. Headquarters for corporate giants like Coca-Cola and Delta Air Lines, Atlanta was the unofficial capital of the New South. During that racially fraught period, it stood apart from other southern cities like Birmingham and Montgomery, Alabama, becoming known as "the City Too Busy to Hate." I would open a Smith Barney branch. And using my Duke connections, my skill at golf, and my own grit, gumption, and charm, I would cultivate affluent clients—doctors, lawyers, businessmen, commercial real estate developers—and sell them stocks and bonds.

This was a volatile time in the economy. President Lyndon Johnson was spending a lot of money—more than the Treasury was taking in—on two fronts: the ongoing Vietnam War abroad and the Great Society programs at home. The biggest worry for men my age in 1968 was the war. I was called up for the draft right out of college, but I had cracked the C4 vertebra in my neck playing football at Duke, and the draft board rejected me. I was glad I didn't have to go to Vietnam, but if I had passed the physical, I would have served. I had friends from high school and college who were injured or died in the Vietnam War. I knew how lucky I was.

Through the Great Society and its war on poverty, the federal government attempted to solve urban and rural problems. Starting in the mid-1960s, inflation began to ratchet up, eroding the value of the savings accounts where many Americans kept their money.

It was also a boom time for America. Astronauts were walking in outer space. People were investing in the country. A surging middle class wanted to own a piece of the companies that undergirded the US economy—corporations like Xerox, IBM, General Foods, and the Ford Motor Company, which had unveiled its sexy Mustang at the 1964 World's Fair in New York. Millions of Americans jumped into the stock market.

On Wall Street, the volume picked up so dramatically and the markets were so popular that in three years the number of transactions on the New York Stock Exchange (NYSE) more than doubled. In 1965, there were five million a day. By 1968, there were twelve million. But the system wasn't automated. I can remember seeing hordes of messengers racing around Wall Street delivering paper stock certificates by hand. Computers were just starting to be used, and back offices couldn't keep track of all the trades. You could buy a stock and not get confirmation on it. If there was a mistake, it would be hard to get it corrected. There were trades that you couldn't assign to a purchaser or a seller. These trades were called DKs—don't know the trade.

At one point, unprocessed transactions added up to $4 billion.

People on the Street often referred to this problem as "the paperwork crunch."

It got so bad that in August 1968, when I started at Smith Barney, the NYSE was closed every Wednesday just to battle the massive paper pileup, and sometimes it had to close early on other days.

As is almost always the case, what was unfortunate for some people was a boon for others. Newspapers at the time claimed that while many employees labored into the night, eating not just lunch but also dinner at their desks, some stockbrokers used the free hours to shave strokes off their golf handicaps. The Smith Barney trainees—me included—were not among those out on the links. Wednesdays found us stuck in the back office, processing transactions with paper and pen.

This lasted through the end of the year. Even after the NYSE went back to a five-day-a-week schedule in January 1969, it still closed early on Wednesday afternoons to clear the paper jam. This continued until July.

The problem got ironed out. But not without enormous, and sometimes calamitous, disruption. Around a hundred member firms on the NYSE—a sixth of the total—were forced to merge or close, putting thousands of people out of work. Not since the Great Depression had Wall Street seen such carnage. The survivors: the big firms with lots of money that could buy computers and hire the staff to run them.

By the time my twenty-fifth birthday came around in November 1969, I had learned something that would be true for the rest of my career: you have to recognize change. You have to embrace the hard choices that change demands. Most of all, you have to do your best to look into the future to get out ahead of whatever is coming.

Otherwise, you will fail. This is as true on Main Street as it is on Wall Street.

JOHN MACK

Because of the paperwork crunch, the NYSE asked member firms like Smith Barney not to open any new offices. There went my opportunity to set up the Atlanta branch and my dreams of playing golf at the Atlanta Athletic Club.

On the other hand, to judge from the interest I was attracting from Smith Barney offices around the country, I was a standout trainee. I was recruited to go to Philadelphia as a retail broker, and the manager of the San Francisco office flew me out, too.

While I was considering these offers, I had a career-changing conversation with one of the senior Smith Barney managers who was the head of training, George Wilder. After graduating from Princeton University, he had served in the navy during World War II and was a devoted golfer who commuted into the city from West Orange, New Jersey. George was a former municipal bond salesman. He invited me to have a beer with him one night after work at Fraunces Tavern, a popular Wall Street watering hole that had been around since George Washington drank ale there. "John," he said, "I see you in the bond business. You're a born salesman. You know how to talk to people. You know how to get people on your side. Most of all, you know how to close. *That* is what selling is all about."

It takes a salesman to know a salesman. George was pushing hard. "San Francisco is filled with hippies," he said, his voice dripping with disgust. "Philadelphia hasn't been the big time since Ben Franklin was running the show. I think you'd be fantastic selling muni bonds to banks and institutions here at HQ, not shilling stocks to scotch-guzzling golfers at some country club in Bryn Mawr."

I listened closely to what George was saying. I trusted him. And by the time we paid the tab, I'd made up my mind to switch from retail to municipal bonds.

Muni bonds are issued by state and local governments to raise money for schools, roads, airports, and other public projects. Let's say the New York State Thruway Authority needed money to build a spur off a highway near Rochester. It would finance the project by selling municipal bonds, which pay interest, to investors. Another appealing aspect of muni bonds: they are exempt from federal taxes.

The final step in the Smith Barney training program was to take what was then known as the Series 7 test. We were given three hours and forty-five minutes to complete a 125-question exam. You had to get 72 percent—ninety questions—correct to work in the securities industry.

My scores were middle of the pack. But I promised George, "I'm going to be the best bond salesman you've got."

I screwed up almost immediately.

I went out to lunch with some Smith Barney colleagues and a couple of executives from a firm we worked with, C. J. Devine, the leading dealer in government bonds. After several bottles of wine, we moved on to a bright yellow Italian liqueur called Strega, the Italian word for witch. Served straight up in aperitif glasses, it's sweet and lethal—eighty proof. I was hammered and in no condition to return to the office, but I did.

That afternoon, several brokers needed bonds to sell to clients. To accommodate them, I had to make a trade. My math was off. This was just before the handheld calculator was introduced.

I cost the firm a little less than $1,000, equivalent to about $7,000 today. By the standards of Wall Street, it wasn't a lot. But to me, my error and the amount were huge. Huge. I wasn't supposed to lose money, I was supposed to make it. I didn't sleep that night. I thought I might be fired. I couldn't face the idea of having to move home to Mooresville and ask my cousin for a job in the stockroom at John Mack & Son.

The next day, Kenneth Siebel, a Smith Barney executive in San Francisco, called me. He wanted a blow-by-blow account so he could understand what went wrong.

I did the only thing anyone should do in a situation like this. I looked at the phone, I took a deep breath, and I told him the truth, right down to the multiple glasses of Strega.

Yes, the adults around me when I was growing up—my parents, my teachers, the Catholic priests—always emphasized the importance of telling the truth. But this wasn't just about moral rectitude or the Ten Commandments.

You can't fudge the truth in business, especially about money. It is the fuel that every business runs on, especially the financial services business. At the end of the day, numbers don't lie. The balance sheet has to add up.

After I finished describing the events that led to my calculation error, all I heard was the crackle of the long-distance line. The seconds felt like days as I sat waiting for Ken to say something. "Eh, don't sweat it," he told me. "We'll work it out. Everybody screws up sometimes, particularly when they start. It was an honest mistake. Hope the lunch was fun."

I've never forgotten his understanding.

I was working on the Fixed Income trading floor, buying and selling municipal bonds. This was no boring desk job. It was pandemonium: deafening, thick with cigarette and cigar smoke, every other word "fucking this" and "fucking that." Chinese takeout containers, empty pizza boxes, and abandoned, half-drunk cardboard cups of coffee littered every surface.

I had a phone to my ear and an eye on what all the other muni bond salesmen and traders were doing. The louder and more chaotic it was, the more my adrenaline flowed. I'd get really pumped up. It's very competitive. You play off each other. If I made a big sale, the guy next to me would bellow, "Goddamn it, John Mack just did that!" Then he would try to make an even bigger sale. Every day was something different.

This is where I got the Wall Street bug. I loved it, and I was good at it.

———————

NEW YORK HAD become home. In a city filled with people from all over the world, my Lebanese background blended right in. I had often felt like an outsider growing up in Mooresville. As a teenager, standing on the free-throw line in my basketball shorts, I was embarrassed that I was so much darker and hairier than the other boys. My parents insisted that I make the sign of the cross before I took a shot, thus identifying me as one of a handful of Catholics in a town of Southern Baptists.

In Manhattan, I wasn't like some southerners I knew, who, as the writer Willie Morris observes in his memoir *North Toward Home*, had severed their connections to wherever they'd grown up and lived like expatriates in a new country. There were others who couldn't pry themselves away; they always knew the score of last Friday night's high school football game. I was comfortably in the middle. I didn't miss Mooresville, or even North Carolina. But I still called my mother long-distance nearly every day.

I also didn't downplay my Tar Heel roots. Just the opposite—I'd sit down with eight people around a table or at a bar, and they'd say, "Where are you from? Where'd you grow up? What's that accent I hear?" Or they'd make fun of me. That was fine with me. I knew that when I got a couple of drinks in me, I could sound like a twanging banjo. I didn't care if people thought I was from Hick Alley. I thought it gave me an advantage. People remembered me.

Mercifully, a studio apartment opened up on the nineteenth floor in my cousin Ray's building. It was one of two twenty-story skyscrapers in the enormous Kips Bay Plaza complex, which occupies three city blocks. The towers, designed by renowned modernist architect

I. M. Pei, were airy—with a lot of glass. I snapped the place up. It cost $186 a month and faced east, toward the borough of Queens. Standing in the window, sipping a cup of coffee, I loved to watch the planes take off and land at LaGuardia Airport.

I didn't mind living alone. I had a lot of friends in New York from Duke, and my social circle expanded even more when Ray started taking me to Southampton, the exclusive beach town toward the end of Long Island.

The Hamptons opened my eyes. I had never seen such wealth. I gawked at the magnificent old estates, with their sweeping oyster-shell driveways in front and huge porches overlooking the Atlantic Ocean in back. This was not honky-tonk Myrtle Beach, South Carolina, with its fry shacks, motels, and mini golf, where my family had vacationed.

By my second summer, I was able to afford a half share—six weekends—in a small, run-down rental house out there. I got to know Ray's friends in advertising. They were older than me—people who had built successful careers on Madison Avenue. The memorable slogans and visuals they created were reshaping the way Americans saw themselves. Likewise, the people, right out of *Mad Men*, left a lasting impression on me.

A lot of the guys on the trading floor were equally foul-mouthed and coarse off the floor, and the parties I went to when I first arrived in New York were an extension of my time in college—a noisy crush of drunk guys pounding down beer from a keg.

I realized that was not what I wanted.

The ad folks were part of a different social stratum. They knew how to dress, how to entertain, and how to behave. I observed how they lived and how they interacted. There was an elegance to the way they did things. At parties, they easily mixed business with pleasure. I was impressed with them. They taught me how to act like an adult.

My clothes, my haircuts, and my manners improved. You can learn a lot from people if you don't let yourself be intimidated.

Do I sound like a square? You betcha. I was part of the hippie generation, but I had no interest in turning on, tuning in, or dropping out, as countercultural guru Timothy Leary suggested. I wasn't moving to some commune up in Vermont. A lot of people my age were questioning American capitalism. That wasn't my scene.

But I wasn't oblivious to changes happening in society. I listened when my women friends talked about feminism, and I learned about how boxed in they felt by gender stereotypes. Most of all, I recognized that the Civil Rights Movement was long overdue. Racial injustice had been sewn into the fabric of Mooresville for two centuries. Black families lived in a segregated area across the railroad tracks and had to attend a different school. When I was twelve, I saw about a dozen white-robed, hooded members of the Ku Klux Klan march down Main Street, past John Mack & Son. My olive-skinned parents, always anxious about their own tenuous position in the social order, never discussed race. Few people did, even though sit-ins started in 1960 at a Woolworth's counter in Greensboro, just seventy-five miles away.

———————

BACK AT 20 Broad Street, Smith Barney decided it wanted to go into corporate bonds: bonds that companies issue to raise capital so they can grow, either by expanding or by buying other companies. The new manager assured me, "This is a great opportunity, John. It's better than muni bonds. You'll get commissions."

He was right about one thing: it was a great opportunity. I developed relationships with new clients at banks and pension funds. But after I had been on the corporate bond desk for eight months, I hadn't seen a single commission check.

I have zero patience with people who don't do what they say they'll do. So I quit.

John McDougall, who ran Smith Barney's Fixed Income Department, was shocked at my decision. "I can't believe you're leaving," he said. "You have to talk to Fred." J. Frederick Van Vranken Jr. was one of Smith Barney's senior executives. "He'll give you what you need to make you stay."

"Fred hasn't spoken to me since the day I got here," I said. "Why would I talk to him now?" But out of respect for McDougall, I did make an appointment to see Van Vranken.

I sat down in his spacious office. "I don't like the way you're doing things," I told him. "I've done a great job selling corporate bonds. I've made a lot of money for Smith Barney. You made a commitment to me to pay commissions, and you didn't deliver."

Then I quit again.

After I left Smith Barney, I traveled to Lebanon on the cheap with Mitchell. My father and Uncle Side sometimes talked to each other about their homeland, but they never tried to give the next generation any insight into the country. I don't know if it was too painful or if they had just moved on, that they wanted us to assimilate as fully American and not be tied to their Lebanese past. It was only on that trip to Lebanon, my first one, that I developed a much richer appreciation of the people, the landscape, and my heritage. The way we gathered in the backyard and ate food with friends and relatives in North Carolina and South Carolina was our version of the Lebanese *hafli*. For the first time, I understood why my parents were so drawn to the North Carolina mountains. When you're on the beach in Beirut, the mountains come down practically to the sand.

It wasn't until I took a job in Fixed Income at F. S. Smithers in 1970, selling corporate and Treasury bonds, that I started making real money. One afternoon, I did a transaction and my commission was

$8,000—almost $54,000 these days. I was so excited that I called my mother. "Mom, I just made $8,000!" I blurted out. "Start packing your suitcase. You can finally go home and visit your family in Lebanon!"

My mother let out a whoop. "You did good, Johnnie!" she shouted into the phone.

With my windfall at Smithers, I also gave my mother money to remodel the three-bedroom brick house I grew up in. There hadn't been a single change made to it since I was four. Having money let me do that. I saw money as a way to reach my goals: to be independent, to be respected, and to help people. These things were important to me, and I worked hard to achieve them.

DURING THE TWO years I worked at Smithers, I often looked out the trading room window at the Statue of Liberty. In November and December, when the sun set early, I would see her lit torch blazing.

I thought of the legendary Cornelius Vanderbilt, who had plied the waters of New York Harbor that roiled just in front of me. He had started his first business as a teenager, ferrying customers from Staten Island to Manhattan on his way to astronomical wealth in shipping and railroads.

The Statue of Liberty wasn't just about my family's past—the risks they took and the promise for their future.

It was also about my future and the risks and rewards awaiting me.

I was all in.

CHAPTER THREE

M r. Mack, she's the one," Marcel whispered to me halfway through dinner.

At A La Fourchette, an authentic French bistro on West Forty-Sixth Street, I knew all the waiters. Proud, middle-aged Frenchmen in tuxedos who served diners with a flourish, they had seen me here with plenty of dates, some more serious than others.

When Christy King walked in on the night of Saturday, May 13, 1972, they were dazzled. I was, too. Christy—tall, willowy, and wearing a long, clingy, white halter dress slit to the knee—was a showstopper. Tanned, with frosted blond hair down to her waist, she was a beauty, with soft brown eyes and a big smile.

I was primed to think Christy would be someone special. Soon after I moved to New York in 1968, I was at a cocktail party at an apartment not far from my own in Kips Bay. It was thrown by a quartet of American Airlines stewardesses, as we called flight attendants back then. Grabbing a beer at a makeshift bar in a living room clouded with cigarette smoke, I found myself elbow-to-elbow with future TV talk show host Charlie Rose. I had known him, a fellow North Carolinian, at Duke. "I want you to meet my wife, Mary," he said. I shook hands with a slim, fine-featured blonde as Otis Redding crooned "Sittin' on the Dock of the Bay."

The longer we chatted, the more I realized that Mary was as smart and down-to-earth as she was gorgeous. Putting my cards faceup on the table, I said, "You're just great! Do you have a sister who's not already taken?"

"As a matter of fact, I do," she said. "My younger sister, Christy."

"The next time she comes up, call me. I'll take her to dinner," I said.

"Well, she's still in college. She's a sophomore at UNC in Chapel Hill."

"I don't care. I want to take her out."

Four years later, the wall phone in my kitchen rang. It was Charlie. Mary got on the line. "You told me you wanted to meet my sister," Mary said. "Are you still single? Christy's coming up for a visit. She'll be staying with Charlie and me."

I had seen Mary and Charlie only once since the cocktail party. They had attended a splashy party that my cousin Ray, his advertising friends, and I had given at a rented mansion on Shinnecock Bay in the Hamptons the previous summer. The elegant event had been written up in *Holiday* magazine.

"I'll call you back," I said on the phone now. As great as I thought Christy would be, I didn't want to get stuck with some girl I'd never met for the entire weekend. So I got a different date for Friday night.

At A La Fourchette on Saturday, the four of us sat at my usual table in a private alcove with leather banquettes and red velvet curtains. I remember every minute of that date. We talked about North Carolina. The King sisters grew up in Greensboro, northeast of Mooresville. Like my hometown, it was known for its textile mills. I learned that Christy and Mary came from a family of five children. Their father, a surgeon, was as exacting at home as he was in the operating room. He demanded that his daughters be both homecoming queens and honor-roll students. His sons had no choice but to be star athletes who achieved academic excellence.

Christy remembers the dinner differently. "Nobody made any effort to include me in the conversation," she says. "You never asked me a thing, John."

According to her, Charlie, Mary, and I obsessed nonstop about President Richard Nixon's recent historic eight-day trip to China and what it might mean for the United States, as well as the renewed American bombing of North Vietnam. Mary had the inside skinny because she worked as a researcher for vaunted journalist Bill Moyers, then at CBS.

Why did I even come out tonight? Christy wondered as Marcel gently placed her sole grenobloise in front of her.

Then Charlie posed the kind of probing question that would make him famous, and China took a back seat. He turned to me. "What kind of girl would you like to marry?"

"She's right here," I replied, looking Christy straight in the eye. I had dated a lot of women, but this night was different. Instead of being a cliché out of the movies, the idea of falling in love at first sight suddenly seemed possible to me.

I thought I noticed the tiniest smile from Christy.

Apparently, I was hallucinating.

According to Christy, her mind was wandering when Charlie asked the big question. What I thought was a shy smile at my answer was in fact Christy smirking. *Yeah, right. What a line*, she thought.

After dinner, we split off from Mary and Charlie. I took Christy to a disco I knew called Le Directoire, on East Forty-Eighth Street. We danced to Motown hits—"My Girl" and "Just My Imagination

(Running Away with Me)." When we took a break, I quizzed her. "What do you like the most about yourself? What's the worst thing you've ever done? What's the best? How do you like to kiss?"

"No one's ever asked me these kinds of questions," Christy said. "Are you really interested?"

"I am," I said. I was being honest.

I invited Christy back to my apartment. We kissed for the first time.

Around 11:30 p.m., I hailed a cab and took Christy back to Charlie and Mary's apartment on the Upper East Side. They were waiting up. I guess the way Christy and I looked at each other—and the way we looked together that first night—said everything. Charlie and Mary later told us that after I left, Mary predicted, "Christy and John are going to get married."

The next day I took Christy to a matinee performance of *Grease*, which was playing on Broadway. She was flying home that night. She had a job as an administrator for a couple of ob-gyns in Chapel Hill. During intermission, I delivered my own monologue, unrehearsed: "I really like you, Christy. I want to get to know you better. Come back next weekend."

She did.

That Saturday night, I had a business dinner with a few work buddies and their wives. I took Christy as my date. She was wearing the same white halter dress. Just before we started eating, one of my coworkers tapped his glass and said, "I want to make a toast." He lifted his glass in Christy's direction and quoted English poet John Keats's famous line from *Endymion*: "A thing of beauty is a joy forever."

She blew everyone away. Blew them away! It was pretty cool.

In the taxi that night, Christy said, "I can't get over your self-confidence, John. You just seem so comfortable in your own skin. I'm not like that at all."

Over Memorial Day weekend, fourteen days into our instantly serious relationship, I flew down to North Carolina and introduced Christy to my mother in Mooresville. That Sunday, the three of us drove a couple of hours up to Boone, in the Blue Ridge Mountains, to spend the afternoon with some of my family. I wanted to introduce Christy to my cousins Madeline and Mitchell and to Mitchell's wife, Delores. Watching me down on the floor roughhousing with their son Jeff and seeing me so engaged with my relatives was a new experience for Christy. "I never knew a family interaction could feel so effortless and easy," she told me that afternoon.

Driving back to Mooresville that evening as the sun sank behind the mountains, my mother was in the back seat and Christy was next to me. I took my eyes off the road long enough to look at Christy. "I love you," I said for the first time.

"I love you, too."

There was no reaction from the back seat.

A couple of weeks later, Christy quit her medical job in Chapel Hill and moved up to New York and into my studio apartment. She found an administrative post at Citicorp. Her parents thought she was staying with Mary and Charlie.

In late June, I was going to Los Angeles to meet with a client, Security Pacific Bank. From there I planned to go to Lake Tahoe to spend the Fourth of July weekend with friends from Smith Barney. There would be three other couples there, and I figured this would be a fun trip for Christy, who had never been west of the Mississippi.

"Come with me," I said.

Instead of saying yes, she said, "No, I think I'll go home and visit my parents. I think you need a break from me. I think all this 'us' is making you uncomfortable." She put air quotes around the word "us." "I think you need some time alone. I'll see you when you get back."

I guess without realizing it or meaning to, I had become a little distant. Christy is a master at reading people. She has an intuitive grasp of what is going on with me. Even though I had just invited her, she sensed there was a small part of me that didn't want her to come. She was giving me an out.

It dawned on me that this freedom and trust were part of my attraction to her. I had dated several women, but inevitably I would start to feel claustrophobic. The more I pulled away, the tighter they gripped. I was used to women being jealous. I couldn't meet an old girlfriend for a cup of coffee without triggering a meltdown. Christy was different. She's independent. Christy gives me a long runway. She later told me, "I trusted you. I was in love with you, and I knew you were in love with me."

Whatever was bothering me lifted. "No, no, no. You're coming!" I said.

At the end of July, we were sitting on the sofa in my studio apartment. Tired from work, we had ordered Chinese takeout. As we waited for our kung pao chicken to arrive, we were watching my little black-and-white TV. A rerun of *Hogan's Heroes*, a sitcom set in a World War II German POW camp, was on. As the Allied prisoners once again outsmarted their inept captors, I turned to Christy.

"I think we should get married."

Silence.

"Are you going to answer me?"

"You didn't ask me a question, John."

"Will you marry me, Christy?" I did not get down on one knee.

To the least romantic, least planned proposal ever, Christy said yes.

WHERE CHRISTY WAS a cool breeze that refreshed my spirit, the other woman in my life, my mother, Alice Azouri Mack, was a blast furnace. She radiated love and warmth, but the heat could be overwhelming. Where Christy let me be myself, my mother was suffocating in her desire to control me.

My mother was a dynamo, no question about it. Born in Lebanon across the valley from my father's village of Roum, Alice Azouri met and married her husband on her own terms.

My parents' "courtship" was old-school.

After his wife died of cancer, Charlie Mack did what widowed immigrants did back then: he wrote a letter to an acquaintance from the old country—in this case, Alice's sister Selma, who had settled in South Carolina. "I've lost my wife. I have four sons. They need a mother, and I need a wife. I would like to meet your sister."

Charlie took the train to meet Alice, age thirty-one. By the standards of the time, she was a spinster who would be expected to employ every feminine wile to snag a husband.

Not Alice. Her trademark directness on full display, she looked down at the forty-five-year-old Charlie—literally. "You're shorter than I am. You're *much* older than I am," she said. "Why would I ever marry you?"

"This is going to work," Charlie insisted to Alice as the visit went on. "I'll give you the wedding you've always wanted—and children."

Charlie and Alice were married in 1939.

Alice had no patience for the way people did things in rural North Carolina. When Frank or I got sick, she scooped us up in our pajamas and drove straight to the pediatrician's office, screeching the tires as she took off from the curb. Bypassing the waiting room and pushing past the nurse, she planted herself and her sick child right outside the doctor's examining room to nab him the nanosecond he came out. This was mortifying and obnoxious. My mother was not a genteel southern matron. She had the sharpest pair of elbows in Mooresville. But she showed me how to get things done. No question, I am my mother's son. I loved her.

As tough as she was, in many ways, my mother was very traditional. She saw herself as a wife, mother, and homemaker. She prided herself on her cooking, hurt if someone dared decline a second helping. "Best I ever made," she'd say proudly, standing at the stove tasting her latest triumph.

However, she also wanted her own money so she could spend as she liked. A talented seamstress, my mother turned our basement into a workshop where she custom-sewed curtains, bedspreads, and linens for other Mooresvillians.

When I was in junior high school, she and another Alice, a local woman, expanded into interior decorating. They called their business the Alicettes and ordered dining tables, chairs, and couches wholesale from the manufacturers in nearby High Point. A hard-driving and charismatic saleswoman, my tart-tongued mother didn't think twice about marching into a client's house and blurting out, "Why did you put that color with this color? Those draperies, they're too short. They're six inches off the floor." She didn't say this to be cruel. She just observed and called out the obvious.

My mother's keen eye went beyond interior design. She was a canny investor. Right after World War II, when my family went to visit my father's sister in Myrtle Beach, my mother immediately sniffed out a moneymaking opportunity. She persuaded my father to buy a couple of oceanfront lots at $2,000 each. He ended up selling them four or five years later for ten times the amount. As always, he needed the money for his wholesale grocery business. But had they held on for twenty or thirty years, after Myrtle Beach exploded as a tourist destination, real estate developers would have paid millions for the lots to build high-rise hotels. My mother resented my father's business because it devoured capital.

I did my first deal with Alice Mack. One morning when I was in high school, she sat down with me at the kitchen table. "Johnnie," she said, "let's go look at land." We got in her two-tone gray Pontiac and drove a few miles outside Mooresville, just east of Interstate 77. In 1959, Duke Power had begun building Lake Norman—a reservoir thirty-three miles long and nine miles wide—as part of the construction of the Cowans Ford Dam to supply electricity to the Piedmont region. Now it was selling lakeside lots. We bought six parcels—four in her name and two in mine—for just $2,700 apiece. My mother used her Alicettes money. I scrounged enough for a down payment and borrowed the rest from the Mooresville branch of Piedmont Bank & Trust.

My father thought she was reckless. "I needed that money for my warehouse," he said to my mother. "We don't have the cash to be speculating on land." My mother ignored him. Years later, I sold my two lots for $150,000 each, a fiftyfold increase.

Money was a stress on their marriage. It wasn't that they were desperately picking coins out of the car seats to pay the electric bill. But they approached financial security in diametrically opposed ways. My mother was willing to take big risks—to buy property and hold on to it, waiting for a payoff that wasn't guaranteed. My father's approach was to keep shoveling money back into his business. The problem was that there was never going to be any sort of payoff with the grocery warehouse.

It was an early lesson in risk and reward.

Perhaps it was no coincidence that my mother was better at cards than my father. On Saturday nights they often played whist—a card game like bridge—with a Lebanese couple in Salisbury, North Carolina, about twenty miles away. The two wives would go up against the two husbands. When the women won, which was most of the time, they rubbed it in, dancing and laughing in victory.

Another difference between them: football. I started playing in the eighth grade. I played both offense and defense. In high school, I had the good luck to be coached by a man named Joe Popp. When he started with the Mooresville Blue Devils in 1958, the team had endured a thirty-two-game losing streak. By 1960, when I was a freshman, we had an undefeated season. The next year he led us to the school's first and only state football championship title. It was huge for a small town like Mooresville to beat Asheboro, three times the size and with a team that had a much deeper bench. Popp eventually coached at the college level at the University of North Carolina at Chapel Hill, Wake Forest, and Georgia Tech. Later he became an assistant coach with the Cleveland Browns.

The games were on Friday nights, and it wasn't just students who packed into the stadium—everyone in town came. The next day all these people would come into the warehouse and say, "Mr. Mack, you should have seen what Johnnie did on the field last night!" My father liked hearing good things about me, but he thought sports were a waste of time. He saw me play just once. My mother, in contrast, never missed a game, home or away. The crowd and the cheerleaders loved her. With her coiffed white hair, she was a sight in the stands. She bayed for blood, screaming, "Let's go! Hit 'em, Johnnie!" When I was named all-state my senior year, there wasn't a backyard gathering in either of the Carolinas where she wasn't boasting about "My Johnnie."

My parents were united on one thing, however: their sons doing well in school. It was their absolute top priority. I worked hard to exceed their high expectations. I had a lengthy and diverse list of achievements in the 1963 Mooresville Senior High School yearbook, *Pitchfork*. I was president of the student council, I was on the honor roll, and I played the clarinet. My parents were proud.

But the award that meant the most to me? In senior year, my girlfriend, Camille, and I were voted most popular. Of course, in a graduating class of ninety students, the competition wasn't exactly stiff.

There was no resting on my laurels where my mother was concerned. She set two goals for my future, and they were nonnegotiable. From my earliest childhood, she instructed me: "You are going to medical school. You will become a doctor." Maybe it didn't matter as much to my father because his oldest son, Theodore, was a physician. But Alice was adamant. She wrapped up a toy doctor's bag and put it under the Christmas tree, one of the first gifts I remember. Being a doctor was the most prestigious position in Mooresville. She wanted that for me, and she wanted bragging rights for herself.

Another subject my mother pounded me on practically from birth: I had to marry a Lebanese Catholic girl. It wasn't just me. She did this to all her sons and stepsons. I had witnessed firsthand how implacable she could be when defied on this front. I'll never forget the rehearsal dinner for my half brother Lewis and his bride, Dottie, who was neither Catholic nor Lebanese. Like a queen in exile, Alice sat with her back to everyone, glaring into the distance. Silent. Fuming.

My mother constantly told me how to think, what to do, who to say hello to, what to wear. I'm a big believer that people have to be who they are, and they shouldn't be pushed. "Leave me alone!" I'd say to my mother. "I'm going to do what I want to do, period."

And that's what I did.

CHRISTY'S FATHER, DR. Walter King, was just as fixated on dictating how Christy should live her life. "Growing up, I often felt I wasn't his daughter, I was his project," Christy told me early in our relationship.

With a scouting report like that, you'd think I'd be a little apprehensive when I drove into the Kings' driveway in Greensboro and parked my car behind their redbrick two-story V-shaped house the first weekend of August 1972. I wasn't. I had a goal, and I wasn't leaving until I achieved it.

Soon after that romantic moment in front of *Hogan's Heroes*, Christy had quit her job at Citicorp and gone home to plan our wedding—a wedding no one in Greensboro knew was happening because Christy hadn't told her parents we were engaged. She told them the person she was supposed to replace at Citicorp had decided not to leave after all. Mary was sure Dr. King would call up Citicorp and demand that his daughter get her job back, but he never did.

On the first night of my visit, we had finished up our turkey divan casserole but had not yet left the table in the turquoise-colored kitchen when, out of nowhere, Dr. King began waxing on about how crucial loyalty was to marital happiness. Seizing this opportunity, I interrupted. "While we're on the subject," I said, "I'd like to marry your daughter."

Dr. King stood up. He circled his chair. Once. Twice. Then he sat down and looked at me. "Do you want to say that again?"

"I'd like to marry Christy," I repeated.

That's when the real interrogation began. He looked at me and commenced an unscheduled, out-of-office medical intake. "Tell me about your parents. How old are they? What is their current physical condition?"

"My dad died of colon cancer when he was seventy-two," I said. "It happened at the end of my junior year at Duke, in 1966. He went quickly. But my mother, who is sixty-four, is going strong. Grandfather Mack made it to age seventy-eight. I was a baby when he died."

Three and a half hours later, when he was running out of steam and questions, Dr. King said, "I just want to make sure you've sown your wild oats."

"Yes, sir, I have."

"I also want to make sure that you're not gay. I took care of a lot of football players in my time, and some of them were gay."

"No, sir. I guarantee you. I am not gay."

"You better be a one-woman man, son, because my daughter is a one-man woman."

"Yes, sir, I am."

Finally, he turned to Mrs. King. "Mother," he said, "I'm done. Do you have any questions?"

"I just hope she knows what she's doing," she answered, her lips looking like she'd sucked on a lemon. An especially sour one. She couldn't be pleased that this was being sprung on her.

Later, Dr. King pulled Christy into his home office. "You do realize that your children will be very dark and very hairy," he stated. He had a clinical way of looking at things.

"And?" Christy replied.

———

ALMOST SIX MONTHS to the day we met, on November 11, 1972, Christy and I were married in a Catholic church in Greensboro. A distant relative who was a professional opera singer, Linda Zoghby, brought me to tears as she filled the nave with her rich soprano, performing Roberta Flack's "The First Time Ever I Saw Your Face." I will never forget how Christy looked coming down the aisle on Dr. King's arm. Her hair was loose, and I thought she was the most beautiful woman in the world. I still do.

After the wedding, the Kings hosted two hundred people at a reception at their home. Then a core group of family and out-oftowners moved on to a dinner-dance at the historic Jefferson-Pilot Building downtown. We danced the hora, a Middle Eastern circle dance, until I kicked off my shoes. I knew my mother, in her heart of hearts, was still wishing I had chosen a Lebanese girl. But looking elegant in a full-length, emerald-green raw silk dress embroidered with gold that she'd had hand-sewn in Beirut, she kept that to herself.

That night, Christy and I were lying in bed when she turned to me.

"Are you scared?"

"Yes," I said.

"So am I," she replied. "But at least we're in love with each other."

CHAPTER FOUR

I'm flattered," I said. "I feel like the sky has parted, and a hand is reaching out from the clouds. I've been chosen. But I don't believe that a kid from Mooresville, North Carolina, has a chance at Morgan Stanley. All you guys went to Harvard, Princeton, or Yale. I went to Duke. I majored in history, not economics. I don't have an MBA. I'll never fit in here."

Like my mother, I believe in being direct.

I sat across a white-linen-covered table from Richard Fisher and William Black. We were in the mahogany-paneled Morgan Stanley executive dining room at 140 Broadway, an oil portrait of one of the original partners hanging behind us and a basket of hot, fresh Parker House rolls sitting in front of us.

Dick Fisher, Princeton class of '57 and Harvard Business School class of '62, came right back at me. "You're wrong about that, John," he said emphatically. "I promise you you'll fit in. If you don't, if the people at this firm hold your background against you, I'll resign. Morgan Stanley is a meritocracy."

Bill Black, Yale class of '54 and Dick's boss, nodded in agreement.

It was spring 1972. I was making a real name for myself at F. S. Smithers. My biggest account was Mellon Bank in Pittsburgh. Mellon managed two massive pension funds: teachers' and state employees' for the commonwealth of Pennsylvania. I was selling corporate bonds to Mellon when they had money to invest and buying bonds when Mellon needed to raise money. I worked on commission.

But I was restless at Smithers. As a small firm, it didn't have the capital to compete, especially as Wall Street took on more and more risk. A number of the top producers had already left. I was open to offers.

Blue-blood Morgan Stanley was in the midst of a revolution, and Dick Fisher, a thirty-five-year-old partner, was playing a big part. In charge of the firm's brand-new Sales and Trading group, he put a lucrative job offer on the table. Black, a forty-one-year-old Atlanta native with a soft southern drawl, was known within the firm as a power broker. He was there to emphasize the firm's serious interest in me.

Morgan Stanley had been carved out of J. P. Morgan & Co. in 1935, after the passage of the Glass-Steagall Act two years earlier. The law was designed to be a shield against future bank failures like the ones that occurred during the Great Depression. Some commercial banks had used depositors' money to buy speculative Wall Street stocks. When the stock market crashed, customers' money vanished. Panicked Americans swarmed teller windows, desperate to retrieve their savings. These bank runs overwhelmed the system. Glass-Steagall forbade firms from being both commercial banks, which took deposits and made loans, and investment banks, which supplied capital to corporations in the form of stocks and bonds.

Banks had to choose. J. P. Morgan & Co., founded in 1895 and arguably the most powerful financial institution in American history, remained a commercial bank. Along with four other partners and several employees, founder J. Pierpont Morgan's grandson Henry S. Morgan, age thirty-five, and Harold Stanley, age fifty, resigned from J. P. Morgan to form an investment bank, Morgan Stanley. The J. P. Morgan company stayed at 23 Wall Street, while Morgan Stanley opened at 2 Wall Street, a hundred yards away. The Morgan Stanley founders brought their pedigrees and their traditions with them. Bankers at both firms wore three-piece suits—shirtsleeves buttoned, jackets on at all times (this was before air-conditioning)—and sat at slender-legged, mahogany rolltop desks custom-built in England. Each desk had call buttons to summon an office boy, a switchboard operator, or a secretary.

Thanks to its influential parent, Morgan Stanley had deep connections to the highest echelons of the American economy: railroads, telephones, automobiles, steel, manufacturing, and oil, as well as to foreign governments around the world. Among its clients: American Telephone & Telegraph, DuPont, and U.S. Steel—the blue-chip companies that built modern America.

Morgan Stanley had stood unchallenged at the summit of American finance for nearly four decades. If IBM gave Morgan Stanley the mandate to raise $500 million, Morgan Stanley would underwrite— that is, issue—the shares to make that happen. The partners then invited other Wall Street firms into a syndicate to help distribute— that is, sell—the stock. Morgan Stanley made its money from the difference between the underwritten price and the price at which the securities sold.

Financial services back then had strict, if unspoken, rules. Because Texaco was a Morgan Stanley client, for instance, it was understood that the relationship was exclusive. Other investment banks would not solicit the oil company for business.

But in the 1960s and '70s, trading houses overthrew the status quo. They began aggressively calling on the top management of previously unapproachable companies like General Electric and General Motors. "We can do a lot of things a traditional investment bank like Morgan Stanley can't do," they pitched the chief financial officers, presenting them with creative new ways to manage their balance sheets and raise capital. Salomon Brothers, Merrill Lynch, and others wielded their prowess in the secondary markets—trading securities that had already been issued—as a weapon. This was a battlefield where Morgan Stanley was untested.

The assault worked. The trading houses began to cut into Morgan Stanley's foundational relationships. Overnight, sedate Wall Street became fiercely competitive. Morgan Stanley, shaken, suddenly needed to become more nimble and innovative in terms of the kinds of financial instruments and services it could offer its bread-and-butter clients—the users of capital. The firm that had been able to pick and choose now had to be solicitous and eager to please.

To survive, it also had to focus on the suppliers of capital—institutional investors like insurance companies, banks, and pension funds. Before, these groups had bought bonds and held on to them for decades. Now they were actively managing their investments. One of the reasons: inflation was eating into the value of long-term bonds.

To capture this secondary business, Morgan Stanley needed to create a Sales and Trading division from scratch. Many, if not most, of the older partners were opposed to entering this arena. A trading floor went against everything Morgan Stanley was known for. Its partners drank dry sherry and advised titans of industry. Traders were considered to be greedy, grubby, even uncouth.

Things came to a head at a 1971 partnership strategy meeting. Robert H. B. Baldwin, the farsighted, hardheaded lead partner, was adamant about modernizing the firm. "We made one decision," Dick

Fisher later said in Morgan Stanley's *Fiftieth Anniversary Review*, "and that simple decision led to all the subsequent growth of our firm." Baldwin tapped Fisher to head up the new group.

That's why I was having lunch with Dick and Bill. As a corporate bond salesman, my résumé would have gone right in the trash can just a couple of years earlier. But because Morgan Stanley was now elbowing into the secondary markets, I was a hot commodity. "I'll think about the job, Dick," I told Fisher as we finished our coffee.

He had impressed me. He was not what I expected. Dick had contracted polio at age eight and walked with a cane but had wrestled on his high school team. He had a soft-spoken, welcoming manner. In that way, he reminded me of my dad. Unlike my father, he was fired up with ambition, burning to take on Wall Street. He and five other recently named partners were known around Morgan Stanley as the Irreverent Group of Six. They were determined to keep Morgan Stanley on top by forcing change.

I called Dick the next day. "Thank you," I said, "but I have to say no." I was tempted by this opportunity. Dick was offering me entrée into a rarefied sphere. But I think I was intimidated. I wasn't sure that with my non–Ivy League education and Lebanese immigrant parents I would fit in.

"Well, you're making the wrong decision, John," he said. Dick was pleasant but firm.

Instead I went to Loeb Rhoades & Co., a successful firm formed by the 1937 merger of two prestigious brokerage houses. When I worked there, the firm, at 42 Wall Street, had a private elevator waiting in the lobby for its employees' convenience. I liked what I was doing, and the money was good—very good, actually. I was bringing in $110,000—almost $700,000 today.

But I kept comparing Loeb Rhoades with Morgan Stanley. I was sharp, aggressive. At Loeb Rhoades, my coworkers were content to rock along with second-tier clients. There was no growth, no drive. My colleagues and I were not a team. We were all just guns for hire, looking for the biggest payout. Morgan Stanley, on the other hand, was focused on serving its clients' best interests. I hadn't thought about the culture of an organization before. Now I did. I realized that not all firms were the same.

I'm not sure what took me so long to figure this out. I had understood this distinction as a senior in high school when both UNC–Chapel Hill and Duke recruited me to play football. There was nothing wrong with UNC, and my parents could afford to send me there without a scholarship. But Duke had an edge academically and socially, and I wanted to reach as high as I could.

An older friend from Smithers, Damon Mezzacappa, who had recently landed a senior position at Morgan Stanley, was hounding me to join him. "You've gotta come here," he'd press me every time we met for a drink. "You're selling yourself short, John. Believe me, I know what I'm talking about. If you were here, you'd be killing it every single day."

I kept going back to a story that Dick Fisher, who came from modest beginnings, had told me over lunch about Frank Petito. Like me, Petito was a first-generation American. His father, a janitor, had come from Italy and settled in Trenton, New Jersey. After attending Princeton on scholarship, Petito joined Morgan Stanley in 1937. He quickly impressed everyone. But when he hit the one-year mark, he stopped coming to work. One of the partners found him in Princeton, New Jersey, pumping gas for a living. Asked why he had left Morgan Stanley, Petito said, "You told me that you were hiring me for a year."

"Come back," the partner insisted. Petito returned to the firm and rose quickly through the ranks. Now he was one of two senior leaders, along with Bob Baldwin.

I had my doubts that the Frank Petito story was 100 percent true.

But the moral was clear: a kid from an immigrant family could thrive at Morgan Stanley.

I lasted six months at Loeb Rhoades. In my four years on Wall Street, I had already worked at three firms, which was unusual then. I kept switching jobs because I wanted to work with people who made me stretch. I didn't want to feel like I was settling.

The lesson here: never sell yourself short.

In mid-October, a month before I left for Greensboro to marry Christy, I sat at my desk in Loeb Rhoades's deserted trading room. It was late afternoon, and the market had closed. I picked up the phone. I had turned Morgan Stanley down, and I was prepared to live with that decision if I had to. Not everyone gets a second chance. But I also wasn't going to let pride keep me from going after what I now realized I really wanted: to work at a first-class firm and to be around smart, ethical, competitive people.

People like Dick Fisher. I knew I could learn from him.

When his secretary put me through, I got right to the point. "Dick," I said, "I made a mistake. If the sales job is still open, I'd love the opportunity."

"I knew you'd change your mind, John," he said. "Welcome aboard."

Two weeks later, on October 24, 1972, I walked past Isamu Noguchi's landmark red rhombus sculpture in front of the Marine Midland Building, where Morgan Stanley had its offices. It was an unseasonably warm fall morning, and cloudy.

But I still felt that the skies had parted.

CHAPTER FIVE

T o walk into Morgan Stanley was to time travel. With its customs, culture, and horse-and-hound decor, the firm I joined
in 1972 wasn't all that different from the Morgan Stanley founded
in 1935. There was an air of formality. Twelve of the famous rolltop
desks stood in an area called the platform, raised eight inches off the
floor to discreetly hide the cables beneath.

The partners sat at these desks looking at their Quotron machines,
which gave stock quotes. Their demeanors were as buttoned-up as
their Brooks Brothers jackets. I shook hands with Morgan Stanley's
first president, now emeritus—a stately gentleman named Samuel
Burton Payne. With his chalk-white hair and formidable brow, he
could have been chiseled out of marble and put on-site as a founder
of America.

With offices in New York and Paris and an outpost in Tokyo, the firm
was so small that its 350 employees could fit on the first-class deck of a
luxury ocean liner. And the service was comparable. Every day at 9:00
a.m. sharp, a deferential clerk presented me with a form to fill out. Did I

want sliced beef fillet or fresh cod for lunch, along with soup and dessert? Was that not to my liking? No problem, I could order a sandwich from Wolf's Deli on Beekman Street. Or if I had a yearning for Chinese, say, or French or Italian? I could order from any number of restaurants in lower Manhattan. Morgan Stanley picked up the tab. And the meal was served to me in an elegant dining room on the top floor of the Marine Midland Building by uniformed waiters wearing white gloves. On windy days, the chandeliers swayed slightly back and forth.

This daily ritual and attention to my well-being—the whole sense of tradition and status—made me feel that I was stepping into something bigger than myself and my career. I loved being part of an organization with such a storied culture. Not to mention that the caliber and caloric intake were a big step up from the tuna fish sandwiches on toast from the Clover Deli.

At 10:00 a.m. on my first day at Morgan Stanley, I saw how flawlessly the partnership worked. The firm was pricing a $100 million bond issue for AT&T. Every New York partner sat at the big boardroom table. Every partner spoke. Every partner was heard. They debated vigorously but respectfully. Then, one by one, they went around the table and voted. Whatever the price, it had to be a majority. This is because the partners were risking their own money. At the end of the meeting, they set the coupon—the annual interest rate paid on the bond—at seven and an eighth. I had never observed anything like this before. I felt that Morgan Stanley was completely committed to its clients' success.

Over the next months, I witnessed this commitment to excellence again and again. I realized that investment banking was an intense, cerebral business that required extraordinary attention to detail. Every Morgan Stanley document was checked and rechecked. Every number was prepared by one person and recalculated by another. There could be no typos, no errors. Nothing went out that wasn't perfect.

This cool, severe atmosphere, where voices were always hushed, permeated every corner of the firm.

Almost.

It stopped at the door of the trading floor where I worked. A former conference room newly converted for Dick's Sales and Trading group, this glassed-off bullpen was raucous and smoke-filled. Between the cables, the machines, and a dozen traders and salesmen yelling (in the early '70s, it was *all* men), the room would heat up fast. My jacket came off the moment I stepped inside at 7:30 a.m., and I loosened my tie by lunch.

Forget the rolltops. We jammed utilitarian black metal desks together to form a single surface. When we needed more space, we stuck another desk at one end or the other. Every day was game day in the Sales and Trading room. As I pitched corporate bonds to my clients, I kept my eye on the electronic feed that ran around the sides of the room. It tracked stock ticker symbols and the changing prices coming off Wall Street second by second.

In the firm's early days, Harold Stanley famously asked partners to leave a meeting for muttering the word "damn." But inside the trading room, the f-word in all its manifestations was a favorite. Sometimes the partners stepped down from the platform, poked their heads into the trading room, and stared at us, amazed, as we barked, "Buy this, sell that," and then slammed the phones down. We lacked the *Mayflower* manners of their previous hires. We were a different breed. We had different skills. I'm sure the bankers looked down their noses at us, but no one said anything.

The yin-yang was working. Morgan Stanley was now on both sides of the market. Instead of just underwriting securities, the firm was now buying and selling them.

Here's an example: After oil was discovered in Alaska's North Slope in 1968, oil companies wanted to build a pipeline. It was to start in Prudhoe Bay, above the Arctic Circle, and end 798 icy miles south, in the ice-free port of Valdez. There, tankers would be loaded with crude oil to be taken to refineries in the lower forty-eight states.

Working with British Petroleum and Standard Oil of Ohio, Morgan Stanley served as the investment banker for the gargantuan deal. It raised a record $1.75 billion in financing for the project.

Seventy-six institutional investors were involved, led by the Prudential Insurance Company, which committed to buying $250 million in bonds. We worked on the sale for months. I can't believe I remember this, but I think the coupon was ten and five-eighths. Morgan Stanley's Investment Bank side earned fees for setting up the deal, and the Sales side earned commissions for placing the bonds. The deal was completed in 1975, after which construction began. Crude started pumping through the Trans-Alaska Pipeline System in 1977.

Energy was flowing through Morgan Stanley, too. Spearheaded by Bob Baldwin and Dick, the firm was changing at a breakneck pace. In 1973, it added a Research team under ex-Marine Barton Biggs. Some partners opposed this expansion because Research would offer objective evaluations of corporations, including Morgan Stanley clients, to institutional investors. It opened up the distinct possibility that our clients would be angered by our analysts' cold-eyed assessments. The firm also launched Wall Street's first dedicated Mergers and Acquisitions team—an advisory role it had always done for free—headed by Bob Greenhill. The son of a Swedish immigrant, he was famous for the flamboyant dollar-sign suspenders that his daughter needlepointed for him. His work ethic and win-at-all-costs ruthlessness helped transform how the Street saw Morgan Stanley.

New faces and new names were everywhere. By August 1973, we had a new address in the Exxon Building at 1251 Avenue of the Americas, near Rockefeller Center. Morgan Stanley built a larger trading floor with enough space for the wiring and computers needed to handle the growing number of transactions. It was more efficient to build the floor in a new skyscraper than to retrofit a Wall Street dinosaur. Plus, we wanted to be closer to our clients, many of whom were in Midtown.

We were growing with such speed that Bob Baldwin had his secretary distribute a typewritten memo stating that from then on, last names rather than simply initials were required in all internal office communications. The dictum came from RHBB.

I loved the old aristocratic traditions, but I also loved the new spirit of creativity, change, and growth. The work was demanding and the people inspiring.

I had found my professional home.

CHAPTER SIX

Too bad they didn't have frequent-flier points in 1973, because once I had established myself on Morgan Stanley's trading floor, I was in the air an awful lot. During the workweek I called on clients upstate in Albany, New York, down in Tallahassee, Florida, and out west in California.

Then, many Saturdays at noon Christy and I would hail a yellow cab and head to LaGuardia Airport. We would grab lunch in the first-class lounge and board the 1:35 p.m. TWA flight to Pittsburgh, home to Mellon Bank, which I held on to when I moved from Smithers to Loeb Rhoades and then to Morgan Stanley. It remained my most lucrative account.

Founded in 1869, Mellon was a towering financial presence in the United States, handling huge pensions and trust assets as well as having a vast base of bank deposits. Every firm had salespeople assigned to pitch corporate bonds to Mellon: Goldman Sachs; Salomon Brothers; Loeb Rhoades; international banks. Everyone was competing for the same business. The scorecard was your commission; how many dollars they invested with you instead of with the other guy.

I could tell a client that I had AT&T bonds at X price. Then Salomon might call up and say, "I have AT&T bonds at Y price." X could be slightly cheaper or slightly richer than Y. Clients will always tell you a deal is predicated on price, but they're kidding themselves. They don't take the subconscious into account. Price is important, and relationships are important. But looking back on my career, I would say relationships have the edge. This isn't the case with every client, but it's true with a large majority. If you are creative and come up with good ideas, you get in the door, but relationships always win out over time.

Take Dick Van Scoy, who handled investing at Mellon for the Pennsylvania teachers and state employee pensions. I originally got the account at Smithers because in a world of easygoing, backslapping bond guys, he could be a real hard-ass. He knew the pension business inside out and never let anyone forget it. Nobody jollied him into buying bonds he didn't want. I liked the challenge.

Van Scoy had certain strategies. He liked to corner as many bonds as he could in a sinking fund—bonds designed to be retired—until he owned the majority. Then, because the bond issuer had to retire a certain number of bonds each year, Van Scoy used his leverage to approach the issuer and demand a higher price.

I learned that with every client there's a key that unlocks the relationship. It varies, depending on the client, and I worked to find it. With Van Scoy, the key was honesty. I had to be straight down the middle. I was also dependable. I did what I said I would. That's the way I dealt with Van Scoy. When I called him, I asked him what the pension funds needed. I really listened.

Then I told him what I thought he should do. Van Scoy usually turned down my recommendations. But he knew I wasn't holding back; I was telling him what I really thought was best for him and Mellon, not what would enrich my bottom line.

This is a real lesson: don't avoid the hard things or the difficult people. I forced myself to call Van Scoy again and again. It was not easy for me to pitch him because he had forgotten more about bonds than I knew back then. But in winning Van Scoy's trust, I launched my career.

———

THE OLD MAGISTERIAL Morgan Stanley summoned clients to its Wall Street headquarters. In this new era, Morgan Stanley traveled to meet with clients on their turf. That's why Christy and I went to Pittsburgh so often.

We would get off the plane, pick up a Pontiac Firebird coupe in the Hertz lot, and head over to the Marriott Downtown. A swank high-rise built in the modern style of the 1960s, the hotel had spectacular views of the hilly city. It was a few blocks from the confluence of the famed Monongahela and Allegheny Rivers, which meet to form the head of the Ohio River, which flows into the Mississippi.

As a history major at Duke, I'd always had a soft spot for Pittsburgh. It had been around for centuries. Originally Fort Duquesne, it was fought over by the French and British in the French and Indian War. After the British won, it was renamed for William Pitt the Elder, once prime minister of Great Britain. Pittsburgh went on to become a frontier town known as the Gateway to the West for the pioneers who set out from there to settle a new country.

By 1972, Pittsburgh was a proud, gritty, industrial powerhouse. The steel mills that had built America and made Andrew Carnegie his colossal fortune in the nineteenth century were still smelting iron full throttle. The factories stamped out steel twenty-four hours a day, six days a week. Driving in from the airport, Christy and I saw huge, gray clouds billowing from the steel mills' smokestacks. The people were just as hardworking.

I took Christy to Pittsburgh so many times, she might as well have registered to vote in Pennsylvania rather than in New York. Christy and I had started going to Pittsburgh for my business, but we had become close friends with the Mellon asset managers and their families. Van Scoy had left Mellon, replaced by Jerry Elm and Sally Yeh. It was work, but it was fun.

After we dropped our bags at the Marriott, Christy and I beelined to Jerry's house. Then Jerry and I headed off to the liquor store, where I bought enough handles of Wolfschmidt vodka, Bacardi rum, Canadian Club whiskey, and Dewar's scotch to last a month, along with Kahlua, a couple of cases of beer, and Yago sangria and Chablis for the women. All that booze was Morgan Stanley's treat.

Jerry had a patio in his backyard, and some of my happiest memories from Christy's and my early days of marriage are of sitting out there or in the den, drinks in hand, just shooting the breeze. We would fly in live lobsters from Beal's Lobster Pier in Maine and gorge on seafood, T-bone steaks, corn, and baked potatoes. It would be Christy and me, Jerry and his family, Sally and her family, and the rest of the Mellon team.

The Steelers, the legendary football franchise that united Pittsburgh, was the most exciting team in the pros in those days. With superstars like Terry Bradshaw, Franco Harris, and Mean Joe Greene, the team was starting its run-up to its 1975 Super Bowl championship, and it was pretty much invincible. All these victories made seats at Three Rivers Stadium almost impossible to snag. But some Sundays, I'd score eight or ten tickets courtesy of my old Duke teammates who were now in the NFL and had come to play the Steelers. I'd take my Mellon friends. Then Christy and I would treat them and their wives to dinner. They loved it.

They also loved my bride. Christy was an unbelievable partner and asset—a hit with the guys, their wives, and their kids. They'd all joke, "John, you stay back in New York! We only want Christy to come!"

Christy was game. She went with the flow.

I have hard evidence of this.

Following the most flat-footed marriage proposal in the history of humankind, I topped myself with the honeymoon from hell. Our plan was to spend a week in San Andrés, a little island off the east coast of Nicaragua in the Caribbean. I had read a story about San Andrés in an American Express magazine.

The island looked remote, simple, and quiet—exactly what we were hoping for. We flew from Greensboro to Miami. After a long layover, we went on to San José, Costa Rica. Then we hopped on a small cargo plane, where we strapped ourselves onto bench seats for the last leg. From the tiny airport, we took a taxi to the hotel I had booked based on the magazine spread depicting romantic outdoor dining next to a sparkling azure sea. When we finally reached our destination, I sat in the back of the cab, dumbstruck. I almost didn't open the door.

The place was a dump. We decided to make the best of it and checked in. Then we rented motorbikes to explore San Andrés. That took five minutes. The beaches were deserted. We soon discovered why. The shoreline teemed with spiky, poisonous sea urchins, making it impossible to wade in. That night, we discovered that mice had eaten holes in our bedsheets. The next morning, we found ants in Christy's suitcase. At breakfast, we watched a scrawny, rabid-looking dog wander into the hotel kitchen and never come back out. "Don't look now," I said to Christy, "but I think I just saw a cockroach pull a switchblade on a rat and take its cheese. Let's get out of here!"

I bought two tickets on Condor airlines and we flew to Miami. I called a buddy and asked whether he knew of an available condo that a couple of honeymooning drifters could rent in Fort Lauderdale. "My dad has a place," my friend said. "Use it as long as you'd like. The guy at the front desk will give you the key."

Plan B sounded pretty great. That is, until we walked into the condo to screams: "Who's there? Who are you?" It just so happened that my friend's married uncle was there with a woman who wasn't his wife. I don't know which couple was more mortified.

We hatched Plan C. Walt Disney World had opened a year earlier. It was supposed to be even more amazing than Disneyland in California. So we drove our rental car to Orlando.

We tried to get into the Contemporary Hotel, the brand-new, space-agey resort on the Disney World property that had a monorail zipping straight to the Magic Kingdom through its lobby concourse. It was sold out. We had to settle for a room at a hotel about four miles outside of the park. Then I had a brain flash. "Hey, Christy," I said, "let's call your parents and see if they want to come down. They planned and paid for that beautiful wedding. They deserve a vacation!"

Dr. and Mrs. King flew down from Greensboro. The four of us hammed it up with Minnie and Mickey and rode through the Small World tunnel. We swam in the hotel pool and went out to eat at a restaurant encircled by tiki torches. Christy's mother was delightful, and her father lightened up.

As I said, Christy was game. When we got home to New York City, I picked her up and carried her in my arms across the threshold of our new one-bedroom apartment in the same Kips Bay building I'd been living in since 1968.

But there was an underlying reason Christy was such a good sport about Pittsburgh. She was having a hard time adjusting to living in

New York. And we were just getting to know each other. No sooner had we gotten engaged than Christy had moved back to Greensboro to plan the wedding.

It was a difficult first year. In trying to establish the patterns of our life together, we battled over monumental issues. Like butter.

I expected the butter to be kept in the refrigerator, chilled. That's what my mother did. Christy liked it soft, at room temperature. She expected it to be kept on the counter so that it was easy to spread on toast. The Kings—a family of seven—easily went through a stick just at breakfast. Because there were just two of us, the butter went into the fridge.

Navigating our social life was much tougher. Christy was plunged into my established circle of friends. Most of them worked on Wall Street or were clients. They were older and had been married for a while. Some had kids. These were sophisticated New Yorkers who had lived, worked, and traveled all over the world. Our trip to Lake Tahoe was Christy's first foray to the West Coast. When her family did travel, they attached a little trailer to their station wagon.

I'd call her up and say, "Hey, honey! We've been invited to dinner at La Côte Basque with so-and-so. I'll pick you up at seven. You'll love them!" She would hang up the phone and immediately go into a funk; depressed, nervous, on edge. *What am I going to say to these people?* she would think. *I don't know them. I'm not going to measure up.*

When I'd get home, excited to go out and show off my beautiful bride, she'd be in the bedroom, subdued. "What's the matter?" I'd say as I sat down to switch out my wing tips for loafers.

"I don't want to go. I have nothing in common with them, John."

"Christy, fuck my friends! I didn't marry my friends, I married you. If they don't like you, fuck 'em, but they're going to love you!" It wasn't that Christy was an introvert; she just allowed herself to be intimidated by people who weren't nearly as smart and special as she was.

Honesty had been the key to my relationship with Dick Van Scoy. Here the key was persistence. Some nights when we got into bed, I sensed that Christy was upset. "What's the matter?" I'd ask.

"Nothing."

"Something's wrong. Tell me what's wrong."

"Nothing."

I'd get close, put my head next to hers on the pillow, look into her eyes, and say, "We are not going to sleep until you tell me what's wrong."

Christy had grown up in a family that didn't allow her to share her thoughts or express her emotions. She was expected to present an impassive facade, no matter what. She had almost no experience articulating what she wanted or didn't want. I held nothing back, sometimes to a fault. Whether at work or at home, I wanted to know what other people were thinking and feeling, especially my wife. "We're not going to sleep until we talk," I would say. "Talk to me. Talk to me."

Finally, Christy would confess that *I* was the problem! That I had been brusque, even rude, to her. I had to learn that I had to leave the voice and manner I used on the trading floor at the front door of our apartment. Compounding the hurt, there were many days in the early months of our marriage that I was the only person Christy talked to. It was a conundrum for her: she was deeply in love but achingly lonely.

By the time our first anniversary rolled around on November 11, 1973, Christy had become friends with a lot of our neighbors at Kips Bay Plaza, and our marriage had gone through a big growth spurt. We learned the importance of communication—a tool we've relied on ever since, but it's not always easy. To really communicate, I've learned it requires putting aside your ego and really hearing what the other person is saying, not just waiting for your turn to speak.

———————

MELLON WASN'T MY only big account. I had landed U.S. Trust. The asset manager ran a huge portfolio—the New York State employees' pension. A good guy, he was an ex-Marine who had fought in World War II. He was a huge fan of the Fighting Irish of Notre Dame.

I had been at Morgan Stanley for about a year when I took him out to lunch at a restaurant near Wall Street called Chez Yvonne. I say "lunch," but what I remember are the martinis—ice-cold gin, a splash of dry vermouth, and two olives.

We sat down at noon, and the asset manager promptly ordered a cocktail. Polishing it off, he immediately called for another. The bartender at Chez Yvonne kept the drinks coming as the "meal" went on for three or four hours. We drank. We talked, we bullshitted about college football, with the client yanking my chain about Duke. I don't know how many martinis he consumed, but I must have had a minimum of three and maybe four or five silver bullets just trying to keep up.

Yes, this was a weekday at noon. Times were different then.

If I wanted to get close to the client, I couldn't sit there and sip ginger ale while he pounded down one martini after another. My credo: if the client liked to drink, I liked to drink. But when dealing with clients, you also have to know where to draw the line.

Finally, the check paid, I poured myself out of Chez Yvonne and into a taxi. Remembering through a fog of gin my Strega lunch, I knew I shouldn't go back to the office.

I opened the door to our apartment, staggered in, and said to Christy, "I am so fucking drunk!" I lay down on the parquet floor, closed my eyes, and didn't move for the next eight hours. Christy told me later that at one point she took a mirror and put it under my nose to see if I was still alive.

I DIDN'T DO all my business out of town or at drunken lunches. I often worked on the trading floor. The first thing I would do every morning was talk to the traders. "What are your positions? What are you trying to accomplish?" I listened to their goals. Did they have bonds they needed to move?

Next, I called my clients. "What are you thinking today? Do you have cash you want to invest? Do you need to raise money?" I was the conduit between the two groups.

Here's one of my greatest triumphs: after wooing Chase Manhattan for a long time, Morgan Stanley finally convinced the commercial bank to give us a big piece of business. We got an order to raise money by selling five-year-maturity certificates of deposit (CDs). We were all excited. Because it was my job to alert clients to any new investment opportunity, I immediately called Jerry Elm. "We just priced $100 million in CDs for Chase Manhattan," I said when he picked up. "Any interest?"

"Hang on, let me look at our investment sheet," Jerry said. This was a list of the money Mellon Bank wanted to put to work. Usually when I made a call like this, Jerry would say, "John, we're fully invested. We're going to pass."

I waited, tapping a pen against the metal desk. He had me on hold longer than usual. Finally, Jerry got back on the line. "John," he said, "it's your lucky day! We've got huge liquidity. Give me $20 million worth of CDs."

I was floored. This was the biggest sale of my career—by a multiple of ten.

You would have thought the first thing I'd do was high-five the guy sitting next to me.

I didn't. In those days, there was a lot of camaraderie on the trading floor, but no high-fiving. In fact, that hadn't yet become a thing. It didn't start until the late 1970s, when athletes began slapping each other's raised palms after a great play. Before high-fiving came into vogue, we were more low-key. Sometimes after a sale Dick came into the glass trading room. "That was a great trade, John," he would say, patting me on the back. These compliments always meant a lot.

But the Jerry Elm/Chase Manhattan CD sale was out of the ordinary. When Dick walked onto the trading floor that day, a dozen other managing directors were right behind him. This was a first. Some had never actually entered the trading room. They gathered around me. "Well done! Excellent!" they exclaimed. That sale marked me as an up-and-comer.

SOME PEOPLE PICK up salesmanship immediately, but not everyone is cut out for it. I think you can be taught to be a *better* salesperson, but to be good at it, some traits are nonnegotiable. You have to be comfortable talking with strangers. You have to have the confidence to speak up. You have to have the ability to get people on your side. The most important characteristic: you have to like people and show a genuine interest in them.

When I meet a stranger, I introduce myself. I start with simple questions: Do you have a family? How long have you been working here? Where did you go to school? What I'm talking about is not shock and awe. I'm making conversation using tried-and-true topics just to get people to open up. How old are your kids? Where do you go on vacation? Over time, I get a little more personal. You have to get to know people. How do you get to know people? You engage with them. You show interest. You look beyond the job they're doing at the moment and talk to them as one person to another. I might ask someone working at a restaurant or a taxi driver, how's business? Do you like what you do?

I'm lucky. I had no problem making a cold call. When I was given a new account, I would get the client on the phone and say, "I'm John Mack from Morgan Stanley. Your account was assigned to me. I'd like to come and introduce myself to see what your goals are and how I can help."

I tailored what I was offering to my audience. At the first meeting, I showed the client boilerplate bonds—straightforward, conservative offerings. Over time, I offered them more exotic bonds. They may not buy what you're selling. You keep trying. You never give up. You could say that about anything in life.

But clients can be difficult. Very difficult.

There was an organization for teachers' pension funds. Every year this group held a convention for the state employees in charge of handling the funds. They came from all fifty states, plus Washington, DC. It was a huge boondoggle—they could bring their wives and children. Every major investment firm sent representatives. The reason to attend this convention was to build relationships as you wined and dined the state employees. I wanted to make sure that if the manager of the Ohio pension fund had $50 million to invest, he immediately thought of John Mack and Morgan Stanley. Salomon Brothers, known as the Bond Gurus of Wall Street, dominated the pension market at the time, and it was my greatest ambition to elbow them out of the way.

I attended the convention in 1974, when it was in Hawaii. Back then, a trip to Hawaii was out of reach for most Americans. It was expensive and exotic, and it took a long time to get there. Christy—pregnant with our first child, Stephen—came along. We were real partners. She worked just as hard as I did to make sure everybody was having fun.

I chartered a plane to fly some of the conventioneers and their families to five of the main Hawaiian Islands. When we refueled on Kauai, this guy from the state of Georgia teachers' fund walked over to me with his kid. "My son here wants a pack of Nabs," he drawled, handing me a cellophane sleeve of bright orange crackers filled with peanut butter. "I'd like you to pay for them."

And I did. As a salesman, I was at the beck and call of the client. I understood that keeping them happy was Job One. Well, within reason.

The worst moment came on the final leg of the flight back to Honolulu. Exhausted, Christy and I were sitting in front, counting down the seconds until we could escape from these pension managers.

Suddenly I sensed a shadow looming over me.

"Vinny is throwing up," a nasal voice said.

I looked up at this guy sporting a garish Hawaiian shirt and a puka-shell necklace staring down at me.

"What?" I said.

"Vinny is throwing up," he repeated.

"Well, what do you want me to do about it?" I snapped. "Tell him to grab an airsick bag. That's what they're there for."

The lesson here: you're not going to love every client, and sometimes there is no gratitude. But the convention paid off, even though I drew the line at cleaning up the vomit. My Hawaiian tan hadn't faded when the phone rang on the trading floor.

"For you, Mr. Mack," the assistant said.

It was a headhunter. At this point in my career, I was getting a lot of these calls. But this time it was from the biggest hitter, Salomon Brothers. Between the asset manager at U.S. Trust and Jerry Elm at Mellon, I had really been slicing into Salomon's territory. I realized it was no coincidence that at the convention an overly friendly Salomon bond manager had insisted on buying me a mai tai at the bar of the famous pink Royal Hawaiian hotel. He wouldn't take no for an answer.

"Salomon Brothers is very interested in you," the headhunter said. "Can I set up a meeting?"

I politely declined. I wasn't going anywhere.

A year later, something happened that still makes me laugh out loud. I had become friends with a man named George Poliszczuk, who ran the Investment Department at Mellon Bank. He had a thick Eastern European accent and an amazing backstory. He had fled Ukraine as a teenager during World War II and eventually wound up in Pittsburgh. He was as straitlaced as they come.

George walked onto the enormous Salomon Brothers trading floor in New York. He was looking for Jackie Kugler. Kugler, who had started at Salomon in 1957, was the long-reigning king of bonds. He covered Bankers Trust, Mellon Bank, all the big ones. He was a bulldog.

"Hey, Jackie!" George boomed. No one on the trading floor could miss hearing him. "How does it feel to be number two?

"And you know who's number one?

"John Mack!"

CHAPTER SEVEN

W ith one backhand stroke, I swept off papers, coffee cups, pens, staplers, telephones, ashtrays, cigarette butts—you name it. All of it crashed to the floor. There were four desks arranged in the shape of a cross—a turret, we called it. I cleared each desk with the same destructive force.

Everyone on the trading floor stopped to stare at me. Silence, except for the bleating of a phone off the hook lying on the floor.

It was the late 1970s. I had moved up from salesman to sales manager. Standing on the trading floor on my first day, I addressed my new team. "At all times," I told them, "I want at least one of the four of you manning the turret. No exceptions, no excuses, no bathroom breaks. From the second the market opens to the second it closes, I want someone to answer the phones and be ready to execute transactions."

I wasn't an ogre. I understood that people had to deposit their paychecks, go to the dentist, get something to eat during business hours. But that didn't change my rule: the sales desk always had to be covered. There were four intelligent people. They could figure it out.

Yet one afternoon I walked in to find everything perfectly in place—everything, that is, except the people. My team's turret was empty. Unanswered phones were jangling. This was not the "first-class business in a first-class way"—Morgan Stanley's ethos—I had vowed to deliver to clients.

Today, if you want to reach someone, there are multiple ways to do it. But back in the 1970s, there were no pagers, no cell phones, no email, no texts. We had three methods of communicating: letters, landlines, and in person. Mail was too slow. So we were either on the phone with clients or meeting with them. Voice mail was in limited use, but I can't think of a single situation where it would be okay to send a client's call to a recording. I believe that to this day. The client relationship is fragile. It has to be constantly watched over and nurtured. Rival salespeople from other firms circle, hawklike, ready to snatch up any opportunity. An unanswered call loses business.

The entire foundation of sales and trading is managing the flow of inquiries and turning them into transactions. That's why if Jerry Elm at Mellon Bank or any other client called the trading floor, a human being had to answer the phone. Why not just hire a secretary to pick up the phones? Because a secretary hadn't passed the Series 7 exams and couldn't move money.

I shoved everything off the turret. Then I planted myself amid the rubble, arms crossed. Waiting.

I still remember how shell-shocked the guilty salesman looked when he returned. "I was just running a quick errand, John," he stammered. Nor can I forget the glares the other three salespeople cast at the designated holding-down-the-fort guy as they picked up their stuff.

I said nothing. I didn't have to.

I never found the turret unmanned again.

Looking back now, I'm torn. On the one hand, I had made myself clear. I wasn't going to allow Morgan Stanley to be harmed by anyone, least of all by some kid right out of college who wanted to flirt with someone down the hall. I could have just called out my salespeople when they got back to their desks, but that wouldn't have had the same impact. Unpredictability was my secret weapon. I never wanted my underlings to think they could anticipate what I was going to do next. Keeping people off-balance sharpened them up.

On the other hand, I had punished four salespeople for a mistake only one had made.

None of the salespeople ever confronted me, demanding, "Why'd you do that?" But I got wind of their anger, sense of injustice, and fear.

And they were right. You don't do that.

That's not how you manage people.

TOO OFTEN BUSINESSES, Wall Street included, promote the biggest moneymakers. But being the best producer doesn't mean you'll be the best manager. Or even a halfway decent one. Promoting people into positions they can't handle happens so often, there's a name for it: the Peter Principle. But whether or not they'll be good at the new job, few people can resist the temptation of a bigger title, a fatter paycheck, and more power.

I loved selling, and George Poliszczuk had told the Street that I was the best. If I had remained in sales, I would have made a boatload of money on commissions. But I wanted more: I wanted to rise at Morgan Stanley. I wanted to prove that I could manage and motivate a team. Today sales is a path to becoming a managing director at Morgan Stanley, but back then you had to have management experience to get the nod. When my immediate boss, Damon Mezzacappa, was promoted, I took his place as sales manager. At first I kept my best accounts, including Mellon and U.S. Trust, but I eventually handed them off to my team.

But while selling came naturally to me, managing people did not.

I had to learn to manage myself first.

In a way, I started with a deficit as a manager. I intimidated a lot of people before I even opened my mouth. Since my football days at Duke, I've always been a big, strong guy. I'm six foot one, and in those days I weighed 220 pounds. I have thick black eyebrows that can make me look angry even when I'm not. And I have a resting scowl face. When I got mad, I also used to do this thing with my right hand where I made a fist and pressed my thumb onto my index finger. I didn't even think about it. But Christy, who saw it for the first time when someone irked me at our rehearsal dinner, told me it was scary, even threatening.

The trading floor is filled with off-the-scale intense types like me. Add to that the fact that large amounts of money are in play and decisions have to be made in split seconds. The result is a boiling cauldron of stress. But my emotional thermometer hit scald faster than most people's. I didn't know how to control my temper.

Granted, keeping a bunch of hotshot salespeople in line wasn't easy. You hear the words "prima donna" and you think of a movie star or a pop star. You don't think it applies to someone in a pin-striped suit.

There you're wrong.

Some salespeople developed a close relationship with a big client, and they thought this made them untouchable. They were making a lot of money, so they didn't bother to cultivate their smaller accounts. They were satisfied, but I wasn't.

"You're tying up accounts that should be producing a lot more!" I told them.

Expecting and demanding more was my job.

The problem was that when people told me they hadn't made such-and-such a sale, I called them out in front of the whole trading floor. I also had only one way of doing things: my way. I had a blueprint in my mind of how salespeople should do their jobs, and I accepted no deviation.

I got my comeuppance.

———

EVERY MORNING, MY eyes darted from the clock to the empty chair at one of the turrets. It was always the same desk. It was supposed to be occupied by a top recruit fresh out of Columbia Business School, Joanne de Asis. 7:35, 7:40, 7:45, 7:50. Alternating between irritation and concern, I couldn't concentrate. *Where is she? Did she have an accident? Is she okay?* New York wasn't the safest city in 1977. Finally, she rushed in at 7:57, apologizing once again for not being able to hail a cab.

One of my nonnegotiable demands is punctuality. I remember making it clear to her that the workday started at 7:30 sharp. (She does not recall this.) But Joanne's tardiness continued.

A few days before Christmas, I told Joanne I'd like to speak with her off the trading floor. I didn't have an office back then. We sat down in a small conference room. "You're a nice person, Joanne," I told her. "But you're not working out. I'm going to North Carolina for the holidays. I'll need your seat when I get back."

I was quick, firm, and polite. Joanne's face crumpled as my words hit their target. Fired.

When I returned to the office on January 2, however, there sat Joanne, in her seat, early for once. I marched straight to Dick's office to find out what was going on. "You're not firing her, John," he told me matter-of-factly. "We're giving her a second chance. You need to mentor her."

While I was on vacation, Joanne had clearly gone around me. I was angry but, unusual for me, I held my tongue. I walked back to the trading floor and over to Joanne's desk. "I'm moving you," I said, not bothering with hello. "You're sitting next to me now." If I couldn't get rid of her, I was determined to keep my eyes—and ears—trained on her. I put Joanne at my turret with my sales assistant and Peter Karches, another Columbia MBA. Brooklyn-born, Peter had supported himself as a waiter when he was an undergrad at Georgetown University. More blue-collar than blue-blood, he shared my scorched-earth approach. One of the reasons I immediately took to Peter was that holding back was not in his DNA. He told me exactly what he thought. And he was ruthlessly efficient. When I asked Peter to do something, he wrote it down on his yellow legal pad. By the end of the day, there was a checkmark next to it. No questions asked. No hand-holding needed. I never had to think about it again.

To my annoyance, I noticed that Joanne was always on the phone chatting away in languages I didn't understand. Peter and I periodically glanced at each other. "Who the hell is she talking to?" he mouthed to me.

Then I looked at the sales ledger. To my astonishment, Joanne was doing a brisk business selling bonds to Portuguese and Spanish banks in the United States. This was a lucrative niche that no one else on my team even knew about, much less tapped. She was fluent in Spanish, Portuguese, and Tagalog, the language of the Philippines, where she grew up. Sometimes I also recognized French.

I remember sitting around in a semicircle at our daily 8:00 a.m. sales meeting. I was pushing the team to sell Venezuela Eights of '88—eight-year Venezuelan government bonds that paid 8 percent interest. "Who the fuck wants to buy Venezuelan bonds?" one salesperson blurted out. "Venezuela? Nobody even goes there on vacation!"

The next morning, Joanne took her seat just as our meeting began. "John, the Central Bank of Malaysia will buy the Venezuela Eights of '88 at full price," she announced.

Incredulous, I asked, "I give up. How in the world did you do that?"

"I telephoned Mr. Ramly bin Ahmad, the deputy governor of Bank Negara Malaysia, at eight o'clock last night—nine a.m. on Tuesday, their time. They're thirteen hours ahead of New York, you know. I said to him, 'Sir, there's oil in Venezuela, just like in Malaysia. The bonds are rated AAA.'

"I didn't have to say any more. Malaysia has *a lot* of money. Its economy is growing very fast."

She gave me, Peter, and the other salespeople a satisfied smile.

Joanne was making so many client calls to Southeast Asia at night that soon Morgan Stanley installed a dedicated phone line in her apartment. Next, to accommodate her increasing international client trips, we had to switch travel agencies—the agent we used had never heard of Kuala Lumpur and had no clue what airline flew there. Back then, you couldn't just say, "Siri, who flies to the capital of Malaysia?"

Joanne made me realize that not everyone on my sales team had to be just like me. She widened my lens as a manager. When I first supervised her, I failed to see that Joanne had unique skills. Dick had been right to keep her. Watching her succeed made me realize that it was *my* job to help amplify *her* talents.

I had other lessons to learn. Once, when I was looking for an assistant, I set up an interview with a candidate. As we had agreed on the phone, the woman came to Morgan Stanley's headquarters in the Exxon Building at 1:00 p.m. I was putting out a dozen fires on the trading floor. We had a huge bond issue that day, and the salespeople needed to move them. I had completely forgotten about the appointment. When the prospective assistant arrived, I told the receptionist to put her on the phone. "Listen, I can't see you today," I said, my annoyance at the disruption blasting through the line. "You have to come back some other time."

I hung up.

That afternoon, my phone rang. When I answered, I heard the deep voice that had made admirals quake. LBJ's onetime undersecretary of the Navy—a former World War II naval officer—was on the other end. "John, I got an angry call from Philippa Pierce,"* Bob Baldwin said.

I searched my memory, wondering, *Who the hell is Philippa Pierce?*

Bob read my mind. "The young lady you were supposed to interview at one o'clock today. She took her lunch hour to come see you. She said you were a no-show, John. She said you were rude. She said you didn't apologize or give her an explanation for canceling. Listen, I understand that business can get hairy on the trading floor. She's a family friend, John. But that's not the point. You can't treat people that way."

I called Philippa Pierce, explained why I had canceled, and apologized. I brought her back in for an interview a few days later. I didn't hire her, but she wound up with another job at the firm.

Bob reminded me that I'm no better than anyone else, that you've got to treat everyone with respect, no matter who they are.

My father would never have treated anyone the way I treated Philippa Pierce.

One incident illustrates what kind of man he was. He had stopped by to say hello to J. P. Cavin, a friend who owned the funeral home in

---

* Philippa Pierce is a pseudonym.

Mooresville, and noticed a casket ready for burial with no flowers on top. "Where are the flowers for that casket, J. P.?" he asked.

"That family doesn't have any money," Cavin said. "They can barely pay for the pine box, Charlie."

"I want them to have flowers," my dad insisted, handing Cavin a $20 bill. "From now on, if a family can't buy flowers, I want to know. I'll pay for them."

That was Charlie Mack. I learned compassion from him.

It bothered me that I had forgotten my father's example. Caught up in the urgency of the moment and my intense desire to succeed at Morgan Stanley, I had abandoned everything else. That included courtesy and consideration for other people's time and feelings. I was taking out my stress on Philippa.

Pressure was and is a constant on Wall Street. And the higher I rose, the more stress I would encounter. Bob was right. You can't be dismissive of people. You can't excuse lashing out just because you're under the gun. This doesn't apply only to Wall Street.

———

BOB BALDWIN WASN'T the only superior to teach me a lesson. I was also slapped down by others, usually with good reason.

In 1977, a partner named James Lewis, who was on a recruiting trip at his alma mater, the University of Chicago Business School, invited a soon-to-be graduate named Joe Hill to New York for a follow-up interview. The day he came to town I interviewed Joe, a razor-sharp Texan. I offered him a job on the spot. "How much are you planning to pay me?" Joe asked.

I felt that people should snap up a Morgan Stanley job regardless of the salary. "Between zero and a million dollars," I replied. "After that question, it's trending toward zero."

Joe came right back at me: "I trust you. I accept."

He returned to Chicago, packed up his stuff, and moved to New York ready to start work on the trading floor. But on his first day he ran into a buzz saw—one I had accidentally set up and plugged in.

"Let me show you where things are," I told Joe. I could tell he was pumped: he was looking sharp in a three-piece suit and shined wing tips, sporting a crisp haircut. First I introduced Joe to Luis Mendez, the head of Trading.

A few months earlier, Luis and I had flown out to Los Angeles to see one of my clients, Security Pacific Bank. We were meeting in a conference room when the client began to make fun of Luis's Cuban accent. I reached across the table and grabbed the guy by the collar. "If you want to make fun of anyone," I hissed at him, "make fun of me." That shut him up. Sometimes my size and my temper were assets.

Now, holding a lit cigar in one hand, Luis graciously extended the other hand to Joe. "So glad to have you here," he said.

Next stop: Damon Mezzacappa, the head of Sales. "Who is this fucking guy?" he shouted at me, pointing to Joe.

"I'm a new salesman," Joe said. "John hired me."

"I don't know how in the hell you got hired without me seeing you first," Damon spat. "You two," he said, jerking his thumb over his shoulder. "Into my office. Now." Suddenly I remembered that Damon had been out of the office the day I offered Joe a job.

We followed Damon and sat down. He grabbed a beer from his mini fridge, popped the ring tab, took a gulp, put his feet up on his desk, crossed them, and exhaled. "All right," he said. "So what the fuck are you going to do here? Do you have any clue whatsoever? What did Mack tell you?"

Joe looked my way. I felt a bead of sweat form at my hairline. It started to trickle down. "I have no clue," Joe said. "But whatever it is you do, I want to do it. I want to drink beer at ten a.m."

"Get out of here, you two," Damon said. "Mack, I want you back here in ten minutes to talk about Joe."

As we walked away, I turned to Joe. "You know what? I don't know if that was the stupidest thing or the ballsiest thing I've ever seen anybody do, but I liked it."

It's true. I like ballsy. But when I returned to Damon's office, I realized I'd been too ballsy. I should never have hired Joe without Damon's sign-off. It's not that I didn't have hiring and firing responsibilities, but I still reported to Damon. It was a matter of courtesy. I would go ballistic if anyone ever tried that with me. He had every right to veto my offer to Joe, leaving him jobless in New York.

I apologized. "He can stay," Damon said. "But don't ever pull a stunt like that again."

Joe turned out to be every bit the producer I thought he could be. Within a year, he landed a monster account no one had ever heard of: the MacArthur Foundation. With a billion dollars in assets from the estate of John D. MacArthur, a real estate and insurance magnate who had just died, it was loaded with cash. The foundation would become famous for awarding the MacArthur Fellowships—aka Genius Grants. The person in charge of investments, a guy named Norbert, was buying millions in preferred stocks from Joe, who was delirious. He kept repeating, "This is like gold, I've found gold!" Joe did so well, we sent him back to Chicago, where he put Morgan Stanley's Bond Department on the map.

The Joe Hill–Damon Mezzacappa imbroglio was a minor transgression—nothing compared to the time I blew up at Dick Fisher on the trading floor. Now, I can't remember what set me off, but I lost control. I started shouting at him in front of a group of people. The fact that he didn't fire me on the spot is an example of how Dick kept *his* emotions in check. During the twenty-five years we worked together, I never once saw him lose his cool.

Dick did not ignore my bad behavior. He summoned me into his office, looked me in the eye, and said coldly, "You were out of line. I like hearing what you think, and I encourage you to speak up, John. I believe you have a chance at a great career here at Morgan Stanley. But do not *ever* shout at me in public again." Then Dick picked up the phone and made a call, gesturing for me to leave.

I pride myself on never making the same mistake twice. I never yelled at Dick in public again. But I continued to speak my mind with him.

When I tell people what I think, it can be uncomfortable, harsh, painful—for me and for them. But honesty and directness define who I am. And I knew that Dick appreciated these traits in me. He often said, "I can always trust John to tell me the truth."

My early years as a manager were sometimes rocky. I realized I had to develop more self-control. I learned that if people made mistakes— and they did—I needed to pull them aside and talk to them one-on-one, not in front of people.

Let me be clear: I still told people the truth. I still did it loudly.

I just did it in my office or theirs, with the door closed.

CHAPTER EIGHT

I admit it: occasionally as a new manager, I missed my old life. I missed my clients. I missed the rush of selling. I missed shooting the breeze on the phone. I had given the Mellon account to one of my top salespeople, Kirk Materne, who grew up in Richmond, Virginia, and came to Morgan Stanley straight from Virginia Military Institute. He was a born southern teller of tall tales. I got wistful hearing Kirk on the phone talking bonds and bourbon with Jerry Elm. Sometimes managing seemed more about solving my team's personnel problems than doing business.

But this nostalgia never lasted long. I let nothing distract me from my overriding goal: to build the strongest, most cohesive, and most productive sales team on Wall Street.

Boosting my team's confidence and sales skills was Job One. I often accompanied my people on client visits in town and around the country. Afterward, I critiqued their performance. I never soft-soaped my employees. Almost all of them had trouble with closing: the moment you ask the client directly for the buy. I tried to explain when and how you do it.

But lectures went only so far. I know I'm a talker, but I tried to become a listener. I asked a lot of questions: What do you need? What does your client need? What's keeping you from doing more business? How can I help you?

Job Two was creating an environment where people felt comfortable telling me what they thought of *my* performance. It wasn't enough to tell others the truth; I wanted to hear the truth from them. Otherwise, I wouldn't improve as a manager. I said, "When you come into my office, as long as you shut the door, you can tell me I'm stupid. You can tell me I'm the worst person you've ever worked for. You can tell me you hate me. You can tell me my ideas are shit. I don't care; as long as you say it to my face in my office, I won't hold any grudges."

And I didn't. I think a lot of problems in management come from not opening yourself up to criticism. Telling bosses the unvarnished truth about how they're doing is counterintuitive. Most people won't say anything, for fear of repercussions. I wanted to change that. I really worked on getting my team to give me genuine feedback.

I didn't want to hear only what they thought about me; I wanted to know what they thought about the business. Morgan Stanley poured resources into hiring the very best people. But this talent was squandered if we muzzled them. I wanted my team to feel confident about speaking up in meetings. If everyone just sits around nodding and agreeing with me, that's a shitty meeting. "I don't want sheep," I told them. "I don't have all the answers. That's why we hired you. You're smart people. You see things that I don't see. Tell me."

Where did they think the markets were heading? Why was such-and-such a bond issue tanking? I wasn't blinded by the illusion that I was the smartest guy in the room. I often asked the newest member of the group to talk first because that person had a fresh perspective.

Something I knew from my own experience: conflict was a way of life on the trading floor. There's an inherent tension between salespeople and traders. It's baked in. People in sales want to give their clients the best deal, whereas it's the traders' job to protect and manage the firm's capital. To my mind, traders could be overly cautious, often stubbornly refusing to take a risk that my team needed to make a sale. I had to fight for the salespeople. Every day was a battle. As their manager, I defended the fort—I supplied the salespeople with the mental armor they needed to return victorious.

I'd inherited some people and hired others. There were Ivy Leaguers who tripped over their tongues bragging about where they'd gone to college. They might speak three or four languages but didn't have a clue that their arrogance alienated clients. Some were frat-house charm balls who needed a motivating kick in the ass. Still others craved recognition. I had grown up in a family that didn't hand out compliments. I learned to praise people, sometimes one-on-one and sometimes on the trading floor or in a meeting.

Besides understanding my salespeople as individuals, I had another task. I had to build esprit de corps, to take disparate personalities and shape them into a team.

I am an incorrigible prankster. I have been planning and playing jokes on people since elementary school, when I shorted my brother Frank's bedsheets in the bedroom we shared at home. If I'm a passenger in your car, I view every stop sign and stoplight as a chance to sneak your car's transmission into neutral. Every closet offers an opportunity to jump out of it. Every desk is a place to hide under.

One Saturday morning, I asked the groundskeeper at the Blind Brook Club in Purchase, New York, where I played golf, for a bag of sand. The next afternoon I went to the office and poured sand into my team members' desk drawers, all the way up to the rim. First thing Monday morning, an early bird opened his drawer. "What the hell?" he shouted. "Aw fuck!" Like dominoes, the scenario played out one after another as people showed up at work. When they saw that everyone was a victim, the trading floor erupted into howls of laughter. "Just another day at the beach!" I told them. This was me, trying to turn the release valve on the furnace that is the trading floor. There were a lot of smashed phones and more than a few thrown chairs.

I innately grasped that teasing people helps put things in perspective. There was one salesperson who brushed his teeth, then flossed and gargled meticulously every day after lunch. When he emerged from the men's room, we all got a whiff of his minty breath. When he thought no one was looking, he'd periodically spray Binaca. He popped Tic Tacs all day long.

We couldn't resist.

One afternoon when he was getting lunch, we unscrewed the handset on his phone, stuffed a piece of salmon sushi into the mouthpiece, and screwed it back on. Three days later, he was sitting there, breathing into his hand. You could just tell he was worried sick. *Is it me?* He went to the bathroom every three minutes to brush. Finally, during one of these breath-freshening trips, we removed the now-decayed fish. Eventually, before the guy wore off his tooth enamel, we let him in on our shenanigans. He laughed the hardest of all.

My coworkers weren't my only victims. Not long after Stephen was born, Christy and I signed up to take a Chinese cooking class so we could spend time together—a sort of date night. Along with three other couples, we met at the teacher's apartment on the Upper West Side. It was a hoot. When I was chopping raw meat with a cleaver, I would flip it over to the dull side. Then I would slam the cleaver down and start screaming about my hand.

I did it just to shake everyone up. I had a great time. But after

I disrupted class after class, I suspected the teacher wanted to chop me up.

BY NOW, CHRISTY and I had three kids under the age of five: Stephen was born in September 1974; John in December 1976; and our newborn, Jenna, in October 1978. We chose the name Stephen because it was one that Christy and I both liked, and we named John to honor my grandfather. Jenna is named for my great-grandmother, who raised my mother in Lebanon.

About a month after Jenna arrived, Dick called me. "Could you come downstairs to Bill Black's office?" When I walked in, there stood the two men who had recruited me. "Congratulations, John," Dick said in his understated way. "We'd like to invite you to become a Morgan Stanley partner." He clasped me on the shoulder, and Bill shook my hand. I had advanced quickly at Morgan Stanley. I made vice president in 1976 and principal just a year later, so this promotion wasn't a complete surprise. But that didn't lessen the pride I felt. Mooresville is a long way from Morgan Stanley. Other than marrying Christy and having our kids, this was the most meaningful event of my life up to then.

CHAPTER NINE

I was so excited when I opened up the little brass mailbox in the lobby of my Kips Bay apartment building. Inside was my first passport—its green cover stiff, its twenty-four pages pristine. It was 1970. Gripping it as I took the elevator to my studio apartment on the nineteenth floor, I thought about how much promise and adventure this little booklet held. I had gone to the post office near Smith Barney to apply for it. I was twenty-five years old, and I was getting ready to visit Lebanon with my cousin Mitchell. Now, a decade and a half later, I had a new passport, and every page was covered in entry and exit stamps and stickers. It was so full, I had to ask the passport office to add pages.

From my first months at the firm in 1972, I had traveled a lot for Morgan Stanley. But it was always domestic—Albany, Boston, Tallahassee and Jacksonville, Pittsburgh, Columbus, Los Angeles, Honolulu, and Deadhorse, Alaska. By 1979, I had also started taking international trips. Wall Street now reached far beyond the United States' borders.

Frank Petito, Morgan Stanley's chairman from 1973 to 1979, had had the vision to see opportunities for Morgan Stanley abroad. Maybe his worldly view came from the fact that his parents had immigrated from Italy. As early as 1966, Petito had negotiated a $600 million deal with Banca d'Italia. Another advocate for global expansion was Bill Black. His father, Eugene Black, had been the president of the World Bank from 1949 to 1962.

Morgan Stanley wasn't alone in its international push. Every investment bank was angling for business in other countries. American pension funds and institutional investors were becoming much more sophisticated. If the payout was higher, they chose a UK bond over a US bond. Or a bond out of Hong Kong. The marketplace had gone global.

Two forces were driving this change: deregulation and technology. Here's an example: in 1970, when Mitchell and I were visiting my mother's sister in Beirut, I asked my aunt Marie, "How long has it been since you talked to my mom?"

She looked at me like I had suggested a quick trip to Saturn. "Johnnie, I cannot talk to Alice in America. I write her letters."

I picked up the phone and dialed the operator, who then put through the long-distance call to Mooresville collect. "Hi, Mom, it's Johnnie. Yep, everything's fine. Yep, I know this is expensive. Don't worry, I'll take care of the cost. Hold on, I have someone here who wants to talk to you." I handed the receiver to my aunt. "*Marhabaan?*" Aunt Marie said tentatively—Arabic for hello. As soon as she heard my mother's voice, my aunt broke into a huge smile. No translation necessary.

Back then, most people would never simply call another country unless it was a life-or-death emergency. But phone technology changed rapidly in the 1970s because of transatlantic and transpacific cables. The costs dropped, and the quality soared.

Morgan Stanley bankers could now conduct business in real time by phone around the globe.

Equally important was the telex machine, which received electronic messages and typed them out automatically at a brisk pace, with a loud, clacking *ch-ch-ch* sound to match. Consisting of a keyboard and a roll of paper—like a self-typing typewriter (and later, a self-typing computer)—they allowed businesses to communicate with one another anywhere in the world. In the early 1980s, fax machines, which made transmitting documents as easy as making a photocopy, replaced telex machines.

There was also deregulation. Nations began to open their previously walled-off financial markets to foreign investors. Gradually, these individual markets became connected. Although I didn't realize it at the time, this was a revolution. Globalization was the future. It would transform the financial services business.

ON MY FIRST trip to Japan in 1980, I didn't know what to expect. Although I had flown first-class on Pan Am, I was wrung out from the fourteen-hour time change and the long flight. But my trip was easy compared to previous generations of Morgan Stanley partners, who had had to take a train to the West Coast and then board a steamer to Hawaii, where they caught a plane to Tokyo.

As soon as I passed through customs at Narita International Airport, a well-dressed Japanese man in his mid-thirties approached me. "Welcome, Mr. Mack," he said, bowing. He was Kenji Munemura, a salesman from Morgan Stanley's Tokyo office. Kenji drove me to the Hotel Okura, in the most exclusive part of the city. It mixed traditional Japanese architecture with sleek, modern design from the early 1960s. I instantly got why Presidents Richard Nixon and Gerald Ford—as well as 007—had stayed at this storied hotel. The lobby was featured in the 1967 James Bond thriller *You Only Live Twice.*

I was new to Japan, but Morgan Stanley had a deep history there, going back to its J. P. Morgan & Co. roots. Senior partner Thomas Lamont first visited Japan in 1920. From its founding in 1935 until World War II, Morgan Stanley had an ongoing relationship with the Japanese government. After the war, it was decades before the firm renewed its ties.

In 1970, two years before I joined, Morgan Stanley became the first international investment bank to open a representative office in Tokyo. Although it was just two people, the Tokyo office was a powerhouse, thanks to the man who ran it, David Phillips. Born Satoshi Sugiyama in 1933, he moved to Long Beach, California, as a teenager to live with an American family. He took their last name when they adopted him and changed his first name to David. He spoke English as smoothly as he spoke Japanese.

With this skill set, he put together an amazing career. After Phillips graduated from the University of California, Berkeley, he joined Morgan Guaranty in New York in 1960, then worked for the bank in Japan. Told he'd never make vice president because he wasn't white, he applied to Morgan Stanley, which snapped him up. The very formal Phillips was a huge asset for the firm—"[a] fully bilingual, bicultural man who wore expensively tailored suits and cufflinks and smoked Dunhills," as Ron Chernow puts it in *The House of Morgan*. Phillips knew everyone who mattered in Japan—he was a real connector. He signed up the Industrial Bank of Japan, Hitachi, Nippon Steel, Mitsubishi, and other clients. When Sony decided to make a private placement of bonds, investment banks fought like wolf packs to get the business. According to the *New York Times*, "Goldman, Sachs & Company reportedly had Henry Kissinger talk with Akio Morita, Sony's chairman, on its behalf." That didn't do the trick. David Phillips and Morgan Stanley won. In 1977, the firm elected him its first nonwhite partner, and Phillips later became president of Morgan Stanley Japan.

By the time I visited, the Tokyo office had grown a lot. The manager was an American named Geoffrey Picard, but most of the employees were Japanese. Unlike Goldman Sachs, which staffed its foreign offices largely with Americans, Morgan Stanley established a strong tradition of hiring people from the country where the office was located.

We doubled our talent pool by hiring both sexes—most Japanese corporations didn't accept women as professionals. But Japanese women from elite families often had extraordinary résumés: they had attended Ivy League universities and earned their MBAs at top business schools. Having lived in the United States, they spoke flawless English. Although they had a grasp of American business culture, their real gift was their social connections to the top men at Japanese banks and insurance companies. Some worked in derivatives and others were crackerjack salespeople.

Japan had rebounded from defeat in World War II to become an economic superpower that increasingly seemed on track to surpass the United States. Consumers around the world couldn't get enough of Japan's TVs, camcorders, stereo systems, portable cassette players, and cars. When I first started going to Tokyo, the banks and insurance companies we dealt with were conservative investors. They were interested only in AAA-rated bonds from blue-chip American corporations. But as the 1980s progressed, the Japanese developed a voracious appetite for US assets. A Japanese tire manufacturer acquired the Firestone Tire & Rubber Company in Akron, Ohio. Mitsubishi Estate bought an 80 percent stake in Rockefeller Center in New York for $1.4 billion. A Japanese real estate developer paid $841 million for Pebble Beach Company, including the famed Pebble Beach Golf course near Carmel, California. Japanese companies were purchasing junk bonds and other structured securities that gave them more yield and more leverage. They were aggressive. They wanted to spend money, and we were helping them.

I had the same agenda in Tokyo as I did in New York. I grilled my salespeople there the way I grilled my New York team. "Who's your toughest client? What do you need from me?" I boosted sales by accompanying them on client visits. It meant a lot to Japanese executives that a head honcho would jet in from New York to meet with them. I relied on the same techniques that worked for me at home: I made it a point to sit across from the client at an angle so that I could watch their body language. Were they fidgeting? Looking at their watch? Checked out? If I picked up on something that my salesperson was not delivering, I jumped in.

But there were differences between New York and Tokyo. I found that the Japanese often told me what they thought I wanted to hear. It didn't matter if it was a tuxedo-clad hotel concierge or the CEO of a major life insurance company. You want a dinner reservation at X restaurant? Of course. You're asking us to buy $1 million in bonds? Absolutely. Reality emerges when the restaurant reservation fails to materialize or the deal isn't signed. "It is particularly difficult to do business in this country without knowing the behind-the-scenes business customs," David Phillips once told a journalist. "A lot of it is instinct, a feel. The formal statement someone makes in a business deal in Japan is one thing, but the substance is often another thing altogether."

I knew that I was not going to crack the code of this ancient and sophisticated culture. I hadn't studied Japanese history at Duke, nor did I speak the language. I had to use a translator. But I tried my best. Before meetings, the businessmen took off their shoes and put on a pair of guest slippers. So I did the same, even though the slippers were often too small for my size eleven-and-a-half-C feet. At dinner, my Japanese host usually made a short speech welcoming me, then raised his ceramic cup of sake and shouted "*Kanpai!*"—"Cheers!" I noticed that only then did anyone take a sip.

The business "day" usually extended late into the night. Socializing was even more important than meeting around a conference room table. After dinner, we went out drinking on the Ginza. By day, it is Tokyo's famous shopping district. When the sun sets, it is ablaze with a thousand neon-lit signs—Times Square on New Year's Eve, but even brighter. Wives and girlfriends were never included. That was the culture.

In business, you have to be flexible, to try to fit in. But I had my limits. One day I was at lunch at a super-expensive Tokyo restaurant with Kenji Munemura and clients from the Industrial Bank of Japan. With a flourish, the waiter brought out the specialty of the house: a platter of palm-sized prawns. They were still alive and flip-flopping on the plate set in front of me. My stomach heaved. I just couldn't do it. So I picked up the prawns one at a time with my chopsticks, pretended to nibble, vigorously nodded my approval, then secretly dropped them on the floor.

———

IN 1985, I was promoted to head of Worldwide Taxable Fixed Income. Besides expanding our presence in Tokyo, Morgan Stanley was opening offices in other cities around the world. Part of my mandate was to make sure I put the right Fixed Income manager in each international office. I also continued to meet with clients, flying to Australia, New Zealand, Singapore, Korea, and Hong Kong.

Usually when I traveled, I stayed two days; three days, tops, even if I was halfway around the world. While I was on these trips, I turned jet lag to my advantage. I barely let myself sleep. I fit in as many meetings as the salespeople could arrange. Then I'd board an international flight, I'd hear the pilot turn on the engines, and I'd be out until the flight attendant opened the shades shortly before we landed at JFK Airport.

I wanted to get home to Christy and our kids.

No matter how grueling my schedule was, I knew Christy was carrying the heavier load. She had high standards for Stephen, John, and Jenna. She picked out articles from the *New York Times* to read out loud while they ate breakfast. She was the teacher, the cook, the chauffeur, the coach, the scheduler, the chief of operations and home maintenance, the disciplinarian, the health and hygiene inspector, and the safety warden.

Several years earlier, we had bought a piece of property in Purchase, a New York City suburb. Our two-and-a-half-acre lot, lush with old-growth trees, was about a mile from the PepsiCo headquarters, which had a wonderful public sculpture garden where we could take the kids on weekends.

We were thrilled!

Until we moved in.

Our house was beautiful to look at, but the beams were wood, not steel, and the basement flooded every time it rained. We eventually had to rebuild a lot of the house.

Despite this money pit, we loved being outside the city. There was one downside. Instead of walking or taking the crosstown bus to the Exxon Building, I now faced an hour commute by car each way. And that was on a good day.

I decided to hire a driver who picked me up at 6:30 a.m. and drove me back home at night. Often that was after a client dinner. Having a driver was unusual in those days. Most Morgan Stanley partners took the train into the city. Dick Fisher rode the subway to and from Brooklyn Heights. Having a driver made me a target for ribbing. Seeing me get out of the car one morning, a trader called out, "Do you have a gold toilet too, John?" But I was unapologetic. I didn't want to waste my time driving when I could be reading the *Wall Street Journal* and planning out the day. For about a year, I gave Ken deRegt, a smart young Fixed Income trader, a ride so I could get to know him better and pick his brain. Sometimes I also drove in with Barton Biggs, who established Morgan Stanley's Research Department. Barton was a famed Wall Street investment strategist. Notoriously thrifty, he drove an old station wagon with a broken-out rear window that he duct-taped over instead of replacing.

We met in a mutually convenient parking lot where Barton left his junker. One evening he couldn't find his car. Then his phone rang. "I'm the police chief of Cottonmouth, Tennessee," said a voice on the other end of the line. "We have your car here, Mr. Biggs. Somebody must have stolen it. Can you come on down south and get it?"

Barton was trying to book a flight to this Cottonmouth when I revealed the truth: "Your car is in my garage."

Christy never complained about late nights with clients or business travel. She had grown up in a home where everyone tiptoed around her demanding father, so she made sure our house was relaxed and welcoming. Sometimes I was jealous that she got to spend so much time with Stephen, John, and Jenna. I'd call in the middle of the day and ask, "Can you put them on the phone?"

Once we moved to Purchase, we started entertaining more. We kept it casual, mixing Morgan Stanley colleagues and clients. I loved it. I am a true extrovert. Christy always jokes that she married America's Host, so she had to become America's Hostess. She was a natural. Plus, having big backyard barbecues reminded me of the weekend *haflis* my parents used to have with our Lebanese relatives.

Christy did have limits to her patience, however. After we installed an electric garage door at our house in Purchase, she spent hours warning the kids, "Never play with the garage door button. It's not a toy. It can kill somebody. The door will crush you if you get caught under it as it's coming down."

The next Sunday, Christy pulled the car out of the garage with the kids in the back seat so we could go to church. I turned the burglar alarm on, locked the kitchen door, and pushed the garage door button. With four pairs of eyes glued on me, I limboed under the door as it lowered. I got in the passenger seat, and Christy turned to me. "John, I have a button to close the door right here on the sun visor," she said. "You just undid in two seconds what I've been trying to teach these kids *not to do* for two weeks."

The five of us started laughing.

As I got out of the car at night, I made a conscious decision to try to compartmentalize the day's ups and downs. Not that I was always successful. I was greeted at the door by my three young kids jumping up and down ready to play-wrestle with me. It was the best way to end my workday. Later, after the kids were in bed, Christy and I talked. She sat at the kitchen island, and I sat at the table. I told her about my day, and she listened; she told me about her day, and I listened. This was and is the secret sauce of our marriage: communicate, communicate, communicate.

When I traveled, my mind was never far from home. I'd always take an hour or so to shop for presents. I didn't want to just pick up some overpriced souvenirs at the airport. In Tokyo, I bought Christy a strand of pearls. They were beautiful. And about the same price as a child's plastic version at a US toy store. Each pearl was selling for two American dollars. An unimaginable deal.

I traveled a lot with Joanne de Asis, who had become a star. When we were in Seoul, South Korea, to call on the central bank and an insurance company, she took me to a market that sold Gucci and Louis Vuitton knockoff handbags. The etiquette in Korea was that you negotiated the price back and forth. It was a game. As I paid and the salesperson wrapped up the purse, she complimented me: "Good job!" A few days later, after Joanne and I had arrived in Hong Kong, she took me to the Lanes—a famous shopping area. We were looking at quilted jackets for Christy and Jenna.

I tried to show off my bartering skill again. It didn't go well. "You not gentleman," the store owner said acidly. "You leave."

A mortified Joanne put on her sunglasses and pretended she didn't know me.

The incident didn't keep Joanne from asking me to attend a conference of Asian bankers and business leaders in Zurich, Switzerland. "Mr. Ramly bin Ahmad from Bank Negara Malaysia will be there," she told me, "and the head of Singapore Airlines. Coming to Zurich will save you a trip to Singapore."

The conference was at the Dolder Grand, an opulent five-star hotel that opened in 1899. When the stuffy concierge took us to our rooms, he unlocked the door to a grand suite with a magnificent view of the Alps. "This is for you, Herr Mack," he said in his German-accented English.

"Where is my colleague staying?" I asked.

"Let me show you." We walked down the hall to a tiny, dark maid's room. "This is for the lady," he said.

"Give her the big room," I said. "I'll stay here."

"Herr Mack, you are a true gentleman," he said with a little bow.

If only the shopkeeper in the Lanes could have heard that.

The next morning over Swiss muesli, I said to Joanne, "Hey, I got all these calls from your boyfriends last night. Who's Mr. Green?"

"Sorry, John, they all have code names—'Mr. Black, Mr. Green, Mr. Brown,'" she answered sassily. "You will never know who they are."

The reality was, I knew there was no boyfriend, only a fiancé—Dr. Jose Conrado "Joly" Benitez, a cabinet minister in Ferdinand Marcos's government. Joanne and Joly invited Christy and me to their wedding in New York, where I got a hoot out of dancing with Imelda Marcos, the infamous first lady of the Philippines known for her astonishing shoe collection—she owned three thousand pairs—who was Joanne's matron of honor. When Joanne and Joly's first daughter was born, they asked Christy to be her American godmother.

Joanne and I had come a long way.

For me, the highlight of every business trip was the moment I pulled up in the driveway at home and the kids spilled out of the front door. "Daddy, Daddy, you're home!" they squealed, jumping around with joy and excitement. Seeing them was so great after the loneliness of being away. And, of course, they demanded to see what I had brought them. A particular hit was a little Mickey Mouse hand-held video game—the size of an iPhone—that involved maneuvering pixelated eggs into a basket. If you missed the basket, the eggs cracked open.

Stephen, perhaps because he was the oldest, was becoming increasingly aware of my absences. One night when he was about ten and I was away again, he came downstairs and said to Christy, "We're not a family anymore. We never see Dad. He's always so busy."

When Stephen was a newborn, Christy had brought him to Morgan Stanley one day. Cradling our firstborn, the famously brusque Bob Baldwin had looked at me teary-eyed and said, "Make sure you spend time with your son, John."

I was not going to be one of those Wall Street parents who barely know their children. When the kids were young, Christy and I made a point of taking a two-week vacation at the beach outside Wilmington, North Carolina, every summer with our extended family. We left New York at 7:00 p.m. and drove through the night while the kids slept. Christy and I took turns driving, talking the whole way about the life we were living and our dreams for the future. When we finally got there at 8:00 a.m., we were wrecks, and Stephen, John, and Jenna were ready to hit the beach.

As soon as Christy recounted Stephen's comment about me being gone all the time, I started a tradition on the spot. I decided to take each child on a weekend trip every year, just with me. The deal I made was that they got to choose the destination—anywhere in the United States. That's how I ended up at Disney World seven straight years in a row—Jenna's choice. I had to learn to put the barrette in her hair. I had never been around for that. Perfection was important to Jenna. She'd say, "Daddy, you need to do it again. That's not how Mommy does it." I also carried her purse when we walked around the park talking to Mickey Mouse and Minnie Mouse. I learned a lot about having a little girl. It was really important for us.

Stephen loved *Star Wars*. In the spring of 1983, when Stephen was nine, *Return of the Jedi* was released. I planned to take him to see it that weekend, but that Wednesday night, Christy and I were asleep when Stephen came into our bedroom. "I can't sleep," he said. "I'm too excited about seeing *Return of the Jedi*." The movie had opened that day.

"Grab your coat," I said, getting up and throwing on my jeans. "We're going to the midnight showing."

Naturally, Stephen's first trip had a *Star Wars* theme. We flew to San Francisco and drove seven hours to Crescent City, California, the home of the redwood forests where Lucas had filmed the scenes involving the furry Ewoks.

John always chose sporty trips. We took lessons together at David Leadbetter's golf academy in Orlando and attended basketball camp at Duke. In 1990, we went to the Final Four Tournament in Denver. The Duke Blue Devils went up against the University of Nevada–Las Vegas Runnin' Rebels in the championship game. We cheered our lungs out for Duke and Coach Mike Krzyzewski, and we were deflated when they lost. But what a great time!

These trips reminded me that I couldn't let work overtake my life. It was so important to spend time with my kids and to get to know them as individuals. Sitting beside each child on the plane, I asked questions like, If there's one thing you would like to change about me, what would it be? What's something you like about our relationship? What do you like the most about me as your dad?

Stephen, without hesitating, gave the same answer every year: "Dad, you let me be me."

I can't think of a better compliment for a son to give a father.

FORGING A PERSONAL connection at work was just as valuable.

Everybody thinks money is the only thing that lights a fire under employees. But over the course of my career, I learned that by making an effort to really get to know people, I motivated them. This also helped me build teams.

Thanks to his fantastic relationships with clients, Kenji Munemura was critical to our success in Japan and had risen to become my senior Fixed Income sales manager in Tokyo. Kenji worked really hard. He had an extra spark. I knew this guy had a big future at Morgan Stanley. One day, I called him up from New York. "Hey, I'm coming over in a few days. I'd like to play golf and see some of the country. How about you and me take a road trip?"

Kenji picked me up at Narita Airport, and we drove to an exclusive mountain resort famous for its bubbling, steaming hot-spring pools. We played decent-enough golf and afterward lounged around in the hot springs, Sapporo beers in hand. Kenji had a great sense of humor, and we laughed a lot. At night, to fit in with the other guests at the resort, I wore a kimono. Women in traditional Japanese dress served us dinner on a low table, each of us kneeling on the tatami mat.

It was one of the best times I had in Japan. I got out of my comfort zone, and it was fantastic. I like to see what makes people tick. I liked Kenji. I wanted to bond with him, and we did.

I didn't anticipate the impact our trip would have. When word got around in the Tokyo business community that "John Mack took Kenji golfing," it elevated his reputation. It gave him a lot of "face" with clients. The Japanese felt tremendous communal pride that I took the time to go outside Tokyo to get a richer sense of their country.

In 1986, I successfully advocated for Kenji to be named a managing director. The next year I brought him to the United States to attend a Harvard Advanced Management Studies course and to improve his English. In his place I sent Jeff Salzman to Tokyo. Jeff had joined Morgan Stanley from Merrill Lynch ten years earlier and had done a terrific job building up the Government Bonds Department in Fixed Income.

Kenji and Jeff became great friends. It was just the kind of collaboration we liked at Morgan Stanley. Kenji had insight into what was happening inside Japanese companies, and he and Jeff worked hand in hand to move the Fixed Income business forward. Their dynamic partnership continued to flourish when Kenji spent a second year in the United States, working at Morgan Stanley in New York.

When Jeff first arrived in Japan, we talked every day. Then, as he got more comfortable, we talked two or three times a week. I had supreme confidence in him to get the job done. In turn, Jeff did an excellent job keeping me informed about the inevitable craziness that happens in every office—bad behavior, personality clashes, whatever. He was the best kind of employee because he understood a universal principle: bosses hate surprises.

Jeff and Kenji switched places again in 1989. Back in Tokyo, Kenji, who had worked so hard to improve his English, was determined that his children learn it as well. The following summer, we hosted his teenage son. He lived with us for six weeks and took English language lessons at Manhattanville College, right near our house in Purchase.

It doesn't have to be when you're a teenager, but I can't stress enough: try to live and work overseas at some point. I love America. But it's not the only place where the action is. Whether it's in Europe, Asia, Africa, Latin America—anywhere—what you learn and what you see are invaluable. You become less parochial and more a citizen of the world.

I did have an opportunity to live in London when I was the head of Fixed Income. I said to my family, "What do you think of moving to England for a while?"

The kids answered my question unanimously with a thumbs-down, and Christy and I decided to stay put.

Our family has been fortunate to have been able to take some amazing trips, but you don't get to really know a country and its people until you live there.

I'm not somebody who looks back on my life and thinks of all the things I should have done. I look ahead. But I regret that I didn't seize that opportunity in London.

CHAPTER TEN

March 21, 1986, is not a date that sticks out in many people's minds. It was a Friday, the second day of spring. Many Americans were still stunned by the deaths of teacher Christa McAuliffe and six other crew members in the explosion of the space shuttle *Challenger* almost two months earlier. Super Bowl XX, a contest between the Chicago Bears and the New England Patriots, had been decided, with the Bears winning. The college basketball championship, pitting Duke against the University of Louisville, was ten days away.

But for me and for Morgan Stanley, March 21 marked a seismic change. At the clang of the bell that opened the New York Stock Exchange at 9:30 a.m., outside investors could buy stock in Morgan Stanley, under the ticker symbol MS, for the first time ever. Since Morgan Stanley's founding fifty-one years earlier, the firm had been a privately held partnership. Now it was a publicly traded company. I was part of the seven-person management committee that made the decision to take it public.

Late in 1985, around the time of my forty-first birthday, I was asked to join the committee, along with Anson Beard, who oversaw the Equity Division. This was a meteoric jump for both of us. The invitation recognized that salespeople and traders, still treated with disdain by the investment bankers, were playing a bigger and bigger role at Morgan Stanley. The other members of the committee were now former chairman Bob Baldwin, current chairman Parker Gilbert, President Dick Fisher, Mergers and Acquisitions chief Bob Greenhill, and all-around strategic thinker Lewis Bernard. This was the group that steered Morgan Stanley's future.

Leading up to March 21, Lewis worked with outside underwriters to determine the initial offering price. He told Dick, "I think it should be fifty-seven dollars per share."

Dick, who always saw both sides of a situation, disagreed. "Look, Lewis, you've got to leave a little something on the table so investors benefit. I say the share price should be fifty-four dollars."

"Well, Dick," Lewis answered, "my job is to get the best possible price for the firm. I respect what you're saying, but I'm not leaving very much."

ONLY SIX MONTHS earlier, on September 12, 1985, we celebrated Morgan Stanley's golden anniversary with a black-tie dinner at the Pierpont Morgan Library. Housing J. Pierpont Morgan's world-famous collection of art and books, the library is one of New York's cultural jewels. The same day, Morgan Stanley took out a full-page newspaper ad declaring its commitment to remain a private firm. No sooner had the ad hit print than our certainty about staying private crumbled. All that autumn, we on the management committee wrestled with a decision that was every bit as momentous as splitting off from J. P. Morgan had been in 1935.

Would going public destroy what made Morgan Stanley special?

Or preserve it?

Donaldson, Lufkin & Jenrette, Merrill Lynch, Bear Stearns, and Salomon Brothers, among others, had already gone public. Of the titans, only Goldman Sachs and Lazard remained privately held. (Both firms later went public, the former in 1999 and the latter in 2005.) In the fall of 1985, we unanimously decided to take Morgan Stanley public. Parker Gilbert broke the news to the hundred-plus managing directors.

The firm was of two minds.

The older partners were happy with things as they were. The firm was doing well. If we became a publicly traded company, our books would be open to the public. Analysts from other firms would evaluate whether Morgan Stanley's stock should be bought, held, or sold. Every move we made would be second- or third-guessed. Potentially the most damaging: Would the quarterly earnings report come ahead of the clients' needs? Would going public shatter the traditions of excellence and integrity that we were so proud of?

Nothing illustrated Morgan Stanley's uniqueness more than the financial structure of our partnership. When new partners were elected, they would be told how much money they needed to contribute to Morgan Stanley. When Dick Fisher, who attended high school on scholarship and whose father was an adhesives salesman, had this conversation with Henry S. Morgan, he said, "Mr. Morgan, I'm very sorry, I can't put up the capital."

Mr. Morgan replied, "I'll put it up for you."

It turned out that Mr. Morgan had done that for several partners. The message he was sending was clear: what mattered was talent.

Morgan Stanley's most valuable assets were the people who walked in the door every morning, leather briefcases in hand.

The money the new partners put into the firm earned dividends every year, but there was no immediate payout. Partners were not allowed to withdraw any of their money—either the original capital or the dividends. They didn't earn a return on that capital until five years after their retirement. Then they were paid out based on the five-year Treasury rate. It was a low return and a long disbursement.

This meant that while the partners were working, their salaries were based on how the firm performed. Their bonuses reflected their individual accomplishments. It was only after they retired that they had access to their accumulated wealth.

If Morgan Stanley stayed a private partnership, we weren't in immediate danger. But the operative word was *immediate*. Several of the partners—especially the younger ones like me—could see that long term we had to change, or we would fail. Bob Baldwin famously displayed the "tombstone" newspaper ad from Ford's 1956 initial public offering (IPO) that listed the underwriting firms in that deal's syndicate. He had taken a red pen and slashed through the names of the many firms that had participated and were now out of business.

He often pointed to Kuhn Loeb. Founded in 1867, it was a powerful rival to J. P. Morgan & Co., advising railroads and famous companies like Westinghouse and Western Union. But Kuhn Loeb shied away from risk. In 1977, it merged with Lehman Brothers. By 1984, when the combined firm became part of American Express, the Kuhn Loeb name was dropped. It became a Wall Street ghost. Bob wanted us to understand that a storied past alone was not enough to sustain us in the future.

Besides, Morgan Stanley's finances were not entirely stable. In the early 1970s, the firm had earned record revenues. But in the following years we spent more than we took in because we were growing the business in multiple directions.

In 1970, Morgan Stanley employed 162 people. It had $9 million in capital and $15 million in revenues. The firm had only one business: advising corporations and governments on their capital structure and helping them raise money. Underwriting turned a profit and came with few expenses. Then Dick Fisher launched the Sales and Trading operation in 1971, which required a lot of capital. We were buying and selling stocks and bonds instead of just distributing them through a syndicate. We were now paying salespeople, traders, and the back office, which kept track of these transactions. We also added divisions such as Research and Asset Management. Most costly: funding our international expansion. The price tag was estimated to be $1 billion.

Along with this explosive growth and the corresponding expenses, we were paying out our retiring partners. And the faster we expanded—the more risk we took—the sooner the more wary partners opted for the exit ramp. Previously, such partners were 100 percent comfortable at the firm. "Risk . . . had been foreign to the old Morgan Stanley, which only wanted sure things," writes Chernow in *The House of Morgan*. By the mid-1980s, the subtext at every retirement party was how much capital was leaving the building. The more partners who departed, the less growth we could afford.

We needed more—and a more permanent source of—capital. That was the key. The solution? To go public. In mid-January, the *Wall Street Journal* ran an article with the headline: "Morgan Stanley Planning to Go Public in $200 Million Stock Issue."

———

THE THIRD WEEK of March found me in Deer Valley, Utah. I was trying to keep up with my kids as they raced down the ski slopes. I was keeping a promise to take my family, including my in-laws, skiing on spring break. As every parent knows, school schedules do not bend—even for Morgan Stanley's initial public offering.

Although the signs were promising, there was no guarantee that our IPO would be embraced by Wall Street investors. By that time in my career, I knew the market was unpredictable. Anything could hobble our best-laid plans.

Utah is on Mountain time. Since I couldn't walk the floors of Morgan Stanley, I worked the phones beginning at 5:30 a.m.—7:30 a.m. in New York. "What are you hearing, Jerry?" I asked a golfing pal, Jerry Wood, who worked in Mortgage-Backed Securities. "What do you think's going to happen?"

"John, gimme a break here! The market's not open. You know as much as I do."

Two hours later, I was still in the bedroom on the phone. "What's he doing in there?" I heard Christy's mother whisper. She and Christy were in the kitchen of our rental condo.

"Mom, this is a huge day for Morgan Stanley," Christy answered.

"Well, all I know is that his grits will get cold if he doesn't eat soon!"

"Dad, you promised you would ski with us and not spend the whole vacation talking on the phone," John complained through the closed door. I admit it: even when I was out of the office, I was never really away. George Poliszczuk, who ran the Investment Department at Mellon Bank, once told me, "You're the only person I can reach twenty-four/seven." This was before cell phones. I took it as a compliment, but it drove my family crazy.

"It's like the last day of school," Peter Karches told me. "Not much work getting done. Everyone's just BSing around the water cooler. No one can concentrate."

"Tell those Fixed Income people to get back in their chairs and start calling some clients," I instructed Peter.

"That's not gonna happen today, boss."

Morgan Stanley bankers and traders were used to having millions of dollars cross their desks every day. But now many of them had a personal stake in the outcome of this IPO. Parker Gilbert had devised a formula to apportion shares to partners. The firm also set aside 450,000 shares for nonpartners.

"I kid you not, John, the Equities trading floor is packed," Jerry said when I called him again that afternoon. "They're bug-eyed looking at the stock price!"

The IPO was a roaring success. Investors clawed to get at the 20 percent of stock Morgan Stanley offered to the public. Issued at $56.50 a share, the stock closed that afternoon at $71.25. Before we went public, Morgan Stanley's total book equity value was $305 million. By 4:00 p.m. on March 21, we had sold 5.18 million shares, raising around $300 million. Morgan Stanley's market capitalization—the value of the company's total shares of stock—was now about $1.9 billion.

I made more money in six and a half hours than I had ever dreamed of making over a lifetime. But the truth is, I hadn't worried about money since I joined Smithers in 1970 as a talented salesman on commission. What going public did was to increase my net worth by multiples. Yet what I remember most about March 21 had nothing to do with money. After dinner, we were all sitting around a crackling fire. Stephen turned to me. "Dad," he said, "you have to feel really proud."

I did.

I'm not downplaying the money. But the pride I felt in Morgan Stanley was incredible. I was overwhelmed by the growth and power of the firm. That feeling of success, it pulls you in. I felt so grateful to belong to an organization of such reach and excellence.

We were now a global player.

THE MONDAY AFTER we went public, we got straight back to work.

A major fear of some partners as we debated going public had been, Could we continue to attract the best talent in the country? Before, when associates and midcareer professionals joined Morgan Stanley, there was always the possibility we would go public and make them rich. Would we now lose the top candidates to Goldman Sachs, which remained private?

The answer was no. Morgan Stanley recruiters continued to be mobbed when they visited the top universities and business schools. For every position we filled, we turned away ten knock-it-out-of-the-park applicants.

But did going public change Morgan Stanley?

Yes. We started taking more risks.

When Morgan Stanley was a private firm, if a partner made a bad gamble, the money came out of their division. The drop showed up in their P&L—profit and loss. Their bonus and their team's bonuses went down. As we tallied up the revenues at the end of the year, everyone at the firm felt the loss.

Now the stock price moved on the results of the entire firm, not on any one business or division. If Morgan Stanley didn't do well, the share price dropped. But as a public company, we had millions of dollars from tens of thousands of anonymous stockholders to work with. The losses were spread out across a vast canvas of people and institutions. This allowed us to take more risk without the same severe personal consequences.

I built my career on taking risks. But I am equally certain that as this risk-taking behavior multiplied out exponentially in every publicly traded investment bank on Wall Street, the industry lost the internal financial restraints that had previously curbed dangerous speculation.

This is the single biggest change I witnessed during my forty-three years on Wall Street.

CHAPTER ELEVEN

How did I get my nickname Mack the Knife?

Let's be honest. Overworked headline writers cannot resist putting a blade into the hands of anyone with the name Mack. It's low-hanging fruit, easy to pluck from the 1928 song about a ruthless killer. Both pop singer Bobby Darin and jazz great Louis Armstrong had hits with "Mack the Knife" in the 1950s.

The first time people at Morgan Stanley called me Mack the Knife was in the mid-1980s. I was running the Fixed Income Sales Department. Robert Mulhearn was handling Fixed Income Trading. As I remember, Bob left his position because he was fed up with office politics and Morgan Stanley's cautiousness compared with other Wall Street firms.

He may have been fed up with me as well. We got into it so often that at one point, the management committee—I wasn't a member yet—asked Lewis Bernard to oversee the Fixed Income Division. For a couple of months, Lewis sat on the trading floor listening to us bellow at each other like two bulls.

One morning, Lewis wasn't there. I heard he had reported back to the management committee, saying, "Look, I don't add any value in this situation. I think John and Bob are doing a good job. They're recruiting good people."

"Well, maybe you ought to be there so they don't kill each other," Dick said to Lewis.

"They might," Lewis told him. "But if they kill each other, I'm not going to stop it."

After Bob left, Parker Gilbert and Dick Fisher promoted me to oversee the entire Worldwide Taxable Fixed Income Division—Sales *and* Trading.

This was a huge promotion and challenge for me. I had worked with traders for decades and often feuded with them. Now I was supervising them and their business.

At every investment bank, the traders have the power. The reason: they buy and sell securities with the firm's capital. Salespeople get their inventory from the trading desk. But the traders manage risk for the entire firm. The problem was that about half of Mulhearn's traders thought they were a lot better at their jobs than they were. Plus, they were arrogant and rude to the salespeople and the support staff.

A single bad apple *can* spoil the barrel. I don't put up with bad apples.

Firing people who should be fired is nonnegotiable if you're a boss. Inertia is easier, but it's never good. Not making a decision is making a decision. You end up with a team dominated by bullies and undercut by incompetence. Everyone else is just demoralized. Before I fire anyone, I go through a checklist. Then I make a decision. It may not be the best decision, but it's mine. I own it. I don't like firing people, but if it's warranted, I'll do it in a heartbeat. If it has to be done, I get it done.

One afternoon, after the markets closed, I called the offending traders into my new office one at a time. I gave each a pink slip and a generous severance package. Some leaned across my desk and screamed at me, spittle flying, "You're a fucking asshole, Mack!"

I didn't flinch. And I definitely didn't engage.

That's how I got my nickname.

———————

BEING MACK THE Knife wasn't just about firing people. It was about instilling discipline. The Fixed Income trading room, with its low tiled ceiling and glaring fluorescent lights, was my base of operations. I had spent too much time in mice-infested trading rooms that reeked of yesterday's pad Thai. Now that I was in charge, I vowed mine would be immaculate. "Every turret has to be clean!" I commanded.

I stalked the trading floor. I teased, I poked, I prodded.

"Are you awake?"

"Late night?"

"Did you call your client?"

I shifted between traders and salesmen. I was on the move so much, some days I felt like a shark. The traders sat in a different part of the trading room. I'd talk one-on-one with the head traders of the various departments: Derivatives, Municipal, Corporate, Government Bonds, Money Markets, Global. I'd pull up a chair. "What deals are you doing? What's happening in the market?"

Even after I earned an office, I built a second one made of glass— the Fishbowl, we called it—out on the trading floor. I wanted to be close to the action, seeing and hearing what was going on. That's how I observed the relationship between my salespeople and my traders. Did they respect one another? Were they working together? Often, when traders were losing money, they took out their frustration on salespeople. They tried to get the salespeople to sell bonds to stop the losses. The interaction could be cantankerous and pushy or a lot of fun and laughs. If traders didn't think the sales force was working as hard as it should, they'd say to me, "John, can you get the sales force to pay attention?"

I'd get on the speaker. Pressing the button, I'd announce: "Listen up, people! We're pricing a new issue. It's the most important thing. If you're working on something else, you better call me up and tell me what it is. We've got to move this position."

I wasn't addressing just the Fixed Income team in New York. Thanks to the squawk box—an intercom on people's desks that stayed on 24/7—my North Carolina twang suddenly blared out on trading floors half a world away.

I used the squawk box to praise, to criticize, to light a fire.

I demanded that all my people work their hardest at all times. I wanted traders, salespeople, support staff—everybody—to feel accountable for the advancement of Morgan Stanley. I was determined to pull the best possible work out of people—better, even, than what they thought they were capable of.

My mantra then, and at all points in my career: No excuses. Get it done.

The Fixed Income team met every morning at 8:00 a.m. *sharp.* Managers from each department talked about what they expected to happen in the markets. I wanted a full forecast. Then everyone started working the phones.

One morning, I walked into the office at 7:30 and saw a bunch of employees ripping through the pages of that day's *Wall Street Journal*—group cramming. "This is not the way to start the day, gang," I announced. "I expect you to come in with the *Wall Street Journal* already read. I expect you to show up at work prepared!"

I made my point so "enthusiastically," as Jeff Salzman diplomatically put it, "no one ever forgot."

For my seventieth birthday, my kids shared with me
what they love most about me as their father.

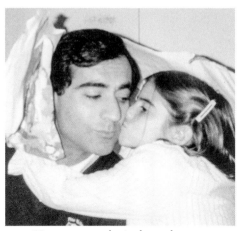

*You gave me the independence to
discover who I am and who I want to
be. It is the greatest gift you could ever
give me. I love you.*
—Jenna

*Thank you for You, and thank
you for my Life.*
—John

*Thank you for always giving me the
support and encouragement to be
whoever I wanted to be.*
—Stephen

Play fighting with my kids after a long day's work, 1983. PERSONAL COLLECTION.

Me with my father, mother, and brother, Frank, on Mother's Day during high school, 1962. PERSONAL COLLECTION.

Peter Karches and me celebrating his career when he retired from Morgan Stanley, 2000. PERSONAL COLLECTION.

My kids, in my office, learning about their investments with Patricia Newman, tax accountant for Morgan Stanley, 1988. PERSONAL COLLECTION.

My mother and me, 1980s.
PERSONAL COLLECTION.

Christy and me at the Forstmann Little Conference, 1999.
ALICE KOELLE PHOTOGRAPHY.

My father's family. Back row, left to right: my father, Charles Mack; my aunt Lucille; my aunt Sophie; and my uncle Side Mack. Front row, left to right: Bahia; my grandfather John Mack; and Nora. PERSONAL COLLECTION.

Middle guard at Duke University, 1965–66.
COURTESY OF DUKE UNIVERSITY ARCHIVES.

Christy and me after getting engaged, 1972. PERSONAL COLLECTION.

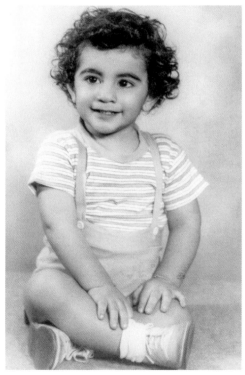

Me at three years old, 1947. PERSONAL COLLECTION.

On the trading floor at Morgan Stanley, 1984. Left to right: Bill Birch, Peter Karches, me, Ernie Werlin, Michael Brown, and Bob Mulhearn.
COURTESY OF MORGAN STANLEY.

Morgan Stanley's Seventy-Fifth Anniversary dinner, 2010. Left to right: former chairmen Bob Baldwin, Parker Gilbert, me, and chairman and CEO James Gorman. COURTESY OF MORGAN STANLEY; PHOTOGRAPH BY LARRY LETTERA.

Dick Fisher, Phil Purcell, and me shaking hands on the Morgan Stanley and Dean Witter merger, 1997. JAMES LEYNSE PHOTOGRAPHY.

There were a lot of things I would not tolerate. If I asked a question, let's just say I was not a fan of the blank look, accompanied by a shrug and "I don't know." That was a big demerit in my book. Far better to respond, "This is what I do know, and I'll get you more info." I wanted the intel by 5:00 p.m. that day. Four o'clock was better.

Most objectionable: lying. I don't lie, and I detest being lied to. It wasn't just me. At Morgan Stanley, you were expected to be honest even—*especially*—when no one was watching. That is why I got so angry when I saw an expense report sitting on my desk. Submitted by someone on my team, it had been returned by the controller's office, which oversaw the firm's accounting.

There were problems. Serious problems. Yellow Post-it notes flagged multiple pages. I had submitted enough expense reports since 1968 to spot obvious padding. This person was expensing personal dinners—with plenty of cocktails and good wine—and passing them off as client meals. Although it was a common practice on Wall Street, Morgan Stanley had a strict policy against it.

I asked the person to come to my office off the trading floor, not the Fishbowl. "I see what you're doing here," I said, holding up the offending expense report. "I don't tolerate it. The controller doesn't tolerate it. Morgan Stanley doesn't tolerate it."

Knowing me well enough not to argue, the person stood up and walked out of my office.

I announced the departure at the top of the 8:00 a.m. meeting the next day. Everyone looked shocked. "When someone cheats the firm," I said, "they're cheating all of us. It's my job to uphold the firm's principles, and it's also yours.

"Now, tell me what the markets are doing."

I DID CUT people slack from time to time.

I still laugh about a weekend sales conference we had. Back then, we drank a lot at these events. After my speech on Saturday night, I was talking with a group of salespeople in the bar. Everyone was sucking up, except for one guy who worked for Jerry Wood in Mortgage-Backed Securities. He kept poking me in the chest, braying, "You've got to pay us more money! We have to make more money as salespeople. I can make a lot more over at Bear Stearns. A lot."

I could hear a chorus behind me, people whispering, "Shut up! Just stop! You're bombed!"

But he went on and on.

The backstory to his complaint was this: Salespeople and traders used to be paid a percentage of the revenue they each generated. When I was put in charge, I changed that. Now people in Fixed Income earned a salary plus a bonus. This was not how the rest of Wall Street operated. But my system forced everyone to work with one another. Instead of "eat what you kill," my team got rewarded for "works and plays well with others." I wanted to make sure everyone in Fixed Income did whatever was possible to help other departments. That included passing on business to other Morgan Stanley divisions to maximize total revenue for the firm.

First thing Monday morning, I called up Jerry Wood. "Bring the Bellyacher to the Fishbowl."

When they got there, I told them, "I thought about what you said Saturday night. I don't want to hold anybody back. You should go to Bear Stearns. I know Jimmy Cayne, Bear's president. I called him, and he said you could have a job. I'm really sorry to see you go." I went on in this way for fifteen minutes. The guy was turning red, turning white, turning red again. He was stammering. Sweating.

Finally, I decided to put him out of his misery. "I'd like you to stay if you want."

Honestly, I didn't know whether the guy wanted to leave. If he was unhappy with the way I did things, best to hit the road.

"I'm sorry, John. I really like it here. I want to stay."

More important—and the reason I had the conversation in the Fishbowl—I was making a point. Working at Morgan Stanley was a privilege. Complainers destroy morale.

There were other times I used a public spectacle to advance my agenda. That's what happened in England. Morgan Stanley had opened a London office in 1977, run by Archibald Cox Jr. The son of the Watergate special prosecutor, Archie built out Morgan Stanley's presence in the City from a small office of twenty to close to a thousand in just eight years. London had become a global financial hub in part because of Prime Minister Margaret Thatcher's drive to deregulate. Oil-producing nations invested their petrodollars in Britain, not the United States. Morgan Stanley was by far the most profitable American firm in Europe.

A funny thing, though: If you called the London office between noon and 2:00 p.m., no one answered. A forty-five-minute lunch, served with Diet Coke, had become the fashion on Wall Street—if you left your desk at all. The Brits were different. A number of people headed to the pub or the wine bar at noon, returning to the office a couple of hours later, a few pints or glasses in.

Another difference between New York and London: On Wall Street, I was an anomaly because I didn't have an MBA. But in London, a lot of the salespeople and traders had not gone to university. Sharp-eyed and street-smart, they'd started working at age sixteen. They tended to be rougher around the edges than the average American investment firm employee.

There was a guy on the Fixed Income side who fit that bill. His drinking habits and his education didn't pose any problems. Nor did his performance: he was practically hoisting money into Morgan

Stanley with a forklift. The problem was his behavior. He was a bully. Women were his particular target. He made sexual innuendos and falsely insinuated that he'd slept with different women in the office. Sometimes he rubbed his face against women's cheeks. "You ought to go out with a real man," he'd announce loudly. After confirming the truth of these reports, I decided to send over a manager from New York. When the bully got wind of these plans, he vowed to quit and take several top staffers with him to a competitor.

Gauntlet thrown.

The guy thought the money he made for Morgan Stanley insulated him. It didn't. I wanted him gone. I knew all I needed to know. I made a decision. I booked the next flight to London—a red-eye. I was sitting at his desk the next morning when he walked into the office.

I stood up. "I came over here because I know you're threatening to leave with a bunch of people. Forget it. You're fired!" I pointed to the exit.

I got a round of applause.

Not every situation called for my intervention. Jerry Wood once came to me complaining about a new trader, Tom. He had come over from Government Bonds to Mortgages.

Mortgages are a different animal than the typical fixed-income bond. Usually, if interest rates go up, the price of the bond goes down. If the rates go down, the price of the bond goes up. In mortgages, that's not what happens. Depending on the structure of the deal, the price might go up or it might go down.

"Tom knows shit about mortgages," Jerry said. "He's a good trader, he's got big *cojones*, and he can handle risk. But he's a know-it-all. No way can I work with this guy."

I gave Jerry a sharp look. "Have you taken Tom out to lunch and talked to him? Do that. Today."

Off Tom and Jerry went. Jerry told Tom: "You don't know what the clients want."

Tom said, "You don't know the pressure I'm under trying to make money."

Forced by me to talk one-on-one, they came to understand what the other was trying to accomplish and what they were up against. They became good friends and great collaborators. Had I stuck my nose in, that would never have happened.

———

BEING MACK THE Knife also meant micromanaging expenses, shaving them when necessary. Take, for example, business dinners. We discovered that a high-end place like La Grenouille, a haute cuisine French restaurant in New York, made many of our Fixed Income clients uncomfortable. Sparks Steak House was a different story. Clients loved being taken out for a sizzling sirloin so huge it flopped over the edges of the plate, accompanied by an equally rich but reasonably priced cabernet. What really got them excited was that this restaurant, on East Forty-Sixth Street, is where Mafia crime boss Paul Castellano was gunned down outside the entrance on December 16, 1985, in a hit ordered by mob rival John Gotti.

I knew all about treating clients right. I had bought plenty of booze and lobsters for the Mellon folks in Pittsburgh. I had had lots of martini and shoot-the-shit lunches. But the point was to have a fun meal that cemented a friendship, not to throw open our wallets in a showy, obnoxious way. That kind of behavior can raise questions in clients' minds about how we were handling *their* money. It was okay to spring for a couple of tickets to *Cats* or *Les Misérables* on Broadway but not to pay a scalper thousands of dollars for a sold-out Madonna concert at Madison Square Garden.

Events didn't have to be extravagant. My favorite example involved Bears football games in Chicago. Joe Hill, who had been promoted to head Fixed Income there, bought a 1953 American LaFrance open-cab fire truck that Anheuser-Busch outfitted with beer taps. On game days, he packed in clients and drove them to the stadium for a tailgate. Then they'd all go to the stands. Afterward, the party started up again, with the players joining. People still marvel about that fire truck.

Once, when I stayed over in Chicago, I took the Fixed Income team to dinner at the original Morton's The Steakhouse. The wine steward came to our table and said, "You've got to try this Bordeaux. We just got it in, and it's delicious!"

"Bring it on," I said. I wanted to show my team some love.

When I got the bill, I was apoplectic. Good wine is one thing, but this was outrageous. I bore a hole into the wine steward with my eyes and cocked my index finger at him. When he came over, I stabbed the bill with that same finger. "I can't fucking believe you did this," I said.

"I'm sorry, sir," he said coolly, looking me right back in the eye. "You're a sophisticated man. I assumed you recognized the label. You should have asked me what it cost. I would have gladly told you."

The guy had a point. It was my responsibility to give the sommelier a price range. There's no embarrassment that way, and you get what you want. I vowed never again to order a bottle of wine without asking the price.

First thing the next morning, even before I had my coffee, I called my assistant in New York. "Send out an all-points bulletin to the division!" I said. "No dinners at Morton's!"

When the memo circulated a few days later, it looked like I had declared war against "Morgan's"—M-O-R-G-A-N-S. The guys in the Chicago office used that typo as a loophole. "We haven't been to Morgan's," they'd say innocently when I demanded to know why Morton's was still showing up on their expense reports.

"You know I meant Morton's."

"John, I always take you literally, not figuratively," Joe Hill insisted, feigning sincerity.

———

KEEPING A CLOSE eye on expenses is easy. And firing someone for bad behavior—you just get it done. But "head-count reductions"—dismissing a group of individuals because there's too much overhead—that's more difficult. This doesn't mean just cutting the mediocre performers. Everyone understands why you're doing that—usually including the people being axed. A head-count reduction means letting go of good people—in-early-stay-late people, solid citizens who, under better circumstances, would be in line for a promotion.

A year or so after I took over Worldwide Taxable Fixed Income, I sensed that our division wasn't as lean as it should be. Earlier, Morgan Stanley had gone on a hiring spree to fill slots. Now I realized we had to scale back. It's the eternal story: hire in haste, repent at leisure.

There was another reason I wanted to slim down our team. The stock market was booming. The growth was so explosive, I suspected it was a bubble. And bubbles always burst. I anticipated that there was going to be a downturn in the American economy and that growth would come from abroad. I wanted our roster to reflect this new reality. I sat down with my managers. "We need to lay off 20 percent of the employees in Fixed Income," I said. We looked at people's records, and I told the managers who I thought they should cut in the United States and London.

Take it from me: when you decide to do a head-count reduction, you gain nothing by putting it off. Rumors circulate, anxiety builds, and no work gets done. The managers laid off salespeople and traders. I handled the more senior people. I had these conversations in my office, not in the Fishbowl. "We've just gotten too big, and I need to make an adjustment. If I can do anything to help, call me."

I remember we cut ninety people.

That night, when I told Christy about my day, she asked me, "Are you upset about the layoffs?"

"No," I said. "It feels awful, but it was the right thing to do for the firm."

Eight months later, the bubble burst, and I was proved right. October 19, 1987, was immediately dubbed Black Monday. The Dow Jones Industrial Average nose-dived 22.6 percent, which remains the largest single-day percentage drop in history—worse than the stock market crash on October 28, 1929, and the pandemic crash on March 16, 2020.

Investors were worried that interest rates were about to skyrocket, as they had during the late 1970s and early '80s. There was turmoil in the Persian Gulf. Congress was taking a hard look at the frenzied M&A industry. Thanks to Ronald Reagan's tax cuts, we'd had a five-year surge on Wall Street. Plus, investment firms were now doing computerized trading.

As soon as the markets opened in Asia, stock prices plummeted. Panicked sellers created a contagion of fear that spread from market to market around the world—Sydney, Auckland, Hong Kong, Tokyo, Frankfurt, Paris, London. The sell-off began in the United States at 9:30 a.m. Black Monday was the first global financial meltdown.

Investors sold their equities and higher-risk corporate bonds, often at huge losses. People were kicking speculative securities out of their portfolios. Needing to put their capital in a safe harbor, they switched to government bonds, the proverbial "flight to quality." We recognized the trend early and bought up T-bills.

Peter Karches walked into my office late that afternoon. Usually brash, ballsy, and tough as nails, he looked broken. "What's wrong, Peter?" I asked, rushing to close the door.

"I'm going to lose everything I've worked for, John. Everything I have," he said. He was teary-eyed.

"Well," I said, "what did you start with?"

"Nothing. Just debt. I borrowed to go to Georgetown and Columbia B-School. I waited tables to pay my rent."

"This isn't the end of the world, Peter," I said, tossing him a box of Kleenex. "Don't worry. You'll make it back."

Christy and I had also lost a considerable chunk of our net worth that day. Morgan Stanley stock, where we kept most of our capital, had dropped significantly. Our other investments were hemorrhaging as well.

Like Peter, I didn't come from money. When I arrived on Wall Street, I had less than ten dollars in my checking account. I'd survived. I'd made a lot of money over the next nineteen years. Now, in six and a half hours, our personal wealth was taking a gut punch. Was it going to change our life? On the margins, yes. I'm a cool guy, but I'm not that cool. I was rattled. But I tried to stay focused. Our kids weren't going to go hungry, and we weren't in danger of losing our house.

As the markets ran red that morning, I made a decision. I was going to look and act confident. I've got a good game face. I put it on and started walking the trading floor. That's what it means to lead. It means being out in front of the troops and keeping them calm. You need to act like everything is going to be okay, even if you're as much in the dark as everyone else.

When I first got into the municipal bond business at Smith Barney in the late 1960s, I sat across from a guy who had been a Marine in Vietnam. He was big, burly, and, to be honest, sometimes obnoxious. Each morning, he came in, sat down, and started bitching and moaning. "John, if I don't get a good bonus, I'm worried I'll lose my house."

He said this every day. *Every single day.*

Finally, I turned to him. "How do you live with this kind of stress?" I asked. "I'm worried about you." I was being sincere. I thought the guy was going to drop dead of a stroke any minute.

He looked at me, amazed. "Are you kidding? This isn't stress. In Vietnam, people were trying to kill me in the fucking jungle all the time. *That's* stress."

His words put everything in perspective for me. I realized that as long as nobody's trying to kill me, I'm in a good place.

In fact, I had experienced true terror in the late 1970s, when I was a sales manager.

Bob Baldwin, proving once again that he was ahead of his time, had put in a gym at the Exxon Building and strongly encouraged Morgan Stanley–ites to exercise. This was long before companies routinely installed gyms and wellness centers. A three-sport athlete at Princeton, Bob remained lean and fit. Famously blunt, he often told people to their faces to lose weight or to quit smoking.

I got into lifting weights and took full advantage of the gym. I bulked up—I was stronger than when I had played football for Duke. One afternoon, I was bench-pressing a lot of weight. Bar off the rack, I sucked in my breath and then strained to push up the loaded barbell.

Suddenly it felt like someone had thrust a spike through my ear and into my brain. I screamed out.

Even though the pain in my head was killing me, I went on a scheduled recruiting trip to California the next day. The agony didn't let up. Worried, when I got back to New York I went to see Frank Petito Jr., a highly respected neurologist and the son of Morgan Stanley's former chairman.

Every test Dr. Petito ran was a little off, and he ran a lot of them. He did a spinal tap, where they inserted a needle between two vertebrae in my lower back and drew out fluid. I had the procedure in the morning and headed right back to the office. Crazy, I know. Around 8:00 p.m., Joe Hill returned to the Exxon Building after dinner. He found me writhing on the trading room floor. "What's the matter, John? Do you need me to call 911?"

"I've got a terrible headache. I had a spinal tap today."

Those results were also a little off.

Now I was frightened—really frightened. Christy and I had three little kids, ages one, three, and five. It wasn't dying that terrified me; it was leaving behind my family. That's all I could think about.

The next test was to inject dye into my brain to look at my blood vessels. It required an overnight stay in the hospital. The night before I checked in, I turned to Christy. "Holy shit," I said. "I am so scared."

In the end, Dr. Petito figured out that I had a burst blood vessel, and the pain subsided on its own. I still lift weights today, though not quite as heavy.

But I've never forgotten the boulder of fear that filled my chest cavity. It had nothing to do with money.

———————

SO, NO. BLACK Monday did not overwhelm me. I was glad I had cut people earlier in the year. Most had landed good jobs, and they were secure. It was a rocky time, though. Every spring, Morgan Stanley hired twenty to thirty new associates. That December, I heard through the grapevine that a group of them were griping about how small their bonuses were.

Boy, was I steamed. I brought them all into the auditorium. Looking out into a sea of suddenly anxious faces, I said, "Some of you have been complaining. Let me walk you through what's going on at other firms. They're firing people! Salomon just kicked half their trainees to the curb. We made a commitment to stick with you. If you don't like your bonus, just think about what shape you'd be in if you were somewhere else. If I were you, I'd be grateful."

Then I walked out. That was Mack the Knife in action.

CHAPTER TWELVE

I've been lucky to know a few real leaders in my lifetime. One in particular was a friend from North Carolina named Bill Lee, a man who inspired me.

In the 1980s and early 1990s, Bill was the legendary CEO of Duke Power Company, headquartered in Charlotte.

Here's a story that sums Bill up.

Duke Power was installing electrical lines wrapped in a new, ultra-thin insulation. The project manager called Bill. "Our linemen won't go up the poles," he reported. "They think the electricity will shock them as it surges through the cable. They're scared."

Bill jumped into his car and drove to the job site twenty-five miles outside Charlotte. As soon as he parked, he put on his hard hat and borrowed kneepads and a pair of crampons from the manager. He headed right over to a utility pole and shimmied up to the top. The middle-aged Bill grabbed the newly wrapped high-voltage power line in both hands and hung there, suspended in midair. Then he climbed down, gave the equipment back to the project manager, and addressed the assembled linemen. "I would never ask you to do anything I thought was dangerous," Bill, a Korean War veteran, said. "And I would never ask you to do anything I wouldn't do myself."

The linemen got to work.

That is leadership.

I got to know Bill in 1978, when we worked together on a deal for Duke Power. A couple of years later, he invited me to go skiing at Hounds Ear, near Boone, North Carolina, in the Blue Ridge Mountains. One Friday, I flew to Charlotte, arriving at about 8:00 p.m. Bill and some other Duke Power guys met me at the airport, and we started driving west. About an hour in, he picked up his hand-held two-way radio. Nobody had cell phones back then. "Connect me with the McGuire nuclear plant," he said. "I want to talk to the head engineer."

I thought, *What is this guy doing?*

"Charlie? Bill Lee here. I know you're getting ready to go active on the plant. I know there's a lot of pressure on you. How are things going, my friend?"

We couldn't hear the other side of the conversation. But we did know that there was a lot of controversy surrounding nuclear power in those days. A partial meltdown at Three Mile Island, a nuclear reactor near Harrisburg, Pennsylvania, in 1979 had fired up strong antinuclear sentiment, leading to demonstrations across the United States.

Next, we heard Bill say, "I want you to know how proud I am of what you're doing. Everyone at Duke Power has confidence in you. We're all with you, Charlie."

I said to myself, *I'd do anything for a boss who makes a call like that.*

Here's a Phi Beta Kappa, magna cum laude civil engineer from Princeton, a worldwide leader in nuclear energy whose grandfather helped found Duke Power. He takes the time to tell the engineer on the job at 9:00 on Friday night that he's thinking of him. This level of consideration and commitment has a ripple effect throughout a company.

Anyone managing other people needs to think about what it means to lead. By the time I was the head of the Worldwide Taxable Fixed Income Division, I was thinking about it *a lot.*

"Leadership" is a word you hear all the time, but it's a tough concept to nail down.

You can't just announce, "I'm a leader." People have to accept you as a leader. The way I saw it, you can't lead people unless you build a team that's ready to follow you.

Every year, I was asked to talk to Morgan Stanley's new crop of recruits. "This is a business of teams," I told them. "It's a business of protecting the person who sits on your left and the person who sits on your right. At Morgan Stanley, every single one of us wants to succeed. Here, you can succeed without having to step on people. It's just the opposite. If you don't work *with* each other, if you don't *help* each other, you will not be successful."

Part of my role as a member of the management committee was to decide who should be promoted to managing director each year. One of the 1990 candidates was Mayree Clark, an Oklahoman who joined Morgan Stanley out of Stanford's business school in 1981. Mayree, a protégé of M&A chief Bob Greenhill, was on the bubble that year to be promoted. In our November 1989 meeting, Greenhill, Parker Gilbert, and Dick Fisher all talked about her many accomplishments. "Mayree should be made a managing director," they said, nodding. "No," I said, "I don't agree. She's done a lot of deals and brought in a lot of revenue. But she's not a team player. We always say we should reward people who work well with others. Mayree doesn't." I lost the argument.

The day after Mayree got her new title, I went to her boss's office. "I'd like to speak with Mayree," I told him. When she came in, I said,

"I want you to know I voted against you. I think you play people off against each other. If you don't get the answer you want, you try to get it from someone else. That's not the way we should do things here." This was a difficult conversation, but I had serious concerns about Mayree.

"Thank you for telling me," she said. "I'm going to prove you wrong."

Maybe she was annoyed, but I suspected Mayree appreciated the fact that I was telling her what I thought. That was the end of it. A year later, Mayree came by my office. "Last year, you voted against me," she said. "This year, I've worked really hard to demonstrate to you and your colleagues that I am a team player."

"I'm impressed," I said. "A lot of people can't take criticism. I know you're sincere because you waited to tell me until after you got your bonus."

I *was* impressed. Instead of resenting me, Mayree changed her behavior. We went on to have a great friendship.

EVEN THOUGH THE Fixed Income Division had swelled to 1,500 employees, I still made every effort to connect. Once, when I spotted a hole in the bottom of a salesman's wing tip, I joked, "What's the matter? Don't you make enough money to be able to fix that?" Then I took him to Brooks Brothers and bought him a pair of tasseled loafers. I knew he could easily afford them, but this was a gesture to show that I noticed and cared about him. This wouldn't work with everyone. Some people liked my pranks and being teased. Others found it off-putting. I was pretty good at figuring out who fit into which category.

To promote interaction with employees, I wore attention-grabbing ties—my favorite was purple and yellow. If someone commented on it, I'd take it off and give it to them. I kept a replacement supply in my drawer. I selected my artwork for the same reason: to provoke a reaction from people. No Currier & Ives winter skating scenes for me. I hung a sculpture by John Woodward on the wall in the Fishbowl, where everyone could see it—and ponder its meaning. It was a head with a spike going right through the forehead, between the eyes. Although it was officially untitled, I called it *High Tension*. I had another sculpture—a three-foot-tall mummy sitting in a basket—on the floor. When people asked me about it, I replied, "This is what happens to people who disappoint me." The truth is, I like to throw people off-balance. You find out a lot about them when you do it.

I never entered a Morgan Stanley elevator without striking up a conversation with my fellow passengers. "How's your day going? Did you get wet out there?" When I saw a group of summer interns or new trainees having lunch, I'd ask if I could join them. I kept an old-fashioned glass jar on my desk, the kind you'd find in my grandfather's dry goods store a century ago. Anyone could come and grab a handful of M&Ms or Tootsie Rolls. I knew people waited until I left my office to dart in and satisfy their sweet tooth before I came back. But sometimes I returned while they were there, catching them with their hand in the candy jar. Looking mortified, they'd rush to say, "I'm sorry! I'm sorry!"

"Don't apologize," I'd say. "It's for you."

The whole reason I had the candy was to encourage these encounters. It was a trap to lure in the shy and the reluctant so we could chat.

When I was sitting at my desk, I often answered my own phone. "John Mack."

"I'm sorry, I expected to get your assistant," the caller often stuttered.

"Well, here I am. What do you need?"

I was as driven and obsessed with profits as anyone on the Street, but I learned that employees worked better if I took steps to release some of the steam out of the pressure cooker that was Fixed Income. I installed a 150-pound heavy bag in the men's room so guys— including me—could punch it instead of each other.

When I was a new partner, I was working with a skeleton crew on July 3, when the stock market was closing early. The weather was sticky and hot, and the few of us who hadn't tacked on a vacation day to the July 4 holiday were wilting. I went down to the street, convinced the Good Humor man to bring his cart up to the trading floor, and paid for people to get whatever ice cream or Popsicle they wanted. I don't know who was happier: the people at Morgan Stanley or the Good Humor guy. But I was pretty thrilled myself when I got a call from Bob Baldwin. "I heard what you did, John," he said. "That was great leadership."

I continued the tradition. A couple of times a year, when I thought people needed a treat, I surprised the Fixed Income Division by calling up the Stage Deli to order sandwiches: pastrami on rye, roast beef, turkey clubs, corned beef. Because we ordered in bulk, the deli couldn't deliver them at lunchtime. Hundreds of sandwiches would arrive at 10:30 a.m. They were gargantuan. I swear they were big enough to feed a family of four. Never mind that we were closer to breakfast than lunch. Employees lined up and descended on the food like ants at the Coddle Creek Church picnic back in Mooresville.

What amazed me was that these people, many making millions of dollars a year, were off-their-pins thrilled to receive free food. Some would scurry back to their desks with *two* sandwiches. I made a point to invite everybody on my floor, from the temp brought in to file paperwork to the highest-paid trader. Nobody likes to be left out. I learned the candy trick from my dad, who was beloved for handing out Hershey's Kisses, Bazooka Bubble Gum, and Tootsie Pops from the trunk of his Pontiac. Alice Mack taught me that food is a powerful gesture of caring.

Fixed Income was killing it. We were on a roll, and the pressure to top ourselves each month kept ratcheting up. It was like playing for a basketball team on a winning streak. People were riding themselves and each other so hard, I instinctively knew I needed to lighten the mood. That's why I started a Monday morning custom. At the start of the 8:00 a.m. meeting, we showed a five-minute clip from a movie or a TV show. Anyone could bring something in. It might be a classic like the Three Stooges, a clip from that weekend's *Saturday Night Live*, or a funny TV news story. The selection was all over the lot. The only rule was that I had to watch it beforehand to make sure it was workplace appropriate.

I know I can be a hard-ass, but I have a sentimental side. I love the holidays, and one of my favorite movies is *White Christmas*. It came out in 1954, when I was ten years old. My father took off from work, and we all went to see it. I couldn't wait to show a clip of Bing Crosby crooning the title song. It was the last Monday in December before the markets closed for Christmas. The rest of the day, no matter where I walked on the trading floor, everyone, including me, was humming, "I'm dreaming of a white Christmas, just like the ones I used to know."

It's one of my happiest memories of Morgan Stanley. I really felt I had built a team.

THEN CAME THE betrayal.

I had just landed at Heathrow Airport, and I was in the car on the way to Morgan Stanley's offices at Canary Wharf in London. I got a frantic call on my brick-sized cell phone. "John! John! They're all gone! We don't have enough people to answer the phones! We can't finance our positions!"

It was the head of Fixed Income Sales in London. I could hear the panic in his voice.

Two months earlier, in December 1991, Bob Diamond, a former trader in charge of Fixed Income International in London, had told me he was leaving Morgan Stanley to head up Credit Suisse First Boston Pacific in Tokyo. I was disappointed to lose Bob, who had been with the firm since 1979, but it was an incredible opportunity for him. "You've conducted yourself as a professional," I told him, "and I wish you luck."

After Bob left, I checked in with his team in New York. I wanted to make sure everyone was happy and to protect Morgan Stanley from losing talented employees to poaching. "My door is open," I emphasized. "Come see me if you need anything. It's my job to help you do your job better."

"We're happy, we're loyal to Morgan Stanley, and we aren't going anywhere," everyone on his old team assured me. A few weeks later, I flew to Tokyo and took a group of Morgan Stanley people, including a brand-new managing director, out to dinner. Not only did I repeat what I had said in New York about my door being open but we also had an in-depth, very candid discussion about the things Morgan Stanley needed to do better. This was a conversation I would never want a competitor to hear.

I got the same response: "We're one hundred percent committed to Morgan Stanley."

The whole time I was talking to them, they sat there smiling and nodding, knowing what was going to happen the moment I was in the air the next day.

Bob launched a synchronized stealth attack on Morgan Stanley across three time zones. The Tokyo team resigned at 4:00 in the afternoon, the London team resigned simultaneously at 8:00 in the morning, and the New York team at 3:00, in the middle of the night. The resignations were timed to coincide with my twelve-hour flight. I was out of contact, ignorant of what was happening, and therefore unable to change anyone's mind. All told, it was about a dozen people, most of them on the Financing desk in London.

In business, raids are common. What I ask is that people tell me about a job offer and give me the chance to match it. If I can't, then Godspeed. I wasn't angry that Bob Diamond left. I wasn't even that angry that he took some of his people. What infuriated me was that I thought they jeopardized the firm. They didn't give us a chance to unwind or finance our trading positions. We had to take out a standby letter of credit so we didn't run out of money in London. To seemingly stab Morgan Stanley on their way out offended me to my core. It still does to this day.

A junior person on the London Financing desk said it best: "At least they could have told us the night before," she told me. "We didn't even have enough people to answer the phones. I can't believe they did that to me! I can't believe they did that to us!" That's exactly how I felt.

Recapping the events at the managers' meeting the next week, I said, "A lot of these people are your friends. I want you to know how they treated you. All of us are professionals. Just remember, the only thing you have in this business—in your life, really—is your reputation. You've got nothing else."

CHAPTER THIRTEEN

I was staring out the airplane window as the sunset reflected off the Wasatch Mountains that tower over Salt Lake City. They are a spare, magnificent range with sharp, snowy peaks that reveal their young geological age. I felt the Delta jet accelerate and lift off. Our kids, on a break from school, were staying behind with Christy in Deer Valley, where we had recently built a house.

I was flying to New York. I had to get back to work. My thoughts about how fast the kids were growing up were interrupted by the man seated next to me. He was talking quietly but audibly to himself. I stared, annoyed. This was not what I expected in first class. I was about to ask the guy to be quiet. Then I began to really listen to him.

"Every organization has an *espoused* theory," he said. "*That's* what an organization *says* it believes in. Then it has an *enacted* theory. This is the one the organization actually uses. These two theories are often very different. When there's a variance between what the organization *says* and what it *does*, that's a *very* good way to lose employees' trust."

"Excuse me!" I called out. "Could you speak a little louder?"

My seatmate stopped. Looking startled, he turned to me. "I'm so sorry," he said apologetically. "Am I disturbing you?"

"No. I'm seriously interested in what you're saying. I'm not kidding. How do you know this stuff?"

"Well," he said, "I study why organizations are dysfunctional and what to do about it. I'm rehearsing a speech I'm giving tomorrow at AT&T in New Jersey."

I leaned toward him, extending my hand. "I'm John Mack. I work at Morgan Stanley," I said. "I'm glad to meet you."

"Tom DeLong," he replied. "I'm an associate dean at Brigham Young University and was a visiting professor at Harvard Business School for a year."

Three hours later, when the pilot announced that we should buckle our seat belts because of turbulence, I realized we had talked nonstop. My new pal Tom was dissecting what leadership is. "It's what happens inside another person when they're with you," he explained. "It's what you do that makes another person feel differently about themselves."

As we landed in New York City, I handed Tom my business card. "You'll hear from me," I told him. "We're going to be friends. Good friends." Tom DeLong had so much to offer. No way was I letting him get away.

"Tom, I haven't forgotten about you and your ideas," I said when I reached him in his office in Provo, Utah, a few weeks later. "I told Dick Fisher, Morgan Stanley's new chairman, all about you. We want you to come to New York and do a consult. Tell us how we're doing and what we can do better."

We flew Tom in and gave him carte blanche to interview people in the Fixed Income Division. "Be honest with this guy," I told my team at the 8:00 a.m. meeting. "Tom's not my spy. He's looking for themes.

It's one thing if an individual pinpoints a problem. It's another if a bunch of people raise the same issue."

Soon Tom was ready to share his findings. He opened with the positive: "John, your team thinks you're fabulous at creating esprit de corps. They love the upbeat atmosphere you've established in Fixed Income. You're informal with them, but you're direct. There's no question about what you expect. Everybody wants to please you."

I beamed at Tom. Then he smacked me with a blunt truth. "Fixed Income is a quasi–old boys' system," Tom told me. "You have your favorites, John. People think that to get ahead, they have to be your friend. I don't know if this is true, but that's what they believe. Another thing, John: you haven't established an objective and balanced evaluation system for promotion. I know you have a 'promotion committee,' but the reality is, people think the committee is a bunch of insiders who rubber-stamp whatever you want. What you say goes."

He continued: "That makes the promotion feel hollow. People want to be promoted because they're achievers, because they know how to play in the same bullpen with others. Not because 'John likes them.'"

I took in what Tom was saying. Morgan Stanley prided itself on being a meritocracy. Dick Fisher and Bill Black had emphasized this when they asked me to join the firm. Frank Petito's immigrant background had become the stuff of legend. As Tom would put it, meritocracy was our *espoused* theory. But the reality in Fixed Income—our *enacted* theory—was that people got ahead based on whether I liked them.

Was this hard for me to hear? Yes. The idea that some people felt I wasn't evenhanded struck me in the heart. I believed I gave everybody a fair shake. But I was determined to be the best leader I could, and I wasn't going to get there by ignoring Tom's expert observations.

I made some immediate changes. Candidates hoping to move up now met first with a ten-person committee. To make sure the committee wasn't viewed as "a bunch of insiders," three members rotated off each year, replaced by three new members. Then I met with the candidates and made the final decision. But I always weighed the committee's recommendations.

The revamped committee opened my eyes. A few candidates who I thought were fantastic team players turned out to be incorrigible credit-snatchers. Others who behaved impeccably around me were reported to scream profanities at analysts, summer associates, and support staff. No way were they going to move up. On the other hand, the committee recommended promotions for people I probably would have overlooked. "This guy is very quiet, but he leads by example," they told me. "He's a utility player. You want him on your team, John." Or "This woman is a superb strategist who never gets the recognition she deserves."

Fixed Income was too large now for me to know every individual. And my role was about to grow a lot bigger.

———

THIS WAS A tumultuous period on Wall Street. Firms were still recovering from the 1987 crash, and Morgan Stanley was not immune. In 1990, Morgan Stanley had laid off fifty people in Investment Banking, a first in our history. Our stock price had dropped. This affected the wealth not just of shareholders but also of Morgan Stanley employees. Morale was tanking, and there was a growing sense that the firm was going sideways. To stop the slide, the managing directors held a multiday off-site meeting in 1992.

The air in the ballroom was crackling with anger and anxiety. In classic Morgan Stanley tradition, managing directors stood up and spoke their minds. They demanded changes in how the firm was managed. The upshot: we established a first-ever firm-wide operating committee.

I was named its chairman.

I moved into a new office in the executive suite. Sharing the space were Dick Fisher and Bob Greenhill. After Parker Gilbert retired in 1990, Dick became the firm's chairman. Bob was Morgan Stanley's president, in line to succeed Dick when the time came. One of the first things the three of us did was to slash our own compensation in half. We did this to boost confidence inside and outside the firm. My new job was to improve the inner workings of all of Morgan Stanley: personnel, day-to-day operations, and expenses. The firm's ten division heads as well as the top people in London and Tokyo reported to me weekly. The payroll had grown to 7,500 employees in twelve countries.

I had been in Fixed Income for two decades and in charge since 1985. Frankly put, it was the most successful and profitable division at Morgan Stanley. In seven years, it grew by 75 percent, and Morgan Stanley's bond revenues quintupled. If you started with a million dollars, you now had five million. I knew Peter Karches would be a killer replacement.

But running Fixed Income hadn't been all *White Christmas* and overstuffed deli sandwiches. One morning I stepped into the revolving door at Morgan Stanley, and instead of getting out in the lobby, I circled back onto the sidewalk. Standing outside, cell phone in hand, I speed-dialed our home number in Purchase. "I can't take this anymore," I said to Christy as soon as she picked up. "I'm quitting."

I can't remember what exactly had riled me up that day.

But I do remember Christy's reaction. She didn't say, "It's not a good idea to quit, John," "Calm down. Let's talk about it tonight," or "Maybe you should sleep on it."

Her response was instantaneous and unambiguous. "Whatever you want to do, John, I'm behind you." I know if I had resigned that morning, Christy would have greeted me at the door that night saying, "You did the right thing."

When I *didn't* quit, she greeted me with "You did the right thing."

That is what unconditional support looks like. Christy has given me that throughout our marriage. It's a lot easier to take risks at work when you have a solid bedrock at home.

I was so grateful that over the years Christy had smoothed out a lot of my rough edges. There were still times, however, that she had to course-correct me. Here's an example: As a boss, I made it clear that I wanted my employees to be leaders in their community. "Do things," I urged them. "Stand up and contribute." One Wednesday night in December, a big deal we had been nursing along suddenly came together. The next day, it was an all-hands-on-deck selling situation. I kept looking around for Jerry Wood. He was AWOL. I needed him, and I was furious. I stalked the trading floor. "Where the hell is Jerry?" I asked everyone. "Has anyone heard from Jerry? Do you know if he's okay? Did he get lost on the goddamn golf course?" I called his house. Crickets.

Friday morning, Jerry showed up in my office, a big smile on his face. "I heard you were looking for me yesterday, boss," he said. "What's up?"

I stood, put my hands palm-side down on my desk, and stared daggers at him. "You weren't here yesterday," I growled. "I needed you. We all needed you. We were scrambling. You let everyone down. I'm going to give you the benefit of the doubt. Were you sick? Did you have a personal issue?"

"Well, yeah. It was kind of personal," he said.

"What's the story?"

"You told us to do things, and I did. I'm the board president at my daughter's school. A nun asked me to play Santa Claus, so I put in for a vacation day. It was the most fun I've had in years. The teachers gave me a cheat sheet so I could predict perfectly what the kids wanted for Christmas. They thought I was the real deal."

"Santa Claus! We've got half a billion bonds to sell, and you're being ho, ho, ho Santa Claus? I can't believe you did that!"

I was seething. I called Christy. "You won't believe what Jerry did." I told her the whole story.

"John," she said with her usual calm, "you can't do that to somebody. You tell people to step up, and then you go ballistic when they do."

She was right. I felt really bad. I was definitely talking out of both sides of my mouth. A good boss doesn't do that. I dialed Jerry's extension. "I'm apologizing to you," I said when he picked up. "But don't come to my office, Santa Claus," I joked. "I don't want your bad judgment rubbing off on me!"

BY 1993, THINGS were bumpy in the executive suite. On Wall Street, the M&A business slowed down, and the division Bob Greenhill had founded shared in the misery. Bob was fixated on repairing the situation and focused on corporate clients. An avid pilot, he often flew his own Cessna Citation X to meet with them. But it was hard to run the firm from the cockpit of a plane, particularly when what Morgan Stanley most needed was attention to detail on the ground.

Things came to a head on Friday, February 26. Bob was on a client ski trip in Colorado when the management committee voted to replace him. Bob was given the title of vice chairman. I was named president. Dick Fisher told Bob about the change when he returned to the office that Monday. On Tuesday, Dick called a managing directors' meeting to announce the change. I walked into the conference room after he spoke. "Thanks, Dick," I said. "I'm looking forward to this." Then I left. My brevity was deliberate. I didn't want to sit there being grilled by the managing directors. I didn't want to appear to gloat or to have to defend how I gained my new position. The message I wanted to send: the firm is moving ahead. *Investment Dealers' Digest* wrote, "If Morgan's executive-suite battles represented the struggles between new and old attitudes, then the deposing of Greenhill was a clear signal that Morgan is finally ready to put its past behind it."

In June, when Dick and I were both traveling on business in Europe, Bob left Morgan Stanley to become chairman and chief executive of Smith Barney, Harris Upham & Co.

One day during this transition, I walked into Mayree Clark's office and stood by the window. Mayree had been the aide-de-camp to Dick, Bob, and me for the past year. "I really am the president now," I said. My eyes filled. It didn't bother me that Mayree saw me being emotional. Since I began at Morgan Stanley in 1972, I had worked so hard. I had joined a firm I wasn't sure I would fit into. My background selling bonds was an unlikely path to the presidency. Now, Dick and I were leading Morgan Stanley.

THE FIRM I was president of was the best financial franchise on Wall Street. But in 1993, Morgan Stanley was also very fragmented—more a collection of fiefdoms feuding over money and power than a unified company. Every division had its own agenda. I had succeeded in creating a cohesive Fixed Income team. Now I wanted to create a cohesive firm. I called up Tom DeLong and asked him to join Morgan Stanley to improve our personnel policies. He found my offer so tempting, he left his job at Brigham Young, sold his nine-acre farm, and moved his wife and teenage daughters to the New York suburbs. Tom had professionalized the way we evaluated and promoted candidates in Fixed Income. I wanted him to apply the same know-how to performance reviews firm-wide. In most divisions, employee evaluations were done haphazardly, if at all.

Performance reviews aren't sexy, but they're crucial. People desperately want to know whether their boss thinks they're doing a good job or a bad job—and whether they have a future at the company. If employees are left to wonder, they squander an enormous amount of emotional energy reading the tea leaves.

Corporate America—the IBMs, the GEs, the GMs—had put formal annual review procedures in place decades earlier. Not Wall Street. I remember the day Tom presented me with cutting-edge research about the importance of giving employees feedback. Next, he shared the information with the managing directors. "I'd like each of you to commit to sit down and talk for thirty minutes once a year with your direct reports about their performance and career goals," Tom said. The managing directors stared at him.

One older director spoke up. "Every November, I call each of my employees into my office. I say, 'Here's your bonus, and here's your salary for next year.' The numbers tell people all they need to know: big bonus, good job. Little bonus, bad job. No bonus, hit the road. It's a numbers game. I'm too busy making money for the firm to waste my time chitchatting with a first-year analyst about their 'aspirations.'" He made air quotes when he spat out the word "aspirations." In other words, no fucking way.

This was the response I expected, but not the response I would accept. The old days of hiring Thoroughbreds and working them hard but never discussing how they were doing or where they wanted to go were over. At least at Morgan Stanley.

I never struggled with giving subordinates feedback. But this was not true for a lot of the managing directors. They groped to find the right words during these obligatory thirty-minute conversations. Finally, Tom hired a company to create videos of actors modeling the conversations we wanted superiors and their reports to have.

The managing directors were even less thrilled when Tom suggested another first on Wall Street: the 360-degree review, when subordinates, peers, and superiors evaluate an employee. Before that, a review, when it happened at all, was purely top-down. You sat across the desk from your boss, and the boss praised or criticized your performance.

Tom's 360-degree review was different. For one thing, it was anonymous. You never found out who had dished. Vice presidents and managing directors at Morgan Stanley weren't used to having their underlings and colleagues weigh in. The point was to improve the way we treated one another up, down, and across the firm. This would create a better working environment.

No one, including me, was above the 360-degree review. When I sat down with Tom, he said, "People describe you as intuitive, inspirational, intimidating. Your employees want to be superhuman, John. You get people to leap tall buildings. Sometimes you do this by manipulating them. People *really* want to please you. You do something that's so unusual. Lots of executives summon employees to meet with them in groups. You go to them, and you interact one-on-one. You physically put yourself in proximity to employees."

Funny he said that. I was just about to launch a new offensive. My target: the Investment Banking division. When I started at Morgan Stanley, certain investment bankers told me I was just a stupid bond salesman. Almost nothing incensed me as much. More than once, I was on the phone with these SOBs and I'd slam down the receiver so hard it broke in half, exposing the wires. I remember a salesperson holding up the broken plastic and saying, "I think this phone's seen its last rodeo."

I still thought investment bankers were a bunch of elitists. But now that I was president, I wanted to get to know them as people and to understand their business. I spent the next eighteen months having dinner with every managing director in Investment Banking, either one-on-one or in small groups. This made me realize how incredibly talented Morgan Stanley's investment bankers were and how integral they were to our success—past, present, and, most important, in the firm's future.

There was another reason: I wanted them to commit to the new direction I was taking Morgan Stanley. We named that direction "The One-Firm Firm." Up to now, as Morgan Stanley had grown, each division had done its own thing. We had eight recruiters from different divisions all at Harvard Business School on the same day—with everyone unaware that the other seven were there. Divisions had their own summer softball teams and holiday parties. People could be as competitive inside Morgan Stanley as they were against our Wall Street rivals.

I was guilty of it myself sometimes. After I was named president, an investment banker confided to me that he preferred to ask for help from a friend in the Fixed Income Division at Goldman Sachs rather than ask me, Peter Karches, or anyone on my team. There had been good reasons for why we were territorial when we first started. The divisional walls erected to protect Fixed Income Sales and Trading were like nurturing a newborn in an incubator. Now it was fully thriving, and we didn't need that protection.

We started having heads of different divisions and departments go to lunch together. We centralized recruiting and encouraged people to move between divisions. This cross-pollination was good for the firm. In the past, if you were hired at Morgan Stanley into one division—Investment Banking, Fixed Income, or Asset Management—there you stayed. Most important, we coordinated contact with clients so that if entrepreneurs did their IPOs with Morgan Stanley, for instance, we followed up to encourage them to invest their newfound millions with us instead of taking the business elsewhere.

———————

AFTER I HAD been named president, Dick Fisher and I went to dinner. We talked business throughout the meal. Then, after coffee was served, Dick gave me a serious look. "John, I want to address a concern I have about you," he said. "You really perform. The people at Morgan Stanley respect you. You are supremely talented." He paused. "But you erode your accomplishments and that respect when you act as tough as you do. You can get anything you want, but you don't have to be a bully.

"You've got the biggest gun in the firm," he continued. "Your goal is never to use it."

We were pouring energy and resources into making Morgan Stanley a better-managed firm. In his economical and elegant way, Dick went right to the crux of my leadership. I needed to manage myself for Morgan Stanley to thrive.

I think about his words every day.

CHAPTER FOURTEEN

J ohn, it's Jack," Christy called from the kitchen.

The phone rang at 7:00 every Sunday night. This call came from the other side of the world. Jack Wadsworth was phoning from his office in Hong Kong, where it was 7:00 on Monday morning.

Jack oversaw Morgan Stanley's operations in Asia. A farsighted banker, he had spent almost a decade in the East, first in Tokyo and now in Hong Kong. As I moved up the ranks, Jack kept telling me, "John, we've got to get into mainland China. China is going to be a juggernaut. Once reform takes hold, there will be huge opportunities for us. We've *got* to get in there." The first sentence of Jack's 1990 business plan for Morgan Stanley Asia reiterated this: "We can get every other country in Asia right, but if we get China wrong, we will fail."

Getting into China had been a Morgan Stanley goal for a long time. Frank Petito had traveled there with David Phillips from the Tokyo office in 1976, just four years after President Richard Nixon's visit. Nixon's historic meetings with China's communist leader, Mao Zedong, inverted the geopolitical landscape. But it wasn't until 1978 that Deng Xiaoping, Mao's successor, launched an economic revolution. While maintaining strict Communist Party control, Deng opened up China to the world—and to capitalism. His bold, market-oriented reforms would eventually spur foreign investment. Jack wanted Morgan Stanley to be first in the door.

Even with the welcome mat out, Jack Wadsworth and Jeff Salzman were in for a shock when they began covering China from Tokyo in the late 1980s. The airport they flew into had a single run-down terminal, with bare light bulbs hanging from wires. The road into Beijing was just a series of separate concrete slabs with grass growing up in between. With the tires dipping down between each slab, a car could bump along at only fifteen miles an hour. Their accommodations were equally rough. Foreigners were restricted to a single hotel. Although the building was seven stories high, Jack and Jeff insisted on first-floor rooms. They were deathly afraid that if there were a fire, they would be stuck in the elevator because the electricity cut off every few hours.

Jeff, on the Fixed Income side, opened the initial foreign currency exchange in China. On the Investment Banking side, Jack traveled to Shanghai and Beijing. China was attempting to privatize its state-owned enterprises, but it wasn't obvious in these early days who, exactly, we should be doing business with. Morgan Stanley conducted some diplomatic outreach on Wall Street, teaching twenty-five Chinese employees at the New York branch of the Bank of China how Fixed Income and the New York Stock Exchange worked.

By the 1990s, the Chinese economy was roaring, with double-digit growth year over year. To build their infrastructure—telephone systems, highways, power grids—China needed access to capital. But it was way behind the West in terms of financial services. Morgan Stanley was determined to fill that gap by becoming the country's go-to investment bank. In a Bloomberg article headlined "Morgan

Stanley's Global Gamble," Dick Fisher summed up our motivation: "High growth rates create wealth. Wealth is what generates business for us."

China was only one of our targets. We also wanted to establish footholds in other promising emerging markets. By the time the '90s ended, Morgan Stanley had become the largest American investment bank in India. We had opened offices in Singapore, South Korea, and Taiwan, as well as scouted opportunities in Thailand, Indonesia, Malaysia, Vietnam, and the Philippines.

But as we scoured the globe, China, with its surging economy and billion-plus population, presented the most possibility. In 1992, when I became head of the operating committee, Jack came to Dick and me with a game-changing proposal: Morgan Stanley should establish a joint venture with the Chinese—the first investment bank in the People's Republic of China.

The idea of the joint venture was hatched by Jack and Edwin Lim, an economist who had opened the World Bank's China office before coming to work at Morgan Stanley. Edwin explained to us why the Chinese leadership might agree to it. "If China wants to grow," he said, "they have to have their own investment banking business and culture. They won't rely on outsiders to come in and fund projects."

I knew Jack and Edwin were right. We had to go for it. We were gambling Morgan Stanley's reputation, throwing in with people and a country that we knew little about and that twenty years earlier the United States had viewed as an existential threat.

No matter. As I told Bloomberg, "It's grow or die. The biggest risk is not to invest."

Our global offensive required me to put in an extraordinary amount of international travel. I was going to China roughly every other month, as well as making frequent trips to Latin America, Europe, Africa, and other Asian countries. The only continent I didn't visit was Antarctica. I know it sounds glamorous. Trust me, it wasn't. I spent a lot of time stuck in foreign airports, grounded by bad weather or mechanical delays, scrambling to reroute. I don't know whether I was a good traveler or a bad one. I just did it. It was the price of getting new business, and that excitement kept me going.

You can be briefed by experts and read a dozen books about a place to get insight, but I knew from long experience that the only way to really educate yourself about a country was to spend time there. I needed to meet in person. No matter where it was in the world, my presence at a conference table signaled the firm's commitment. Language could be a barrier at times, but you can always build relationships. There's no place I traveled where I didn't think I could connect with other people. I would be proven wrong, but you'll have to wait for that story.

THE FIRST TIME I flew to China in 1992, I had to change planes in Tokyo because there were no direct flights from the United States. The airport in Beijing had not been updated since it was built in the 1950s. There was no passport control, no customs agents. As I headed outside to a waiting car, I thought, *Talk about the Wild West. This is it!* Watching the people walking purposefully or pedaling their bikes on the streets of Beijing, I sensed an enormous energy. Buildings were under construction everywhere. This was a city and a country on the move.

I was there to meet with Shi Dazhen, who would soon head up the newly formed Ministry of Power. To describe him as a government bureaucrat would be to underestimate his reach and authority—Chinese officials were often de facto businesspeople. Shi was trying to raise money for a project called Long Yuan Power, and we met eight times to discuss the financing. I knew we were making headway when his boss, Premier Li Peng, attended one meeting. A Russian-trained hydropower engineer, Li was a senior leader in China's ruling hierarchy. He was also infamous as the public face of China's 1989 Tiananmen Square massacre, when government troops fired on protesters. A photographer captured the David-Goliath moment of a man holding shopping bags confronting army tanks. Shocked by the international outcry against the crackdown, Li was "motivated by a deep desire to be seen by history as a reformer," is how the *Wall Street Journal*'s onetime China bureau chief James McGregor puts it in his book *One Billion Customers: Lessons from the Front Lines of Doing Business in China.*

After a year of negotiations, in October 1993, Li and Shi gave Morgan Stanley the mandate to underwrite "Yankee bonds" for Long Yuan Power. It was the first time a People's Republic of China project had ever raised money in US markets. They were called Yankee bonds because they were denominated in American dollars and sold to US investors. Long Yuan Power would be instrumental in funding the massive Three Gorges Dam. Begun in 1994, it took seventeen years to build, even on an expedited schedule. Spanning the Yangtze River, it is the biggest power station in the world and gave the Chinese economy a huge boost. Li asked me to join him on a Yangtze River cruise before they flooded the gorges, but I turned down the invitation because I was so busy. That was a stupid decision. It was a chance to see a landscape that would soon disappear, and I missed it. But when I was in China, I was all business. I never took time to sightsee. I didn't visit the Great Wall until 2009, when I was about to retire.

At the signing ceremony for Long Yuan Power, I sat beside beaming Chinese officials. "So, why did you choose Morgan Stanley instead of the other banks?" I asked, turning to Shi. With a big smile, he replied, "Because you, Mr. Mack, were the only banker who came to meet with us without lawyers. You trust us."

Ironically, it was in China where I became friendly with a top executive at our archrival, Goldman Sachs. Its future CEO Hank Paulson and I were both spending a ton of time there hunting for business. We always bumped into each other walking through the hotel lobby, working out in the hotel gym, or waiting outside different government offices. I developed a lot of respect for Hank, who was a formidable but worthy competitor.

———————

WHILE WE COMPLETED the Yankee bonds for the Long Yuan Power project, Jack and Edwin continued to urge the Chinese to enter into a joint venture with us. The Chinese wanted to associate with an institution that possessed an international reputation for integrity and also had the financial clout to get things done. Morgan Stanley had both.

The key to making the joint venture happen was getting one of the country's go-to problem-solvers on board. Wang Qishan headed up the twenty-four-thousand-branch China Construction Bank. I took an immediate liking to Wang. He was well read, open to fresh ideas, and driven to raise living standards in China. Four years younger than me, Wang was the son of an engineering professor. At age twenty, he became friends with a fifteen-year-old named Xi Jinping—China's future president—when they were both sent to do hard agricultural labor as part of Mao's brutal, anti-intellectual Cultural Revolution in 1968. During this period, universities were shut down. But Wang, who was living in a cave, found a way to study. He never gave up and eventually got a degree in history. Wang had also married up, big-time. His wife was the daughter of a powerful communist leader.

From the moment I met him, I recognized that Wang was astute.

I'm good at reading people and sizing up situations, but this guy's EQ was off the charts, as I learned while negotiating with him to set up what we named the Chinese International Capital Corporation, or CICC.

The project required two years of intense back-and-forth. The Chinese aren't just tough negotiators—they really relish the whole process. In October 1994, we got a handshake deal with Wang and his superior, Zhu Rongji, China's economic czar and the future premier. Although we originally asked for a fifty-fifty arrangement with the Chinese, we ended up as one of five partners. The China Construction Bank owned 42.5 percent, with the Singapore government, the Mingly Corporation from Hong Kong, and China National Investment and Guaranty Corporation each owning around 7 percent. Morgan Stanley, which owned 35 percent, invested $35 million.

The handshake was just the start. We still had to put together a contract. The next ten months required nonstop negotiation on three continents—Asia, North America, and Europe. My team and I went to Beijing, and then we met with Wang in Milan, Italy. We were really making a lot of progress. Our next negotiating session was in my office in New York. But something was off. Wang wasn't himself. He seemed all over the place—tense, twitchy, not at all the focused, determined but likable negotiator. I kept looking at him, trying to pinpoint what was wrong. After about forty minutes, it dawned on me. Wang was a chain-smoker. I put my hands up, signaling a time-out.

"Qishan," I said, "light 'em up!"

"What do you mean?" he asked, his face quizzical.

"Start smoking."

"John, you know I can't do that in New York City. It's against the law."

"It's okay, Qishan. You're in my office. Light 'em up!"

He took out a pack, lit his cigarette, and inhaled deeply. He looked so happy. We got back on track and finished up the deal.

What amazed me about Wang was that he had noticed and was respectful of the laws of New York City. It showed his ability to observe and absorb even the tiniest nuances of cultures not his own. And I have to say, I was pretty proud of my own observational powers in this situation, too.

All our work culminated one evening in August 1995. I was in the back of a limo with Dick Fisher, Jack Wadsworth, Edwin Lim, and others, being driven through the traditional Chinese gate of the Diaoyutai State Guesthouse. Intricately carved and painted, the enormous wooden gate gleamed with gilt. The Diaoyutai complex is where Chinese government officials entertain foreign dignitaries. Blending modern and traditional Chinese architecture, it is one of the "Ten Great Buildings" that Mao commissioned in 1959 to commemorate the tenth anniversary of the founding of the People's Republic of China. The name Diaoyutai means fishing platform. It's where Emperor Zhangzong, who reigned from 1189 to 1208, liked to fish. I was staggered by the centuries-long flow of history.

To celebrate our new joint venture, the Chinese hosted a large, formal state banquet. It's hard to convey how creatively the chefs presented the food, shaping it into flowers, dragons, and water buffalo. There were at least a dozen dishes. I would come to adore the spicy Sichuan cuisine from the southwestern province that is home to the giant panda. At this point I was still a novice when it came to sophisticated Chinese cooking, but I had come a long way from the guy who couldn't eat live prawns in Tokyo. One dish was fish-eyeball soup. I slurped this soup down like it was the best thing I had ever tasted. Otherwise, I would offend my hosts. I also didn't shy away from Maotai. This Chinese hard liquor has since fallen out of favor at banquets. People now prefer wine. But in 1974, Henry Kissinger, the US secretary of state, had told Chinese leader Deng Xiaoping, "I think if we drink enough Maotai, we can solve anything."

I was so accustomed to rushing through my days and nights, I rarely allowed myself to sit back and savor the moment. This was a big deal, and I felt proud to be there. We were pioneers with the founding of CICC. Famous for their slogans, the Chinese hailed Morgan Stanley as "the first person to eat the crab" in recognition of the groundbreaking nature of the venture.

THE VOICE CRACKLED over the phone.

"We have a problem, Mr. Mack," the caller—a Morgan Stanley employee—said. "You need to come to Beijing."

It was Memorial Day weekend, 2000. I had just arrived back in the United States a few days earlier from a grueling trip to China. To relax, Christy and I were in North Carolina, where we had built a beach house. We were celebrating the holiday with friends. It was a warm day, and I was standing on the deck in my bathing suit and a T-shirt. "How did you get this number?" I asked.

"I got the number from Morgan Stanley security," she said. "I know you were just here. It doesn't matter. We cannot wait. You have to return right away."

"We'll talk on Tuesday when I'm back in the office. Good-bye."

I hung up the phone and jumped in the water.

But the calls didn't stop. I got a voice mail every hour. Though annoyed, I had to admire this woman's persistence. She was determined. I gave her that.

Finally, I called her back.

She picked up on the first ring.

"Okay, I'm listening," I said. She explained that unless I was at the conference table in Beijing in three days, the upcoming IPO for China's state-owned oil and gas conglomerate, Sinopec, would collapse.

Her name was Wei Sun Christianson, and she had been working for Morgan Stanley for all of two years. When you're starting out, it's easy to think that every time a deal hits a pothole, the world will come to an end. But her intensity made me wonder, *Maybe she's onto something here.* I had to test her, though. "You know, this better be good, Wei. Otherwise, I'll fire you," I said.

"I know," she said. "I know. You won't have to fire me. I will resign. But if you don't come, Morgan Stanley's reputation in China will be really damaged for many years."

She convinced me. I hung up and called the executive assistant who coordinated flights on Morgan Stanley's new corporate jet. "I have to be in Beijing as soon as possible," I told her. I would be flying thirteen hours each way.

I knew I had put the fear of God in Wei. But I hadn't done what many executives do in similar circumstances: I didn't tell her, "Call somebody else." I didn't brush her off. I learned a long time ago that you're not a leader if you act like a bureaucrat. If this situation was as dire as she said, I couldn't expect someone else to get on the plane. It had to be me. When you're a leader, sometimes you've got to get on that horse and ride into battle. I expected the people who worked for me to take responsibility, which is exactly what Wei was doing. But I also held myself accountable.

Wei Sun Christianson's life spans modern Chinese history. Born in 1956, she grew up under communist rule. Her mother was a doctor and her father, a military official. Wei studied English at the elite Beijing Language University. As Deng opened up China to foreigners, she met an American professor who encouraged her to get a degree at a US college. Taking his advice, she became the first student from the People's Republic of China to graduate from Amherst College, in Massachusetts. From there, Wei went to Columbia Law School, where she met her husband. After the couple moved to Hong Kong in the early nineties, she worked at a government agency, the Securities and Futures Commission. Her job was crafting the regulations that allowed Chinese companies to be listed on international stock exchanges. Deciding she'd rather do deals, Wei joined Morgan Stanley as an investment banker in 1998. That's how she came to be involved with the Sinopec IPO.

Two days later, when I arrived at Beijing Airport, by this time a fully modernized facility, there was Wei. The commanding, impeccably dressed forty-three-year-old banker had come to pick me up. "I want to brief you as we go into the city," she said. "We don't have time to waste." As her driver negotiated the now thick traffic of cars, taxis, trucks, and limousines, Wei laid out what was happening with the deal. "For a year, I have been working with Sinopec and CICC to do this initial public offering," she said. "When we completed the due diligence, we realized that Sinopec shares cannot be listed on any stock exchange. The reason is simple. The price of crude oil and the price of gasoline are set under different policies."

Wei went on: "The price of crude oil is high because it's allowed to fluctuate freely on the global market, and the gasoline price is low because the Chinese state planning commission subsidizes it. This conflict means that Sinopec will never be profitable. We cannot have this company go public. No investor will give it a dime.

"But at the same time, if the government lets the price of gasoline rise, it has huge implications for the country, including the possibility that the taxi drivers will go on strike. So this is a very complex situation.

"Sinopec called me. They said we've got to lobby Zhu Rongji to change the policy. [The economic czar who had green-lighted the joint venture had been elevated to premier.] But Zhu Rongji said the only way he would attend a meeting with Sinopec is to have our number one guy come over." She pointed at me. "You."

Wei concluded, "There's a lot at stake here. I knew if I didn't get you to come back here, this deal is dead. That would be a national humiliation for China. And if Morgan Stanley fails after all this work, we will get a bad reputation. It will set our business back in China for a long time."

I leaned against the leather seat of the Mercedes-Benz. "I'm not going to fire you," I said. "You were one hundred percent right to get me to come, Wei." Then I smiled. "Now, what's the game plan?"

Later, sitting next to Zhu in a reception room, I explained why, if China was trying to reform its economy, the government couldn't interfere with its state enterprises—in this case, by subsidizing the price of gasoline. "The whole point of restructuring state enterprises is to make them market-oriented," I said.

Zhu is a formidable, square-faced man with eyebrows as imposing as my own. He looked at me. "Morgan Stanley is doing this deal, and you're the leader," he said. "I want you to personally give me a commitment that you will do the best you can to make this deal a success."

I put my hand over my heart. "Premier Zhu, I give you my word. I guarantee I will be involved in every detail of this deal, and it will succeed."

I was. And it did. My reputation means nothing without my word.

A few weeks after my trip, the Chinese government allowed the domestic price of gasoline to align with the price of crude oil internationally. On October 19, 2000, Sinopec went public on the New York, London, and Hong Kong stock exchanges, raising $3.5 billion.

If I have only one piece of advice to offer, it is to listen to people who know more than you do and to act on what they tell you. As we prepped for the meeting with Zhu, Wei told me: "There are three things you need to say, and you've got to say them in this order." She knew how I had to act, what I had to say, and, maybe most important, who I had to look at. She understood China in a way that I, or even overseas Chinese, never could. A child of Mao's Cultural Revolution, she knew the people in charge. During this visit, I realized that Wei was invaluable to the future of Morgan Stanley. She's a killer—she's smart, she's direct, she's demanding, she's intuitive. In the war—and believe me, it was a war—to get the best business and thwart Goldman Sachs and other investment firms in China, she was the heavy artillery.

I remember one hideous night in China—maybe in Hangzhou. I was sick with food poisoning. I'll spare you the details, but I couldn't get out of bed, much less attend a banquet. Wei called from the lobby. She and her driver were there to pick me up. "I can't go," I croaked into the phone. "I'm too sick. I can't stop vomiting."

Silence.

Then Wei spoke. "You must go. It's nonnegotiable. Important people in the Chinese government will be there."

I staggered out of bed, took a shower, and got dressed. Meanwhile, Wei sent her driver to buy a bunch of Chinese herbs, which she brewed into a revolting tea. "Here," she said, handing me a cup. "Drink this. All of it."

I looked horrible and felt worse. I was feverish and soaked in sweat. But I went to the banquet with Wei. She's one tough cookie.

I met another steely businesswoman in China. Wu Yajun cofounded Longfor Properties, a vast real estate company spread throughout China. When we pitched Wu to do Longfor's IPO, she was debating whether to use Morgan Stanley or J. P. Morgan. It was a multimillion-dollar deal.

"Maybe I should use J. P. Morgan. They can do the IPO and give us a loan," Wu told me. "You can only do the IPO." I had been my usual delightful self, but I switched off the charm. "I don't think you're very smart," I said. Wei gave me a sharp look like, *Oh my God! What are you doing?* I ignored her. I said again, "You're not smart, because you forgot what this is about. This is about an IPO, and when it comes to an IPO, there is no comparison between Morgan Stanley and J. P. Morgan. You need to think straight. What is your objective, and who has the muscle to achieve it?"

Wu looked shocked. But as I explained that Morgan Stanley did 50 percent of all the IPOs for Chinese corporations, she started to nod in agreement. At the end of the meeting she said, "No one has ever talked to me like that, but I'm giving you the business, Mr. Mack. This is the kind of firm I want; a firm that can be direct and tell me the truth."

I established close ties with people in China. They knew that I was a banker and that I was in the business of making money for Morgan Stanley. But they came to realize that I genuinely cared about them. Once, when Christy, the kids, and I stopped in Hong Kong on our way to Thailand, I took a day trip to see Wang. He had left the China Construction Bank and become the governor of nearby Guangdong Province. I wanted to see how he was doing, to catch up. So I was surprised when I made the news that night on Chinese TV. The newscaster announced, "Morgan Stanley's John Mack comes up to be with Wang Qishan." I didn't visit him hoping to get good publicity. I did it because he was my friend, and that's what you do—you take time out of your schedule to see friends.

I really liked the Chinese I got to know. I found them direct and open. They told me what they thought. Like me, they valued decisiveness. While I might make the wrong decision on occasion, I always make up my mind quickly.

One decision would upend my career.

CHAPTER FIFTEEN

I couldn't believe this day was really happening. I was sitting on the dais in the Equitable Center auditorium on Seventh Avenue in midtown Manhattan. Before me was an audience of three hundred eager financial analysts and business reporters. Newspaper and wire service photographers, crouched on the floor in front, snapped away. TV cameras rolled. More analysts and journalists in Asia, Europe, Africa, and Latin America "attended" the press conference via satellite and telephone.

It was 10:30 a.m. on a rainy Wednesday, February 5, 1997. We were announcing the merger of Morgan Stanley and Dean Witter, Discover & Co. This $10.2 billion jaw-dropper of a deal instantly catapulted us to the top of the financial stratosphere. With more than $270 billion in assets under management, Morgan Stanley Dean Witter, Discover was now the largest financial services firm in the world.

Sitting on the dais between Dick Fisher and me was Philip J. Purcell, the head of Dean Witter. The new colossus united Morgan Stanley's dominance in investment banking and institutional sales and trading with Dean Witter's expansive reach as the third-largest retail brokerage in the United States. In other words, Morgan Stanley's investment bankers would generate the securities, and Dean Witter's 8,700-plus brokers would sell them to American households coast to coast. "This is as close to an ideal merger as there is," Purcell announced.

Phil, Dick, and I shared an easy camaraderie as we joked around on the dais, each flashing a Discover credit card. Dick, who didn't have his own Discover Card, showed off Christy's, concealing her name with his index finger. Among the merger's many positives: there would be few layoffs, since there was little overlap between Morgan Stanley and Dean Witter. Research and back-office administration were the only two areas that overlapped.

I had done a lot of press conferences during my career, and this one was a home run. After our presentation, we took questions from the press. "There are some people who believe you won't play second fiddle," the *Wall Street Journal*'s Anita Raghavan said to me.

"Anita, you don't know me very well," I replied. "It's not about me. It's about building an organization. I only care about what's best for my shareholders and employees. I care about being on the best team. And this is the best team."

Before the merger, Dick, who was retiring, had named me his successor. I had been slated to take over as chairman of Morgan Stanley in June 1997. The board had already signed off.

The merger changed everything.

That's right. I had stepped aside. I agreed to take the number two spot behind Purcell in the newly formed Morgan Stanley Dean Witter, Discover. Phil would be chairman and CEO. I would be president and chief operating officer (COO). The reason? Phil would not agree to the deal unless he was the boss. This made sense. Dean Witter, Discover, with its forty thousand employees, was a lot bigger than Morgan Stanley, with our ten thousand people. Technically they bought Morgan Stanley and paid a hefty stock premium.

I had no problem being second in command. I had worked easily for more than two decades under Dick Fisher. I expected to have the same productive partnership with Phil Purcell. Phil often told people that he hoped for the same.

Phil was a year older than me and grew up in Salt Lake City. He joined the consulting firm McKinsey in 1967 with an MBA from the University of Chicago B-school. Next he went to Sears, a McKinsey client. After Sears bought Dean Witter in 1981, he headed the retail brokerage firm. Phil was best known for successfully launching its revolutionary no-fee, cash-back Discover Card.

In the fall of 1992, Sears decided to spin off Dean Witter, Discover. Phil Duff, a young Morgan Stanley M&A hotshot from Red Wing, Minnesota, by way of Harvard and the Massachusetts Institute of Technology business school who became Morgan Stanley's chief financial officer (CFO) in 1994, had nabbed the Dean Witter account from Goldman Sachs. Working with Dean Witter, Morgan Stanley was the co-underwriter and priced the offering.

Sitting at my desk reading the IPO prospectus, I was blown away by Dean Witter, Discover's revenue flow. Because of credit card transaction fees and the recurrent fees the company earned on its mutual fund business, it covered its overhead within the first four months of the year. Everything from May 1 on was profit. By contrast, Morgan Stanley's business, based on dealmaking and trading, was unpredictable. We didn't cover our overhead until September, or even later. If we merged with Dean Witter, Discover, we would have a steady source of income. I said to Dick, "I don't know why we're doing this transaction for Sears. Why don't we just go to Sears and make a bid for Dean Witter ourselves?"

"John, that's very interesting," Dick said with a smile, "but we serve our clients' desires and ambitions and not necessarily our own. I think we'd upset a few people if we decided this should be an M&A transaction instead of an IPO." But he readily agreed that doing something with Dean Witter had potential.

Dick and I invited Phil Purcell to lunch at Morgan Stanley, where we floated the idea of a merger. I immediately warmed to Purcell, who had an aw-shucks kind of charm. But he nixed the idea. "We've been part of another company"—Sears—"long enough," he told us. "I want to be independent." I totally got that. But Morgan Stanley had a different perspective. We had been operating solo since 1935. Now was the right time for us to form strategic partnerships.

If we go back to May 1, 1975, when the Securities and Exchange Commission forced the New York Stock Exchange to eliminate fixed commissions in favor of negotiated ones, the profit margins in the securities business had been getting skinnier and skinnier. But the financial industry continued to make money because, thanks to globalization, volume continued to grow. Exporting our aggressive, competitive, technologically innovative style of banking, American firms like Morgan Stanley, Goldman Sachs, J. P. Morgan, and Merrill Lynch had dominated finance around the world. That's what the previous decade—the 1980s—had been about.

Things had gone pretty well for Morgan Stanley. But my view was that this momentum would eventually sputter out. We needed to keep innovating; to hunt down new opportunities. The questions we were trying to answer: How do we get more business? How do we diversify our earnings? How do we leapfrog over our rivals?

The answer: scale up. We needed to create a larger financial footprint.

In September 1994, Sir David Scholey reached out to Dick to propose a merger. Scholey was the CEO of S. G. Warburg, the United

Kingdom's largest investment bank. Based in London, it was an off-shoot of a famous German-Jewish banking dynasty. A match would double our size. We were opening brand-new offices throughout Asia and Latin America, but if we combined with S. G. Warburg, Morgan Stanley would crack open the formerly closed doors of elite, established corporate clients in the United Kingdom and Europe.

Warburg also owned 75 percent of a subsidiary called Mercury Asset Management, which had $93 billion in assets under management. This business would provide exactly the steady, recurring fees we wanted. And because we were taking huge risks in emerging markets, it would provide ballast in the form of diversification.

Dick took the lead in the negotiations. I dealt with my counterpart at S. G. Warburg, Lord Simon Cairns. On the surface, we are opposites. He is an aristocrat and a vegetarian who attended Eton, the ultra-prestigious boarding school founded by King Henry VI in 1440. I am a Mooresville High grad who loves nothing more than a pulled pork sandwich topped with coleslaw. But we got along great. Cairns was a principled banker who wanted what was best for his company in the long run. This boded well for us to be co-presidents under Dick as chairman. By early December, our talks had gone so smoothly, we thought we had a deal. The *Wall Street Journal* ran a story under the headline: "Morgan Stanley, S. G. Warburg Discuss Merger: Stock Swap of $7 Billion to Bring Global Reach, $150 Billion Asset Pool." The most-read newspaper on Wall Street deemed the potential merger a "marriage of blue bloods."

But obstacles emerged. The biggest problem was that Mercury Asset Management priced the 25 percent of the company that was public at an absurd 350 percent over its trading price. "We're never going to be able to deal with these people," Dick told Phil Duff. He was right. The deal was doomed. Cairns and I tried to salvage it but couldn't.

IN THE LATE 1980s, corporate America began moving away from providing fixed pensions to retirees, instead offering current employees 401(k) plans. This switch changed Wall Street, as baby boomers invested in stocks and mutual funds. According to Charles Geisst in *Wall Street: A History*, "Between 1990 and 1997, the amount of money invested in mutual funds increased ten times over, and the number of investors buying them almost doubled." We couldn't ignore numbers like that. Morgan Stanley had handled pension funds for decades, but we had no way of reaching average investors. If the firm really was to become a major player, it needed to have access to the single largest pool of assets in the world: US households.

And a specific category of stocks had grabbed these investors' attention: tech.

Morgan Stanley had been present at the creation of the information age. The first time Steve Jobs, the visionary cofounder of Apple Computer, met with Jack Wadsworth—this was several years before Jack moved to Japan—Jobs put his bare feet up on the conference table and asked, "So, what does Morgan Stanley do?" By the end of the meeting, Jack and Jobs had reached an understanding that Morgan Stanley would take Apple public. This happened in 1980.

It was the start of our tech streak. In the first half of the 1990s, we handled IPOs for Intuit and AOL. We had a not-so-secret weapon in Mary Meeker, a Portland, Indiana, native and graduate of the Cornell University Johnson Graduate School of Management. Meeker, who joined Morgan Stanley in 1991, became known as the Queen of the Net for her preternatural ability as a research analyst to spot winning tech companies. Her annual "Internet Trends" report debuted in 1995 and became a must-read. That same year, on August 9, 1995, our client Netscape ignited the dot-com frenzy when its stock price hit the stratosphere in a highly publicized and wildly successful IPO.

All this time I kept thinking about Dean Witter. It had offices across the United States—some, in fact, in Sears stores—and managed hundreds of billions of dollars for American families. I was so curious that Christy and I took a field trip to our local Sears. While she wandered the aisles remembering her family shopping at Sears as a child, I sat down with a broker at the Dean Witter kiosk. You could buy mutual funds as easily as you could purchase a hammer, a pair of dress socks, or a washer-dryer. I thought it was cool and innovative.

Merrill Lynch, then the largest financial services firm in the world, had an average investment banking business. If Morgan Stanley combined our stellar investment banking with Dean Witter's massive retail operation, the result would be a winning formula for shareholders. Plus, we would crush Merrill.

That's why we wanted to do the merger.

After our 1992 lunch, Dick and I continued to pursue Phil Purcell and Dean Witter. In 1995, the publicity frenzy surrounding the Netscape IPO piqued Phil's interest. He told us that when Dean Witter launched a new mutual fund, clients didn't invest *more* money, they simply moved money out of an existing fund they owned and into the new one, thereby cannibalizing their portfolios. But clients viewed tech stocks differently. They were willing to invest more money if it boosted them onto the internet rocket ship.

Purcell started negotiating in earnest in December 1996. I think the catalyst that brought him to the table was another merger. NationsBank—soon to be called Bank of America—bought Boatmen's Bancshares, the biggest bank in St. Louis, Missouri, and the lower Midwest. Purcell must have suddenly recognized that Dean Witter now had another huge national rival. "I'd really like to renew our discussions and see if we can figure out how to put a deal together," he told us on the phone.

That's when the negotiations got serious.

But it wasn't long before they were interrupted.

Christy and I invited three couples to Deer Valley for a long weekend. I was managing my way down the slope when a skier rammed into me from behind, knocking me down and rupturing one of my kidneys. So much for a fun time. I wound up in the hospital all weekend, unable to do anything but lie there. Because Phil owned a ski house not far from ours, Dick offered to fly out to Utah so the three of us could keep the momentum going. But Christy, between visiting me and entertaining our friends, prevailed. "No, we're not going to do that here," she told me. "You're not going to negotiate flat on your back." After I left the hospital, Phil kindly flew Christy and me back to New York on the Dean Witter plane.

The last week of January, Dick, Phil Duff, and I met with Purcell at Dick's Central Park West apartment three nights in a row. We couldn't agree on either the financial terms or who would lead the combined firm. There was no clear path forward on how to put the companies together. I thought Purcell should have reached across the table and shaken hands—that he should have met us halfway. Dick provided a lot of support, but he took the attitude that since he was retiring in May, I should be in charge of the talks.

This was in keeping with the working relationship we had established in recent years. I had been de facto running the firm. Dick had been immersed at Morgan Stanley since 1962. Now age sixty and about to embark on a second marriage, he wanted to spend more time pursuing his interests in philanthropy and the arts with his future wife. I still went to him if there was something I couldn't quite figure out. But that happened less and less.

Friday morning, Dick, Phil Duff, and I got on a conference call with Purcell. "Phil, we should stop," I said. "We've been at this three nights in a row, and we can't get it done." This wasn't a negotiating tactic. I thought the merger was off.

Purcell disagreed. He shot back with good reasons why we should go for it.

After we hung up, Phil Duff came into my office and sat down. "Look, John, we're so bloody close here," he said. "You don't get these opportunities very often. We've talked about the other targets that could be candidates for us. But there are two parts to any merger. First, the strategy has to work. Second, and just as important, you have to have a willing party. Those are not easy to come by. Why don't you call Purcell back and suggest having dinner together, just the two of you."

That night Purcell and I met in a private room at the Box Tree, a tiny, discreet French restaurant on East Forty-Ninth Street.

I got home around midnight. "This is big!" I told Christy, who was waiting up. Next I called Duff. "I got it done! Check your fax machine. I'm sending over a one-pager. It's the term sheet. We hammered out the financials and the exchange ratio between the stocks."

I continued. "We agreed on the leadership of the new firm."

When I went to Dick's apartment the next morning to give him the news, his eyes got a flinty look behind his glasses that I'd seen only a few times in the quarter-century we had worked together. "I don't want you to do this, John," Dick said. "This is a mistake. It's not right for the firm. It's not right for you. You should be CEO, not Phil. You're the stronger leader."

I took in what Dick was telling me. But I felt with all my heart that the benefits of the merger outweighed the downside of giving Phil the top job. This was a once-in-a-lifetime opportunity to create the largest financial services firm in history. As we approached the new millennium, this would position the firm to take a huge step forward. I was willing to give up the CEO title to secure Morgan Stanley's future. "This isn't our firm, Dick," I said, looking at the man who had hired me, who had made my career at Morgan Stanley possible, whose business counsel I had seldom questioned. "It's the shareholders' firm. We have to do what's right for them."

The question of succession was, and remains, a thorny and painful subject. Dick told me that he and Purcell had shaken hands, agreeing that within two or three years Phil would step aside, and I would become CEO of Morgan Stanley Dean Witter, Discover. Purcell says there was no handshake agreement. The bottom line: it was not put in writing that Purcell would turn the CEO title over to me.

That weekend, we performed due diligence on each company. The lawyers were drafting merger agreements and all the related documentation. Our PR team was crafting an announcement. We had to move fast so the news didn't leak. We didn't want anything to affect the stock prices.

All of a sudden, we were getting drafts of new parts of the deal that hadn't been discussed. Among them, Purcell's insistence that 75 percent of the board members would have to vote to fire him rather than 50 percent.

Reading the faxed changes, Duff was aghast. "No way in hell should we agree to those sorts of things," he told me. "It's blasphemous and hypocritical that we're making concessions we would forbid a client to accept."

Only when I was writing this book did I fully realize the depth of Dick's reservations. Tom Nides, another whip-smart Minnesotan, was overseeing Morgan Stanley's media strategy. He recently told me that less than twenty-four hours before the press conference announcing the merger, Dick had summoned him to his office on the fortieth floor of the Morgan Stanley Building. Sitting at his desk, Dick was smoking a cigar. "We shouldn't do the deal," Dick told Tom. "You need to convince John not to do the deal."

"Dick, I think it's too late," Tom replied. "John is doing the deal."

At the Equitable Center auditorium the next morning, Dick, Phil, and I hammed it up for the cameras. My wide grin was 100 percent sincere. I was over the moon that we had pulled the merger off, and by the end of the day, the market was, too: Morgan Stanley's stock jumped up $7.875 a share to $54.25, and Dean Witter's stock rose $2 a share to $40.625.

The merger made headlines around the world. "Wall Street Wants 'The Little Guy' and It Will Merge to Get Him," blared the *Wall Street Journal*. The *New York Times* announced, "A Deal Reaffirms the Strength of the Individual Investor." "Giant Brokerage Is Born," roared the *Charlotte Observer*, with a big photo of Phil and me grinning.

Some commentators fired off cautionary flares. "One firm is white shoe and the other is white socks," the *Washington Post* quoted a Wall Street insider. "They may both have the same philosophy, but they are very different."

"Will This Marriage Work?" asked Bloomberg News.

CHAPTER SIXTEEN

I admit it. It was strange for me to see Phil Purcell settling his six-foot, five-inch frame into Dick Fisher's seat at the head of the conference table. For the first time in the firm's sixty-two-year history, an outsider who knew nothing about our traditions, values, or procedures was running Morgan Stanley.

From the get-go, just as pundits had predicted, the cultures of Morgan Stanley and Dean Witter clashed. We *could* be arrogant assholes, while the Dean Witter employees seemed hell-bent on taking *everything* as an insult. I still remember the first time our combined management committee met. Phil and I went around the table. "Bring us up-to-date on your business unit domestically as well as internationally," I said to the division heads. I really wanted to get to know the new managers and to foster a sense that we were all on the same team.

When the guy running Discover Card started talking about his international business, he described its operations in Canada. Peter Karches, never one to curb his tongue, interrupted. "Listen, it's not international if the number doesn't start with 011!" Everyone from Morgan Stanley laughed. The vibe I picked up from the Dean Witter people was chip-on-the-shoulder hostility, particularly from Purcell. He eyed Peter coldly.

Of course, we knew Canada was foreign. This was Peter being Peter, yanking the guy's chain. I hadn't forgotten that at one point my team had no idea about Venezuelan bonds or what airline flew to Kuala Lumpur. But at this point, we had eighty-four offices around the world. Dean Witter was almost an entirely US-based operation. As the *New York Times* noted, "Morgan Stanley's senior executives, in their tasseled Gucci loafers and expensive Armani suits, make many millions of dollars a year as they jet to Tokyo, London, Frankfurt and other world financial centers to do deals with government ministers and business tycoons. Often graduates of Ivy League universities and top business schools, they are young and often on such a fast track that many are able to retire wealthy before the age of fifty. Their counterparts at Dean Witter, meanwhile, favor Brooks Brothers and Dexter shoes and shuttle around on suburban highways, where even the more successful earn at most several hundred thousand dollars a year hawking mostly plain vanilla mutual funds, stocks and bonds to Main Street America."

It wasn't a question of superior or inferior. If the New York Stock Exchange hadn't prohibited the opening of new branches across the country during the paperwork crunch of 1968, I might have opened a retail office in Atlanta for Smith Barney.

There was fault on both sides. I was staggered to hear that one of my most trusted people, Jeff Salzman, had been publicly humiliated at a meeting with his new boss from Dean Witter, James Higgins. Jeff and a Morgan Stanley colleague from the Private Client Division gave a presentation to bring the Dean Witter Retail execs up to speed on the division's revenue, costs, and margins. When they finished, Higgins turned to his CFO and said, "I don't believe any of this. Check all those numbers and come back to me and tell me what the real story is." Jeff eventually quit. I rehired him as a direct report in Strategic Planning.

We tried to meld the two cultures. Not long after the merger, Purcell and I decided that a golf outing would be a great icebreaker. We took a handful of Morgan Stanley folks and a handful of Dean Witter, Discover folks to play at Muirfield Village Golf Club, an exclusive course designed by Jack Nicklaus with Desmond Muirhead, in Dublin, Ohio. As soon as we reached the "Nineteenth Hole" on the second day, I figured it was time to go home. I didn't give it a thought. I'd made countless trips to China and had never stayed longer than three nights. The Morgan Stanley team, me included, headed to the airport to fly back to New York. The next morning, when I noticed that Phil wasn't in the office, I realized that he and his team had stayed another night in Ohio. Later, when I ran into him, he seemed irritated. "All you guys cared about was getting back on the plane," he said. "I thought we were going to have dinner together."

I was stunned. "Phil, we had work to do."

I picked up on something. In meetings, Purcell did most of the talking. When his subordinates did contribute, they just echoed whatever he was saying. He was undeniably sharp. But I began to believe that he did not want to be challenged. As Morgan Stanley executive Bob Scott told Patricia Beard in *Blue Blood & Mutiny*, "Phil thought that if there were only enough hours in the day, he could do everyone's job better than they could do it." Since he seemed to believe he had all the answers, I thought he looked for personal allegiance from his subordinates. People talked about how Purcell joked, "At Dean Witter, I tell people to turn left, and they turn left. At Morgan Stanley, they look at me and ask why."

I was the opposite. I always knew I wasn't the most brilliant person in the room. I looked for brains and talent in the people I hired.

From my earliest days as a manager, I had encouraged employees to speak up. I had often sent people for training to learn how to speak up in meetings, present their views effectively, and challenge what other people were saying, including me.

Certain style differences were to be expected between Phil and me. I wasn't looking for a twin. I'm an extreme extrovert. Purcell struck me as an introvert. When he got within four blocks of the office, he had his driver call ahead to building security. They reserved an empty elevator for him so he could ride up alone. I had an open-door policy. To see Phil, you needed an appointment.

There were geographic issues. Although Purcell took charge of Dean Witter, located in the heart of Wall Street, in 1982, he never moved his wife and seven sons from the Chicago suburbs to New York. Instead he commuted to New York on a Falcon and later a Gulfstream corporate plane, typically flying in on Monday mornings and flying home on Thursday afternoons. He continued this routine after the merger. Considering the prestige and responsibility of his position, I believed he owed it to the firm and the shareholders to be on-site. Plus, Morgan Stanley, like all Wall Street firms, expected its leaders to be philanthropically engaged with the city. Bob Baldwin had gotten me involved with Columbia-Presbyterian Hospital when I was a young managing director. Others devoted time, energy, and money to the Morgan Library and the Metropolitan Museum of Art.

Besides seemingly remaining aloof from New York City, I thought Phil also appeared not to appreciate what an incredible resource he could have had in Dick Fisher. Dick possessed not just institutional knowledge but true wisdom. After the merger, he chaired the executive committee of the new firm's board of directors, seven from Dean Witter and seven from Morgan Stanley. But the second the merger agreement was signed, it looked to me like Phil went out of his way to snub Dick.

When we moved to the Morgan Stanley Building at 1585 Broadway in 1995, Dick and I put the executive offices on the fortieth floor. But Phil, it seemed, didn't want to be on the same floor as Dick. Spending millions of dollars, he built out the executive suite on thirty-nine and left Dick alone on forty. Because I reported to Purcell, I had to move.

What I considered to be Phil's callous, even cruel, treatment of Dick enraged me. But there was nothing I could do to change his behavior. What made it worse was that on the first anniversary of the merger becoming official—May 31, 1998—Dick was diagnosed with the prostate cancer that would eventually kill him.

I didn't fully appreciate what a unique partnership I had with Dick until I started working with Phil. I never questioned Dick's motives. He never pushed a secret agenda. Our working relationship was as good as you could ever find in any company anywhere. Dick was balanced, brilliant, and gentle—and I don't mean gentle in a soft way. If I went to him with a problem, I knew he would never put me down or preach at me. There was no competitive undercurrent or subtext between us. In retrospect, I was naive to think that I would have the same relationship or level of trust with Purcell.

I was also struck by Phil's decision-making process. He never pulled together a group to hash out pros and cons. Instead, he summoned people one by one to get their input. That was fine. The problem, as I saw it, was that he spent most workdays in his office, door closed, gaming out different business strategies. I thought his slow, cerebral approach led to much theorizing and little execution.

I had a different approach. Here's how I did things.

Around the same time as the Morgan Stanley Dean Witter merger, I also helped engineer a merger between Columbia-Presbyterian Hospital and New York Hospital. We put the two doctors who headed those institutions in charge. Bill Speck of Columbia-Presbyterian became president of the combined hospital, with David Skinner of New York Hospital as the CEO. A few months later, I was at our monthly trustees breakfast at the *Good Housekeeping* dining room with John McGillicuddy, the CEO of Chemical Bank; Frank Bennack, the wise and gracious CEO of media conglomerate Hearst; and Dan Burke of Capital Cities/ABC, an admired TV executive. Somebody said, "Look, this arrangement between Skinner and Speck is not working. The merger's a disaster, and Speck's the problem. He's going around Skinner."

"Let's bring him in here," I said. "We've got to take care of this." I picked up my phone and called Bill Speck. "Hey, Bill," I said, "where are you?"

"I'm in the car going to the hospital," he said.

"Come by. We're on the ninth floor of the Hearst building. We want to talk to you."

As soon as Dr. Speck walked in and sat down, I said, "Bill, we cannot have these conflicts. We cannot have you undercutting David Skinner. This merger has to work. We made a decision. We're going to pay you, but you're fired."

I had worked closely with Bill. I thought he was an excellent doctor and administrator. But the merger's success outweighed my past relationship with him. It was over. He was fired. As soon as Dr. Speck walked out, McGillicuddy looked at me and said, "Where did you come from?"

"That's how you do it," I said. "What's the point of having coffee and doing all the how-are-you bullshit? No, it's 'You have to resign. We'll treat you with respect, but you're gone.' That's the way I run Morgan Stanley."

Bennack, who grew up in San Antonio, Texas, said, "John, you do not take all day to look at a hot horseshoe. You have no difficulty making up your mind, do you?"

LOOKING BACK, I realize that Frank Petito, Bob Baldwin, Parker Gilbert, and Dick Fisher were atypical leaders, especially for their time. They ran Morgan Stanley as a flat hierarchy. The best ideas won on their merits, not on the rank of the people who proposed them. By contrast, Purcell operated Dean Witter as a conventional corporation. The C-suite sat at the top of a pyramid and dictated what should happen below. No one asked for input from the employees on the lower rungs. From where I stood, it appeared that Phil also promoted the old-fashioned way. It seemed that to get ahead, you had to be one of his allies. That's how people thought I ran Fixed Income: that you had to be an F.O.J.—a Friend of John's—to move up. When Tom DeLong alerted me to this problem, I had him create a more objective promotion process. Morgan Stanley was way ahead of Dean Witter in terms of corporate evolution.

There were other differences. One involved teamwork. At Morgan Stanley, it was the essential element. A multibillion-dollar M&A deal couldn't be done by just one individual. It required people to work together, often laboring through the night for months. Traders and salespeople, whose agendas often clashed, had to work in tandem to move bonds. These kinds of experiences bound people together, building esprit de corps. Dean Witter, at its heart, was a network of individual retail brokers. Collaboration didn't advance their careers because the key relationship was broker to client. They were paid on commission. It was "eat what you kill."

In the merger, I was placed in charge of Dean Witter's thousands of retail brokers across the country. The division was headquartered downtown in the World Trade Center. Just as I had put the Fishbowl in the middle of the trading floor, I wanted to interact in person with the retail brokers and their managers. I wanted to know what problems they faced in their business; how I could help with their clients. If I was going to lead them, I needed to get to know them.

"I want to set up an office down at Dean Witter," I told Purcell.

"No," he answered. End of discussion.

Later I found out Phil refused my request because the Dean Witter executives were worried that I would be putting them under a microscope. That's exactly what I had in mind. That was my job. With no choice in the matter, I grudgingly accepted Phil's decision. Still, every time I took a business trip, I tried to fit in a visit to a branch office. I was meeting with the CEO of Safeway, based in Pleasanton, California. Having arrived a couple of hours early, I decided to drop by the nearby Dean Witter branch. I took questions and asked some of my own. "What do you need from us? How can we make your job easier?"

Phil called me into his office the next day. "I understand you went to a Dean Witter branch in Northern California," he said.

"Yeah, it was great. I got some good feedback."

"John, you can't do that."

I was flabbergasted. "Wait, are you telling me I can't stop by a branch office?"

"Yes. As CEO, Ed Brennan would never make an unannounced visit to a Sears store. He always arranged it weeks in advance."

"That's the stupidest thing I've ever heard!" I shouted. "Why? So everyone can put on the right shirt and cut their hair because 'Here comes the boss'? This is not fucking Sears!"

That was the moment I realized I didn't respect Phil Purcell. I thought he was insecure. And that insecurity seemed to make him territorial. Territorial leaders are terrible leaders because they put protecting their personal power base ahead of the institution they're supposed to lead.

In my eyes, Phil focused on strengthening his grip on the board of directors instead of improving Morgan Stanley. Before the merger,

Morgan Stanley's board was a group of hard-nosed thinkers like Donald Rumsfeld and Dick Cheney. As they cycled off, Purcell replaced them with people who were loyal to him—typically midwestern CEOs from manufacturing companies. It seemed to me that he made sure to keep them happy. If a board member needed a ride to his beach house in South Carolina, Phil had the corporate jet fueled up and on the tarmac waiting.

Despite this friction, I never doubted the merger. The numbers backed me up. All our divisions—Wealth Management, Asset Management, Fixed Income, M&A—were booming. We were number one in IPOs. Our stock price was selling at seven times the firm's book value. (Book value is the difference between a company's assets and its liabilities.) We had done what we were supposed to do: deliver for shareholders. At its height, in September 2000, Morgan Stanley stock was trading at $109.38 per share. We were the most profitable securities firm in the United States.

Then the dot-com mania began to cool. Investors realized that many of the just-hatched tech companies were burning through cash without a glimmer of profit on the far horizon. Suddenly the "new economy" was revealed to be similar to the "old economy": you have to have a strong stomach to hold on to stock in a company that is losing value, no matter how cutting-edge and disruptive it claims to be.

Along with others on Wall Street, Morgan Stanley felt the chill. We lost $1 billion on a telecommunications high-yield—aka junk—bond issue. Purcell, who held Peter Karches responsible as the head of Investment Banking and Institutional Securities, forced him out. I went to the board of directors to argue for keeping Peter, but it didn't do any good. I thought Purcell never seemed to understand how a top-tier firm like Morgan Stanley operated: risk was—and is—inherent to investment banking. We had to take risks to make money. It was inevitable that some of those risks resulted in losses. That's just how it is.

But there was another reason for Peter's involuntary exit. From the beginning, he couldn't hide his contempt for Purcell. One day, after Phil did something Peter found especially galling, he told Purcell, "It's like you're playing in the US Open, Phil, and you have a seventeen handicap." In other words, Purcell was out of his league.

Peter and I had been brothers in arms since the day I hired him in 1976. His departure took something out of me. My enthusiasm for coming to work flagged. I had a hard time figuring Phil out. I never knew what he was thinking behind his aviator glasses and his genial facade. I never saw him get angry or confront people. But I observed that if he felt threatened by someone, it was just a matter of time before that person was packing up their office.

As tech companies continued to lose their luster, the same individual investors who couldn't buy shares fast enough when they were hot now fled the stock market altogether. The bull market turned into a bear. Morgan Stanley's stock dropped 45 percent, closing at $65.89 on December 29, 2000.

Anyone who has worked at a company during a downturn knows the drill: factions form, rumors circulate, layoffs loom, the long nights set in. There were fights around allocation of capital. What areas were we going to invest in? I was running the institutional business, including Equity and Fixed Income, which is where all the risk was. Phil wanted to dramatically cut back on risk. He wanted to concentrate on Retail and the credit card business.

I would have done things differently, and that's just what our competitors did. As Phil drew back, Goldman Sachs and J. P. Morgan leaned in, looking for the opportunities that a crisis always creates. They made tremendous inroads in areas where Morgan Stanley had once dominated. To my mind, we lost focus and commitment—and along with it, our leadership position on Wall Street.

But I was not in charge. In fact, I was less and less in charge. In 1998, Phil had taken Asset Management away from my portfolio. Next, in 2000, he took Retail but added the Discover Card. The question of when I would succeed Phil surfaced periodically. We were making the same amount of money, but Phil was running the firm, and I was becoming a figurehead. Dick Fisher worried about what he saw happening at Morgan Stanley Dean Witter.

"You've got to give John more responsibility," he implored Phil. "He should be CEO, and you should be chairman."

Phil gave me something else instead. "I have a private bathroom in my office," he said to me one day. "You should have a bathroom, too." He was trying to placate me by awarding me the trappings of power instead of actual responsibility. It didn't work. Bit by bit it came to me: Purcell was never going to make me CEO.

Outside of conversations with Dick and Christy, I kept my concerns to myself. As I increasingly felt trapped, I decided to consult with a man I deeply admire: savvy, risk-taking billionaire entrepreneur Phil Anschutz. I know Phil is a vault when it comes to keeping confidences. He would also give it to me straight. So I flew to Denver to see him. I met Phil Anschutz in the 1980s, when he acquired Southern Pacific Railroad, and Morgan Stanley helped finance the deal. Anschutz remained a client as he expanded into other businesses, including telecommunications, oil, and entertainment. In the process, we became friends. There are just some guys you like to be around. I had often been Phil's guest at his Colorado ranch, where we went dove hunting.

"I've done everything I can to make the partnership with Phil Purcell work," I told him. "He's a roadblock. I can't get past him. There's no point in staying. But I'm worried about letting the people at Morgan Stanley and our clients down. I don't want them to feel like I'm bailing."

"John, everyone knows that you've given it your all," Phil said. "You gave up the CEO title you deserved. You put yourself in second place. You'll do the right thing. You don't know any other way."

Phil Anschutz gave me the backbone to do what I needed to do. It was painful, but at the same time I thought, *If I'm going to die, I want to die quickly.* Staying at Morgan Stanley, I would have died slowly, with cuts every day.

I had to leave.

———

THIS PERIOD IN my life brought back the memory of another time when I had been desperately unhappy. I always kind of grimace when people talk about college being the best years of their life. Not for me at Duke. At Mooresville High, I had been a top student and an all-state football star. But my freshman year in college was a shock. It showed me that I wasn't as smart as I thought I was—or as athletically gifted. I almost flunked geology my first semester because I didn't attend class for two months and thought I'd just read the textbook. As soon as I switched my major to history and started studying, however, I had no problems academically.

Football was different. I showed up at the first practice thinking I was hot stuff. On the fourth day of practice, I tore the ligaments in my right foot. Because of this injury, I was red-shirted my freshman year. When I got the cast off, the coach put me on the practice team. If we were playing Clemson that Saturday, for instance, my squad ran the plays that we believed the Tigers were likely to use. We were cannon fodder. I got pulverized every single play. I was competing against guys who were bigger, faster, stronger, and just all-around more talented. Some would go on to play in the NFL. I thought I could really add value. Then I looked at the roster and found out I was on the second team. I had the drive but not the ability to make the first team.

I was eighteen years old, and I had no clue what I was doing. During the season, I spent hours dressing out and hitting the practice field. Sometimes there were two practices a day. I remember the psychological pressure. The coaches cared about winning, not about their players. If they didn't win, they got fired. I was killing myself but getting nowhere. No matter how hard I practiced, no matter how much I sweated in the weight room, no matter how much I wanted it, I couldn't change the outcome. I kept asking myself, *What the fuck am I doing?*

Finally, in my junior year, I got to play in a game—Duke versus North Carolina State. I tackled an NC State running back. The crowd cheered. It felt amazing!

Soon after, we were at practice. The coach told me to lower my head, run at the tackling dummy, and smash into it as hard as I could. I executed the play perfectly. Then I felt a ripping pain in my neck and fell to the ground.

I had cracked my C4 vertebra, which is critical to supporting your neck and head. The injury didn't heal. My upper body ached. Every time I tackled someone, my left arm went dead. When I told the team doctor, an orthopedist, that I had lost a lot of the feeling in my left hand, he looked at me sympathetically and said, "Son, your playing days have come to an end."

Adding to my misery, I was constantly strapped for cash. My football scholarship took care of my tuition as well as my room and board. But, especially after my father died my junior year, I had to find a way to pay for everything else, from shaving cream to gas to date money. I came up with a genius move: become a medical guinea pig. I volunteered for psychology tests at fifteen dollars a pop. The Duke medical school paid top dollar. The experiment that stands out had me astride a stationary bike inside a hyperbaric chamber—a submarine-like tube that delivers 100 percent oxygen and is used to treat people with wounds that won't heal and deep-sea divers who get decompression sickness. Wearing nose clips, I had a 16-gauge needle practically the size of a McDonald's straw shoved into my arm. I pedaled as fast as I could while a technician measured the oxygen and carbon dioxide in my blood. Two doctors, watching through the glass portholes, took notes. I said to myself, *I'm a fucking monkey.* As I pedaled, the pressure in the chamber was amped from one atmosphere to two. In other words, I was pedaling in the equivalent of almost thirty-three feet of water. My face got redder, and my breathing got more and more labored. For this pain and humiliation, I got paid $32, which is $235 in today's money. I still have nightmares about this experiment.

One afternoon, I walked over to the Duke Student Health Service Center. The doctor asked me what was wrong. "I'm miserable," I replied. "I have to go to practice to keep my scholarship, but I do stuff like fill up the water buckets and clean off cleats in the equipment room while the rest of the team runs plays. Every Saturday night, I have to drive the game film to High Point and wait for it to be developed. I don't get home until one a.m. I can't sleep. I can't concentrate. I have no appetite. I don't feel like I belong at Duke."

"I think you should talk to somebody," he said gently. "A psychiatrist."

"A shrink? Seriously?"

"Yes, we have a therapy group that meets here in the evenings, and I think you would get something out of it."

Going to my Tuesday therapy group really helped me. Listening to the older people in the group talk about problems with their spouses, their kids, their careers put my issues in perspective. I went a few times and then stopped. I am proud that I decided to go. And believe me, back in 1967, football players from Mooresville, North Carolina, didn't talk about their feelings with therapists and strangers. But take it from me, when things feel overwhelming, get help.

I have never forgotten how bad I felt back then, that sense that I couldn't control what was happening to me. Those hot, humid, miserable days on the field at Duke were decades behind me. But I felt the same way—powerless—sitting down the hall from Phil Purcell on the thirty-ninth floor at Morgan Stanley.

————————

AT DICK'S URGING, I met secretly with three board members at the Hôtel Plaza Athénée, on East Sixty-Fourth Street near Madison Avenue. I didn't go to negotiate. My mind was made up. "Morgan Stanley used to be a meritocracy," I said as soon as we sat down in a private suite. "Morgan Stanley Dean Witter under Phil Purcell is not. It's time for me to leave."

I later found out that Dick tried to get the board to keep me. No longer a director, he came to the Morgan Stanley offices and sat outside the conference room where the board was meeting, waiting to be asked in to speak. Purcell finally stuck his head out and said they had no interest in hearing from him.

On Tuesday, January 23, 2001, I walked into Phil's office. "Clearly, you don't want me here," I said. "And I can't do this anymore."

"Okay," Phil said matter-of-factly.

"I won't do anything to hurt the firm," I continued. "I'll stay positive."

Morgan Stanley announced my exit the next day. My remarks to the staff were followed by a three-minute standing ovation. Then I walked off the stage. The headline in the January 25 *New York Times* read, "Morgan Stanley's President Resigns, Stunning Wall Street."

That night, at Phil's request, I got on a plane to attend an off-site meeting of about seventy Morgan Stanley executives at the Boulders Resort & Spa in Scottsdale, Arizona. I was still a Morgan Stanley shareholder, I had a lot of friends at the firm, and I wanted it to thrive. I put on a big smile and mingled at the opening reception.

At 6:00 a.m. the next day, I opened the door of my casita to grab the *Wall Street Journal*. Bam. The door slammed behind me. There I stood, naked and locked out of my room. It was so ridiculous, I started laughing. I covered myself with the *WSJ* and scrambled up the path leading to reception to get a new key. I was halfway there when I saw a groundskeeper and flagged him down. He drove me back to my casita in his cart and unlocked the door.

Thus ended my time at Morgan Stanley.

You come into this world naked, and I guess that's how you leave it.

CHAPTER SEVENTEEN

I hate this fucking game," I told Christy. I was standing in the door-way of her office at our house in Rye, where we had moved a few years earlier. It was a blue-sky Wednesday afternoon in spring 2001, and I had just come back from playing yet another eighteen holes at the Golf Club of Purchase. I was fifty-six years old, and I'd had a rev-elation: if the most important thing in my life, besides my wife and my kids, was golf, something was off.

Way off.

I was now officially unemployed. On the shelf. I didn't have to worry about money, which was huge. But for the first time in thirty-three years—or maybe since I started boxing up groceries at age eight in my father's warehouse—I was at loose ends. My former self—the one who had supervised tens of thousands of employees around the world—he was gone. That guy got picked up in our circular driveway before dawn. He started making phone calls immediately from the car to staffers monitoring the international desks. At the office, he had two executive assistants who kept his calendar, scheduling his days in fifteen-minute increments. One critical meeting followed another. No phone message went unanswered. Like air traffic controllers, his assistants stacked his calls, so he talked to one person while the next waited on hold to be patched in, and then the next after that. His suitcase was always packed and his passport at hand. He routinely flew across time zones to meet with bankers and world leaders.

This new guy—me—was a clock-watcher. Time had gone from being my scarcest resource, measured out in minutes, to something that I had too much of. I had gone from operating at 200 percent to trying to find ways to occupy myself. Having never forgotten the blistering words of my elementary school choir teacher, who said, "John's voice would scare a horse from its oats," I took singing lessons so I could belt out "Happy Birthday" when the occasion called for it. And I played golf every day. Sometimes twice a day.

I had picked up my first golf club in high school. My family didn't belong to a country club, so my friends taught me the game on a nearby public course. When I came to New York, I realized that golf was the official obsession of Wall Street—other than money, of course. I took lessons, and I got competitive. At my best, I was a twelve handicap. At Morgan Stanley, I'd often put together a foursome of clients and salespeople. Because you're on the course for four hours, golf is a good way to get to know someone. Over the years I've discovered that you're not one person on the green and another at the bargaining table. Someone who cheats at golf is likely to cheat in business.

Smashing a little ball with a big club was a real stress reliever for me.

Naturally, the golf course was center stage for Prankster John. I still laugh my head off when I think about the time I put a golf tee at the bottom of a drinking straw in a friend's iced tea. He turned red trying to suck the liquid up before he noticed that I was doubled over. Another time, at a brand-new, snooty golf course in Dubai, I kept surreptitiously loosening the strap that secured my friend's golf bag every time he putted. Then, as we drove to the next hole, his clubs tumbled out. Concerned, the spiffily uniformed greens attendant ran over to see whether everything was okay. The jig was up when I started howling.

Outings to different courses—around the country and the world—also built and strengthened friendships. I love my wife and kids more than anything. I also love my friends. It's so easy to get caught up in work and family responsibilities. But friendships are essential to me, and they die when you neglect them. I can't stress this enough.

Over the decades, I got really close with three guys from Morgan Stanley: Jerry Wood, Mike Rankowitz, and Mike Cassedy. We took a lot of golfing trips, but sometimes the highlight of our trips had nothing to do with golf. One unforgettable night involved Mike Cassedy, a kick-ass salesman from Chicago whom Peter Karches and I hired for Fixed Income in 1984 and brought to New York. I took the Fixed Income sales force to play two days of golf in a tournament at the National Golf Links of America, an exclusive course in Southampton, on Long Island, where I was a member. It had a clubhouse built in 1911, where you could stay overnight. Because they were short on rooms, we had to double up. Mike and I were roommates in a creepy, creaky little room right out of a horror movie.

I fell asleep in one of the twin beds but woke up at 2:00 a.m. when I heard Mike in the lavatory. Mike turned out the bathroom light and felt his way back to his bed in the dark. Unbeknownst to him, I had moved to his bed. He climbed in and without a second's hesitation murmured, "Maureen?" his wife's name.

"Yes, honey," I said, patting his arm.

"John, you son of a bitch! Get out of my bed!"

I'm an eight-year-old boy at heart.

Another time, Jerry, Rank, and I were heading out for a golfing weekend, hustling to make it through hellacious traffic to the Newark airport on time. We managed to check our luggage and the golf clubs, but when we got to the counter, we found out the flight had been canceled.

"We're not turning back!" I announced. We found another flight leaving in fifteen minutes, but we didn't have our luggage and golf clubs: they were checked with the previous airline. We flagged down a skycap. "I can get back here with your bags in five minutes," he vowed. Rank reached into his pocket for a twenty-dollar bill, saying, "Good, you go get them." I reached out, grabbed the twenty, ripped it in two, and handed him half. "I'll give you the other half when you come back with our stuff," I said.

We made the flight with our clubs, but we got in only one day of golf. There was a huge, unexpected snowstorm. We had tickets to a basketball game that night, but we had nothing to do during the day, so we ended up going bowling. We had such a great time razzing each other, switching bowling shoes, and being complete goofballs.

If you haven't seen someone in twenty years, how much of a friendship is it, really? You don't have to spend a ton of time with people you care about. But it's unbelievably important to reconnect so you remember why you matter to each other, to make new memories.

———

GOLF WAS ONE of the things I used at Morgan Stanley to help level the playing field for women. As I moved up in the firm, I became acutely aware that women, just as smart, well educated, and driven as the men when they joined Morgan Stanley, were not advancing at the same pace as their male counterparts. In early 1992, after I became head of the operating committee, Christy and I invited four promising women employees and their spouses for a weekend at our ski house in Deer Valley to talk about the obstacles in their way—long hours, endless travel, double standards, the issues of pregnancy and childcare. I knew it wasn't in my power to eliminate all these challenges. No question, investment banking was a male-dominated industry that all but demanded one parent stay home.

But as we talked, they often mentioned they weren't invited on the golf outings with clients and superiors that had been so helpful to me. It turned out that none of them had ever picked up a club. "The women said they don't have access to the same accounts as men because they don't know how to play golf," I told Christy as we waited in the lift line. I was going to change that. One of the jobs of a leader is to block and tackle any obstacle in your people's way—anything that keeps them from achieving their goals.

I was all in. The next month I took twenty-five female managers to a resort on Kiawah Island, near Charleston, South Carolina. I brought in a seasoned instructor, Gary Smith, who taught at David Leadbetter's golf academy outside Orlando. (David Leadbetter was and remains *the* golf guru, and Gary later became an ABC and ESPN golf commentator.) A few women already knew how to play. Gary and Jerry helped improve their swings. Others started with the game's fundamentals.

The Kiawah Island weekend wasn't a one-and-done. We took groups of women to the Country Club of Landfall and the Tom Fazio–designed Eagle Point Golf Club, also in North Carolina. Later, we invited a group of women to play at the club in Purchase. Our backyard abutted the golf course's third hole. "The beauty of those events wasn't just playing golf," Carla Harris told me recently. A vice chairman of Global Wealth Management at Morgan Stanley, she explained, "It was an opportunity for me to spend a day or two with the president of the firm. Getting that kind of exposure as a Black woman in investment banking was huge."

Eventually, Morgan Stanley's women began holding an annual golf tournament for their female clients. Each year, when I got my invitation, I felt like a proud parent. But I was equally proud that I was no longer the driving force. People seizing their own initiative on something you started is one of the best things a leader can hope for.

But all that was in the past. Now I was hanging around with a bunch of retirees who did nothing but play golf.

———————

A LOT OF people, especially on Wall Street, have what is known as "the number." This is the amount of money that, once accumulated, allows them to walk away from their jobs. It can be $5 million or $500 million. The sum doesn't matter. The point is, they feel that they're set for life, and they want out. They might be thirty; they might be fifty-five. They love the money but not the job. Some good people at Morgan Stanley felt this way.

I was the opposite. I liked the money a lot, but I was in it for the work. It gave my life purpose and structure. I enjoyed putting on my suits from Savile Row's Henry Poole, a London company that had been in business since before Napoleon met his Waterloo. I sought out opportunities to interact with clients and get to know trainees. I thrived on being the person who led the meetings, made the deals, took responsibility for the tough decisions. I loved the pressure, the risk. Now I was bored. I believed I was in the prime of my career, and I still had a lot to contribute.

Over the winter, I had turned down an opportunity to be appointed chairman of the US Securities and Exchange Commission (SEC). I knew Dick Cheney, George W. Bush's vice president, from his time on the Morgan Stanley board. "I'm flattered, Mr. Vice President," I told him, "but I don't see myself as a regulator."

Where did I see myself? I was feeling out other offers, but none of them grabbed me. Christy looked at this question from a much deeper perspective. "John," she said one day as I was setting down my golf bag in the front hall of our house, "I think it would be good for you to find other interests; to find some balance in your life." She had been invited to a weekend conference at Miraval Resort in Tucson, Arizona, for philanthropists and physicians. The agenda was to make integrative medicine more accessible to patients and doctors. "You should come, John," Christy said.

A couple of weekends later, we were in a corral participating in the resort's Equine Experience. The point was to get the horse in the ring to lift a back hoof through clear and wordless communication. Some human participants never got the horse to react. Some accomplished it only after *a lot* of perseverance. It took a pediatrician in the group an hour.

I took one step inside that corral, and the horse obeyed me. I guess even though I was at loose ends, I was still a boss.

———

ONE AFTERNOON, I got a call. Lionel Pincus was on the line. He was a legendary venture capitalist and chairman of the private equity firm Warburg Pincus. We had done some business together over the years. "I think it would be a good idea if you and Lukas Mühlemann had a chat, John," he said. Mühlemann was the chairman and CEO of the Credit Suisse Group. Founded in 1856, the giant, 145-year-old Swiss bank was based in Zurich. It was one of the world's nine universal banks, offering a full array of commercial and institutional services, on par with Deutsche Bank and HSBC. Although less familiar to most Americans, it was a financial steamroller, with dozens of offices around the world. Its Investment Banking Division, Credit

Suisse First Boston (CSFB), headquartered in Manhattan, was a heavy hitter on Wall Street.

I met Pincus and Mühlemann for lunch at the Four Seasons on East Fifty-Second Street. The spare, elegant restaurant, on the ground floor of the landmark Seagram Building, was the lunchtime spot for Manhattan executives to see and be seen. A journalist describing the restaurant's iconic Grill Room for *Esquire* magazine had coined the phrase "power lunch."

Born in Zurich and armed with both a Swiss law degree and a Harvard MBA, Mühlemann had headed up McKinsey's offices in Switzerland before taking the top job at Credit Suisse Group. He was cool, contained, and formal and wasted no time. "I want you to run Credit Suisse First Boston," he said as I dug into my lunch.

Mühlemann explained that he was planning to replace the current CSFB chief, Allen Wheat. The firm was facing trouble on several fronts, and the chaos was taking a toll on the bank's share price. The SEC and Eliot Spitzer, New York's attorney general, were examining whether to criminally charge several CSFB bankers for kickbacks. Mühlemann needed to bring in a get-it-done, clean-it-up CEO. I suspected that having lunch with me in Manhattan's most closely observed restaurant wasn't just an accident. Things were so rocky at CSFB that I wondered if Mühlemann wanted his board back in Zurich to know he was taking action before they decided to put his neck on the block, too. "You have the executive skill set we're looking for, John," he said. "We need an eight-hundred-pound gorilla, and you're it."

"I'll think about it," I replied. I would never make a big decision like this without talking it over with Christy, but I wasn't going to tell him that. The truth is, there wasn't much for Christy and me to discuss. I had pushed away the CEO crown once, and I don't make the same mistake twice.

Credit Suisse dismissed Wheat on July 11 in London. When my name was announced as CSFB's new CEO on July 12, Credit Suisse's shares rose 5 percent. Under the next day's headline "Wall Street Fears a Big Mack Attack," the *New York Post* reported: "For John Mack, 56, his new job at the helm of Credit Suisse First Boston marks a graceful return to Wall Street." My spirits soared as well. In the days before I started, I wanted to get a handle on my new firm. At night after dinner, as I sat hunched over my yellow pad writing out my to-do list for the next morning, I was energized.

But sometimes I recalled things people had said to me when I told them I was taking the job. Sophia "Ria" Mills was a friend whose judgment I valued. She was the flight attendant on the Morgan Stanley corporate jet, and we had logged hundreds of hours playing gin rummy and talking. Before I hired her, she had flown with her share of Swiss executives. When I told Ria that I was going to work for CSFB, she said, "Well, good luck with the Swiss."

I laughed. "John, I don't think you understand," she went on. "They're different. They make clocks. They're perfectionists. They're cold. They're not flexible."

I also called Jack Wadsworth and asked him to meet me for a drink at the wood-paneled University Club on West Fifty-Fourth Street. Prior to joining Morgan Stanley, Jack had worked at First Boston for fifteen years and was part of the team that negotiated a fifty-fifty joint venture with Credit Suisse in 1978. "What do you think, Jack?" I asked as we sat in the stately bar, talking over a couple of icy beers.

"Well, I have the same impression of the Swiss I had in 1978," he told me. "To survive, John, you have two choices. One is to spin off First Boston and make it an independent company. The other is to move to Zurich.

"Otherwise, they will kill you."

CHAPTER EIGHTEEN

This is going to be fun, I thought to myself as my driver pulled up in front of CSFB's headquarters at 11 Madison Avenue near Twenty-Third Street. Erected in 1933, the thirty-story art deco skyscraper stood majestically in the hazy summer sunlight.

I was taking over as CEO of one of Wall Street's biggest investment banks. For the first time, I was running the show on my own. But I was also inheriting a deeply damaged franchise of twenty-eight thousand employees, a company constantly in the headlines—all of them terrible. Lukas Mühlemann had given me a mandate to clean things up—to impose more rigorous procedures and to slash costs. He wasn't just hiring John Mack; he was bringing in Mack the Knife.

My first hire was Stephen Volk, a lawyer with an impeccable reputation. By doing this, I was sending an unmistakable signal to the regulators in Washington and New York that I took their investigations seriously. Steve and I immediately hired Gary Lynch as CSFB's general counsel. In the 1980s, Gary had headed up the Enforcement Division at the SEC, where he investigated infamous Wall Street figures Michael Milken and Ivan Boesky for insider trading. (Boesky was the model for Gordon Gekko in the movie *Wall Street*, known for his motto, "Greed is good.") One of the first things Gary and I did was fly down to Washington to meet with regulators face-to-face. I promised them, "You're going to get better cooperation."

Many other problems CSFB faced stemmed from its disastrous acquisition of Donaldson, Lufkin & Jenrette (DLJ) for more than $11 billion eleven months earlier. DLJ was a bold, energetic investment firm founded in 1959. But the price tag was absurdly high. My predecessor, Allen Wheat, hadn't reduced head count nearly as much as I thought was necessary. "It's like Noah's Ark!" Steve told me of the investment banking unit. "There are two of everything."

CSFB had also handed out salaries and bonuses that dwarfed what other Wall Street firms paid. I had to stop the bank from hemorrhaging money. The place teemed with MBAs and financial wizards, many trying to tear as much compensation out of the firm as they could. These people didn't seem to care if they killed CSFB in the process. A typical business pays twenty to twenty-five cents out of every dollar of revenue to its employees. Because talent is the primary asset of an investment bank, it usually pays its employees fifty cents on the dollar, with the other half going to shareholders and administrative costs. But at CSFB, sixty cents of every dollar was going to the employees. When you're talking about hundreds of millions of dollars, those ten extra cents add up.

There was another problem. The way the contracts were written, people at CSFB got paid the same amount whether the firm had a good year or a bad year. It made a mockery of the concept of "pay for performance."

Bottom line: CSFB was on track to lose a billion dollars that year.

It wasn't just the salaries. It was the eye-popping perks. Every managing director at DLJ could lease a company-paid luxury car and have an unlimited gas card. If you were on the management commit-tee, your spouse received the same VIP transportation package. Many CSFB executives owned private planes as well.

I had asked Tom Nides, who had overseen media strategy at Morgan Stanley under Dick Fisher and me, to join me at CSFB. He was my Jiminy Cricket—the guy who always called me out when I was about to do something dumb. "Are you fucking crazy?" he'd say. "That's a *terrible* idea!"

One day Tom walked into my office. He looked about to burst. "What dopey thing did I do now, Tom?" I asked. But for once, it wasn't about me. "John, you won't believe this," he said, waving a thick stack of expense reports in the air. "Some of the guys here are filling up their personal airplanes with their gas cards!"

While the A-listers were wallowing in corporate-subsidized luxury, most CSFB employees weren't receiving these kinds of perks, nor were they being paid gargantuan salaries. In fact, the demoralized majority didn't have contracts and were earning far less than they deserved.

I had to dismantle this dysfunctional system.

I called a meeting of the managing directors in the CSFB audito-rium. "I want each of you to give up 25 percent of your contracts," I said. "I also want you to get your employees to do the same. Trust me. I'll remember who's a team player and who's not." My demand went over like cold soup on a cold day. A voice piped up from the seats, "John, will you give up 25 percent of your pay?"

"Yes," I said. That three-letter word cost me $8 million.

A few days later, Bennett Goodman, who ran the Leveraged Finance and Private Equity businesses, came to my office. "My team wants to give back 25 percent of our bonus pool," he told me. I leaned back in my chair, gave him a steady look, and said, "Thanks, Bennett." Then I went back to my Bloomberg terminal.

His face fell. Clearly deflated, he turned and left.

When Bennett got back to his desk, his phone was ringing. His assistant told him, "A guy named Mike Somebody is on the phone."

"Who?" Bennett asked.

"I don't know—he's got a really long, complicated name."

"Ask him how to spell it," he told her.

When his assistant came back saying it was Mike Krzyzewski—the winningest coach in Division One college men's basketball history—Bennett figured someone was playing a practical joke. He picked up the phone and said, "Hey, Coach, how ya doing?" Like he knew him.

It *was* Coach K of Duke fame.

When I first arrived at CSFB, I saw a book by Coach K in Bennett's office. "Are you a Duke fan?" I asked him.

"Avid!" Bennett replied.

Coach K and I had met when I took my son John to the Final Four in Denver in 1990. There are a lot of things that Mike and I share besides our affection for Duke. When we talk, there's no BS. We not only like each other, we respect each other. We both value brutal honesty, and we think being decisive is the essence of leadership. He's a brother to me.

"You should know that John Mack is one of my best friends," Coach K told Bennett. "He's a coldhearted son of a bitch, but you've warmed his heart. He told me he got the greatest piece of news today. He couldn't believe it. You and your guys made a really generous offer to help make the team successful."

Bennett asked, "Why didn't John tell me himself?"

"John's an emotional guy," Coach K answered. "He thought it would mean more to you if it came from me."

———

I INSINUATED MYSELF into every corner of the firm. CSFB had an elegant partners' dining room. The food was unbelievably delicious. There was a communal table where people enjoyed Swiss delicacies like *Zürcher Geschnetzeltes*, a veal stew made with mushrooms and white wine, and kibitzed from noon to 3:00 p.m.

That is, until I started showing up.

"Who'd you call on today?" I'd ask different partners. "What can I do to help with your clients? Put me to work. I'm happy to make a call, have a meeting, or fly anywhere. I'll do anything to help you with your business." I wanted to give CSFB every edge I could.

My directness intimidated some people. Would-be lunchers started phoning the host to ask, "Is Mack there?" If I was, they would eat at their desks. But soon the more ambitious bankers started saying, "I want John in all of my meetings with clients."

One morning I spied another culture-building opportunity. It was mid-August, and yes, Manhattan can be steamy. Did that excuse what I saw as I walked toward the CSFB headquarters? Not for a nanosecond. I couldn't believe it. The guy was coming to work dressed in denim cutoffs, with his hairy legs exposed for all the world to see.

Keeping him in my sights, I followed him to the elevator, carefully noting which floor he punched. When he stepped out, I did, too, and tracked him to his desk. Then I found his boss. "Have you seen what your employee wore to work today?" I asked. "I know it's casual Friday, but there are limits. You've got to suit up for the game, man. You tell him to go to the nearest Gap and buy a decent pair of khakis. I don't want anyone in this building unless they are appropriately dressed."

Was it worth my time to hunt down a fashion miscreant?

Absolutely.

I wanted the people at CSFB to take pride in their work and in how they represented the company. I wanted the boss of "Mr. Cutoffs" to understand that he had to be accountable for his employees.

It was the managers' responsibility to take the culture I was building at the top and push it down to the levels below.

Word got around, just like the time I rebuked the Morgan Stanley trader who kept the breakfast sandwich deliveryman waiting.

———

ON SUNDAY, SEPTEMBER 9, I played a round at the Golf Club of Purchase. I had been at CSFB for eight weeks, and golf had resumed its rightful place in my life—crammed into a busy schedule. I felt great. Things were far worse at CSFB than I had anticipated, but we were making progress.

One mistake a lot of CEOs make when they take control at a new firm is to simply bring in their own people and disregard the employees already there. I eventually hired trusted talents like Wei Christianson, Jeff Salzman, and Jerry Wood from Morgan Stanley. But I was on the lookout within CSFB for gifted people. The more time I spent there, the deeper I found the bench.

I was also looking outside for top-tier talent. On Tuesday, September 11, I was scheduled to have dinner with Brian Finn, a private equity expert. Private equity firms invest in companies and then help run them. Brian had been a wunderkind at First Boston but had left CSFB in 1997. I wanted to lure him back.

Our dinner would be postponed.

That morning, around a quarter to 9:00, I was running the management committee meeting in the executive boardroom on the twenty-seventh floor of the CSFB headquarters. Outside the wide, south-facing windows, we saw thick, dark smoke billowing into the cloudless blue sky downtown. "What the hell is that?" I asked. People spun their chairs around to stare. "Maybe a big fire?" one person suggested. We turned on CNN. A newscaster was saying that a plane had hit the north tower of the World Trade Center.

Then a second plane hit. This time, it was the south tower.

As we stood in stunned silence, I did a quick mental checklist of my family. I knew Christy was okay. She was in Rye. All three kids were now adults and living in Manhattan, but there was no reason for them to be anywhere near Wall Street.

I was worried about our offices in Tower Five, where CSFB had more than eight hundred employees. We learned that the windows had blown out from the impact of the explosions, and the building suffered extensive damage. People were being accounted for and evacuated, but a few employees were missing. Tom Nides was frantically trying to locate them.

In the end, CSFB lost one person. Steven Glick was a forty-two-year-old managing director who had recently returned to the firm so he could spend more time with his family. He had been attending a financial technology seminar at Windows on the World, the landmark restaurant known for its spectacular views from the 106th and 107th floors of the north tower. Steve left behind a wife and two children, ages six and four.

While Tom was on one phone, I grabbed another, instinctively calling Morgan Stanley. The firm where I had spent most of my career was the biggest tenant at the World Trade Center, with close to 3,700 Retail and Asset Management employees. Morgan Stanley lost thirteen people that day. Other firms experienced inconceivable losses. Every single person—658 people total—who came to work on September 11 at Cantor Fitzgerald in 1 World Trade Center died.

The computer systems at many banks were down, which meant that they didn't have information on what they had bought or sold. A firm that had escaped damage but that had the ethics of a skunk could take the favorable trades and reject the unfavorable ones. That's not my style. "We're in pretty good shape," I told my team. "If I catch anybody taking advantage of the competition at a time like this, they're fired."

I'll never forget certain calls I got that morning. Wang Qishan, then vice premier of China, checked to see if I was okay. So did Zhou Xiaochuan, the governor of China's central bank. "John," he said, "I'm seeing what's going on. I'm heartbroken."

As the day went on, people from our downtown office straggled in. Covered in gray ash, they looked shell-shocked. Some were barefoot, having lost their shoes in the stampede out of the building. Because the subway had been shut down almost immediately, the CSFB employees had walked two and a half miles through debris, acrid smoke, and the screaming sirens of emergency vehicles hurtling south. We set up water, food, and phones for them. In this traumatic moment, I knew I had to be visible. This was a time to remember that leadership is an activity, not a position. People needed to see that someone was in charge.

On Wednesday, September 12, the chairman of the NYSE, Dick Grasso, summoned me and other Wall Street CEOs for a meeting. The agenda: How soon could we reopen the markets? I thought it was crucial for the financial system's gears to start turning as quickly as possible. A symbol of American capitalism had been toppled. There was a massive gap in the skyline, and ground zero was still smoldering. One of the best ways to demonstrate our nation's resilience was to resume trading. But because Verizon's underground phone and internet cables that served lower Manhattan had been damaged, the stock market didn't reopen until Monday, September 17.

During these days, I had a hard time keeping my emotions in check. I touched base with Frank "Skip" Bowman, a friend from college who had become a four-star admiral in the US Navy. "You're taught to deal with this in the military," I said. "You understand that some people might not come home. That's part of being in the service. But these were people who went off to work on an ordinary Tuesday morning. Their families never expected they weren't going to return. How do you deal with that?" On *The Charlie Rose Show*, I reiterated my message of encouragement. "I'm really proud to be in this country and see how people pull together," I said. "I think at the end of the day, we're fighters. We're survivors. We're not going to be intimidated." But even as I said these words, I broke down on camera.

IT WAS A couple of weeks before Brian Finn and I finally met for the dinner originally scheduled for September 11. "What do you love about what you're doing right now?" I asked.

"I love the company. I love the people. I love the team," Brian said. "Candidly, the most interesting companies to work with are the ones that are screwed up."

"Brian," I said as I leaned in close, "I've got the biggest, most fucked-up company in the world right here. Come back to CSFB and help me fix it."

He did.

I put another business dinner on the calendar, this one for October 3. I called Frank Quattrone, CSFB's big-name banker for our tech IPOs out of Palo Alto, California. In 2000, he hauled in $120 million. Back then, people made big bucks on Wall Street, but nothing like that. He was earning ten to twenty times more than other people in similar jobs. I told him, "We need to talk."

I had known Frank for a long time. He had come to Morgan Stanley straight out of Wharton in 1977 and rejoined in 1981 after Stanford Business School. Anticipating how computers and the internet would transform the economy and the world, he established Morgan Stanley's Technology team in Silicon Valley. Back in the 1980s, it was a small community. The geeks, the entrepreneurs, the venture capitalists, the lawyers—Frank knew them all.

In 1990, Quattrone handled the Cisco IPO. Five years later, he was the front man for the blockbuster Netscape IPO, which made the world sit up and pay attention to tech stocks. Soon after, Frank came to Dick Fisher and me, demanding that we allow him to build a firm within a firm in California and give him a revenue-sharing deal.

Dick and I instantly recognized that Frank's proposal would give a single managing director way too much power, way too much money, and far too little supervision. It would take a wrecking ball to the "one-firm firm" culture we were building. Our answer was an immediate and unequivocal no.

Frank jumped to Deutsche Bank, where he handled the Amazon IPO in 1997. A year later, he and his group joined CSFB. Frank got a contract that gave him almost complete control over his team—that is, Quattrone, not CSFB, decided who was hired, who was fired, and who was paid what. Quattrone's contract meant that while I might be *called* the CEO of CSFB, I wasn't the boss of Frank or anyone on his team. I had no say over what risks they were taking or what laws and ethics they might be skirting.

I had to install guardrails, and fast.

To understand how critical this was, flash back to the late 1980s. Michael Milken was the superstar of Drexel Burnham Lambert, bringing in billions for himself and the firm by selling junk bonds. Blinded by the outsize profits Milken was generating, the Drexel CEO failed to keep his lone-wolf employee in check. After Milken went to prison for violating federal securities and tax laws, Drexel Burnham was forced into bankruptcy. In 1990, it became the first investment bank to declare Chapter 11 since the Great Depression.

This was not happening to CSFB on my watch.

Steve Volk and I met with Frank in Kansas City, Missouri, halfway between us. I got right to the point. "Look, Frank, I'm not going to continue this arrangement. We have to redo your contracts, or I'm going to just terminate everything."

"You can't do that," Frank replied. "It's a contract."

"I can do it," I said. "I believe I have legal grounds, and I'm prepared to go to court." To me, Quattrone's contract gave him so much control, it violated the rules governing securities firms. I knew where I wanted to end up, and I knew I had to be tough to get there. When you're negotiating, wishy-washy doesn't get you what you want.

By the time we got up from the table, Frank and his team had agreed to work with Steve and Gary Lynch to hammer out a new contract.

But my problems with Quattrone were just beginning. During the tech mania, Frank handled more IPOs than anyone else on Wall Street. In 2001, when the promised internet riches didn't materialize for the average American investor, Quattrone became a target for the public's anger, and in turn for state and federal regulators' investigations. We had to pay out hundreds of millions of dollars in penalties.

Then there were the infamous "Friends of Frank." In September 2002, the *Wall Street Journal* ran a front-page scoop about how his group was giving valuable IPO shares to internet company executives in hopes of snagging their investment banking business. Again, we paid penalties. Still, the headaches didn't stop. Seven months later federal prosecutors charged Quattrone with obstructing justice and witness tampering. The case centered on events in December 2000. After a CSFB lawyer told Quattrone there was a grand jury investigation into his group, Quattrone forwarded an email with the instruction: "Time to clean up those files." Was this simply innocent end-of-the-year digital housekeeping? Or, as prosecutors alleged, was Quattrone telling his people to eliminate evidence?

I asked Gary to look into this. "In my heart of hearts, John," he told me, "I don't think in that message that he was telling people to destroy documents."

That was all I needed to hear. I trusted Gary.

After Quattrone's first trial ended in a mistrial, the next jury found him guilty on all charges, a verdict later reversed on appeal. Ultimately the government dropped the charges and lifted its lifelong ban on Quattrone working in the securities industry.

Regardless of the outcome, Frank's saga proved to me that Dick and I had been right all along. Giving *anyone* a fiefdom is a terrible idea.

THE YEAR 2001 was shaping up to be the worst year for mergers and IPOs in a decade. The week after Steve and I returned from Kansas City, I announced that we had to cut $1 billion in costs and eliminate two thousand jobs in New York and London. I knew I would be inflicting pain, but I had no choice. My marching orders from Zurich were to make the firm run efficiently.

The following spring, I announced a new round of cuts. This time it was three hundred executive jobs, including fifty managing directors. I assigned this burden to my division heads. I had promoted Adebayo Ogunlesi to head Investment Banking. Born in Nigeria and nicknamed Bayo, he had graduated from Oxford University in England and earned both a law degree and an MBA at Harvard. He then clerked for Supreme Court justice Thurgood Marshall, becoming the first non-American to clerk for the US Supreme Court.

These impressive credentials did not make the task I gave him any easier. Bayo had to cut *a lot* of people. "It's gotten to the point that if people see my name on their phone, they won't take my call," he told me. Years later, Bayo shared that he always knew what was in store when he saw *my* name on his phone. If I opened the call with "Hey buddy," it meant our conversation would be pleasant. If I didn't, Bayo knew he was in trouble. It was a tell I didn't know I had.

As I approached my first anniversary at CSFB in July 2002, I was feeling good. But an avalanche of trouble had hit Credit Suisse Group (CS), the parent company of CSFB. DLJ was just one of Lukas Mühlemann's disastrous acquisitions. CS's stock plunged 35 percent that year, the worst performance by a bank in the United States or Europe. Enraged by the losses, CS shareholders were demanding a change at the top.

Looking to quell the rebellion, Mühlemann proposed that he step down as chairman of the company but stay as CEO. He and his board came to New York to explain that they were thinking about bringing in a Swiss academic with a banking background as chairman.

"What do you think?" Lukas asked me over lunch.

I served up an Alice Mack–size helping of candor. "Well, you guys do what you want, but I'll never take this guy to see a client. He's so flat and colorless, he couldn't get a piece of business even if it were handed to him on a silver platter."

The upshot? Mühlemann departed, the academic wasn't hired, and Walter Kielholz, a member of the Credit Suisse board, was elevated to chairman.

I was asked to take over as CEO of CS, a promotion requiring that Christy and I move to Zurich. But at that point we weren't willing to uproot our lives. The CS board also insisted that I learn Swiss German, the dialect they speak in Zurich. "I don't have time to take language lessons," I said.

The board decided to make me co-CEO of CS. Staying put in New York, I would share the job with Oswald Grübel, a German who would be based in Zurich. Ossie, as he is known, was a three-decade veteran of CS with a reputation for being a gruff workaholic. We kept up a stiff regimen of cost-cutting. Eventually, Ossie and I fired ten thousand employees.

After a career of getting along with different people on six continents, I was surprised to find myself stymied by the Swiss. Once, when Ossie, Steve Volk, and I had a meeting with their government regulators, they insisted on speaking only Swiss German. Steve and I had no idea what they were saying, and they didn't provide a translator when I demanded one. That task fell to Ossie. It illustrated how insular and arrogant they were.

I'll give you another example. Switzerland's national airline, Swissair, had overexpanded and was already facing disastrous financial headwinds when 9/11 occurred and people temporarily stopped flying. Soon the business collapsed. Because the airline was a big employer, the Swiss government pressured CS to make large loans to the airline. Even that wasn't enough. By October 3, Swissair ran out of money, and the fleet was grounded. Swiss TV ran coverage of more than forty thousand passengers stranded around the world.

After I was named co-CEO, the government came back asking for more loans. I made my position clear to the board: "You're throwing good money after bad. Absolutely no more loans." Walter Kielholz and the board nonetheless bailed out the airline again. I was apoplectic.

The board also made me angry when we discussed compensation for the people at CSFB. Bennett Goodman and others had given back huge amounts of money in 2001. By 2003, I had returned CSFB to the black, making a profit of $1.4 billion. The Bennetts of the firm trusted me to do right by them. I wanted to reward them for both their success and their earlier financial sacrifice. But the penny-pinchers in Zurich tried to stop me. That's when I called them stupid to their faces.

After witnessing some of these battles, Tom Bell, a friend and fellow southerner I'd brought on the board, sat me down in a hotel bar in Zurich. He had spent decades as a CEO running both real estate and advertising companies. "John, you've got to stop," he said.

"Stop what?" I asked.

"Every compensation meeting, you tell the board they're stupid," he said.

"Tom, I can't help it. They *are* stupid. They have a great franchise, and they're pissing it away."

The mood in New York lightened up now that we were profitable. For a charity event in the summer of 2003, I dressed up head-to-toe in a gray velour shark suit and busted a move dancing and lip-synching to "Mack the Knife." What would have come across as heartless in 2001 was now hilarious. Having righted the ship, I was looking ahead. The logical next step to me was pursuing a merger with another big bank. This would give us more financial firepower. The CS board disagreed.

On the night of June 23, 2004, the CS board gathered in Manhattan for dinner. I had no clue what the board was planning to dish out to me.

First thing the next morning, Tom Bell burst into my office. "John, they're not renewing your contract," he said. "They're voting at the board meeting today."

"Those sons of bitches," I said to Tom.

Then I laughed.

Ossie became the sole CEO of CS, and his protégé, Brady Dougan, replaced me as CEO of CSFB. It was an unceremonious ending to my time with the Swiss. But I'm very proud of what we accomplished. After losing $1 billion in 2001 and $1.2 billion in

2002, I resuscitated the ailing bank. We were turning a huge profit, and we were back on solid ground with the regulators. Would I have liked a few more years there? Probably. Was it my swiftest move to tell the Swiss they were stupid? Probably not.

But just as I had predicted, I'd had a hell of a good time.

CHAPTER NINETEEN

Cold and bright with a slight breeze, Wednesday, January 12, 2005, was a day when the weather did not match the moment. At about 10:30 a.m., Christy and I, wearing black and feeling somber, walked into Riverside Church in New York's Morningside Heights neighborhood on the Upper West Side. We were there for Dick Fisher's memorial service. Dick had died on December 16. Just sixty-eight, he had been diagnosed with prostate cancer six and a half years earlier. He faced his illness the same way he faced everything—unflinchingly. I never once heard Dick complain about—or even acknowledge the existence of—the steel leg braces he wore underneath his trousers because of his childhood polio. Subconsciously, I must have believed that Dick would prevail, that nothing could defeat him. It made it all the harder to grasp that he was gone.

Inside the immense, vaulted Gothic church, designed after the famous thirteenth-century Chartres Cathedral in France, Christy and I watched as first the pews filled and then the aisles. The standing-room-only crowd revealed the affection and admiration Dick had inspired. His cobbler was there, as well as the mayor of New York City, Michael Bloomberg. In addition to Dick's impeccable reputation on Wall Street and his generous support of the arts, he truly liked and enjoyed people. He offered everyone the same warmth, humor, and ready wisdom he had shown me at our first lunch in the Morgan Stanley partners' dining room in 1972. The president of Bard College, Leon Botstein, delivered one of four eulogies. Dick had given the small liberal arts college 110 miles north of New York City both his time and his money. Botstein described Dick's "elegant talent for focusing attention on others." Sitting next to Christy, holding her hand, I thought, *That's exactly right. That's what made Dick so special.*

As we were leaving the church, we stopped to speak to old friends from Morgan Stanley. "This felt like more than just a service for Dick," one told us. "It felt like it marked the end of an era." Others nodded. I didn't say anything. At this point, I had been gone from Morgan Stanley for four years. I had walled off the anguish I felt when I left.

Other long-timers groused: "Did you see that not a single member from the board of directors even bothered to show up?" I had noticed Phil Purcell sitting with Bloomberg and a handful of senior Morgan Stanley people. But there was no one else from the board. I was glad these people who had been so dismissive of Dick had not attended the service, but it shocked me all the same. Tarek Abdel-Meguid (known as Terry Meguid), the head of Investment Banking who had worked at Morgan Stanley for more than twenty-five years, shook my hand. "John," he said, "the place is a mess. We've got to get you back. You need to come run Morgan Stanley."

I wasn't here to talk about Morgan Stanley, Purcell, or the culture of mediocrity that was strangling the firm. I've always believed that once you leave the field, you shouldn't Monday morning quarterback the game. So I just said, "The last time I checked, Terry, someone *is* running Morgan Stanley."

"Well," Terry said, "it's not working."

I didn't foresee then how strong the discontentment percolating among Morgan Stanley's old guard would grow over the next six months. As Lewis Bernard, who knew Morgan Stanley better than pretty much anyone else, said, "It was like the United States in 1860. You could feel a war was coming, but you didn't know how it was going to be resolved."

———

CLEANING UP A firm with tens of thousands of employees, flying to Zurich every month, and battling the Swiss's shortsighted decisions had given me zero time to stop and evaluate much of anything outside of work. After I had left Credit Suisse the previous June, however, I had taken stock of my own life. "I talk to my friends on the phone," I told Christy. "I never see them. I want to spend time with the people I care about." Yes, I saw friends at the golf course, and Christy and I went to dinner with different couples. But a lot of people fell outside that circle.

"Instead of making your sixtieth birthday about turning a year older, why don't we use it as a way to reconnect, John?" she suggested.

My wife is a genius.

For three days in November 2004, we hosted eighty-two people in Paris for a long weekend. We put everyone up at the Hôtel de Crillon, a five-star hotel in an eighteenth-century palace overlooking the Place de la Concorde, at the end of the Champs-Elysées. I loved bringing our friends together to share experiences like this.

We kicked off the celebration with a moonlight boat trip and dinner on the Seine River. The next day we chartered the iconic Venice Simplon-Orient-Express train to Normandy, where a French guide took us to the German bunkers at Pointe du Hoc, then down to Utah and Omaha Beaches, and on to other D-Day landmarks. Our tour culminated at the Normandy American Cemetery and Memorial, on a bluff in Colleville-sur-Mer overlooking Omaha Beach on the English Channel. It is the resting place for 9,386 American soldiers—many of them just on the cusp of manhood—killed during the Allied invasion of France in 1944, the year I was born. Their sacrifice is marked by row upon row of white crosses and Stars of David. Two of my half brothers, George and Philip, had fought in World War II, and both had made it home safely. Our guide pointed out the graves of other brothers who had not been as lucky. As the afternoon wound down, soldiers lowered the American flag to the mournful notes of "Taps" and handed the crisply folded triangle to Peter Karches. I was so glad that Peter and his wife, Susan, could join us, because he was fighting the leukemia that would take his life two years later, at the age of fifty-four. There was not a dry eye in our group. It capped a powerful, poignant day.

The final night, we hosted a black-tie dinner at the top of the Eiffel Tower, with champagne toasts and a video tribute. Watching the video, I thought, *Man, a lot of people think sixty is ancient. They're wrong.* At sixty, I knew I had a ton of energy and experience. I loved the investment banking business, and I wanted to do more of it.

IN JANUARY, AROUND the time of Dick's memorial service, my old friend Art Samberg invited me to come spend time with him at Pequot Capital Management Inc., a $6.5 billion hedge fund. (A hedge fund is an investment pool that uses various strategies to produce a return, even in a volatile or down market.) I met Art through Byron Wien, who joined Morgan Stanley in 1985 as chief US strategist to replace my thrifty carpool buddy Barton Biggs after he was promoted to become the firm's first global strategist. Admired on Wall Street for his acumen and his "Ten Surprises" annual financial forecast, Byron was never shy about voicing his opinions. After Morgan Stanley went public, Byron sat me down. "John, you ought to have someone smart like Art manage your money," he said. Back then, Morgan Stanley shares made up my entire investment portfolio, and Byron strongly believed that I should diversify.

Byron was right about Art. He wasn't just smart, he was a savvy risk-taker. A few years older than me, he was born in the Bronx. Art graduated from the Massachusetts Institute of Technology before going on to Stanford for a master's degree in aeronautical engineering and then to Columbia Business School. Combining a deep grasp of science with investing prowess, Art got into tech stocks early and did well. He and a business partner started Pequot in 1999. Before they split the firm up, Pequot was the largest hedge fund in the world, with $15 billion under management.

Art was also a lot of fun to be around. Although he had an office in Midtown, it was Pequot's headquarters in Westport, Connecticut, that really showed off Art's style. He had designed the offices with an indoor basketball court. Passionate about the game, Art had tried and failed to make his high school team every year. Finally, he got a spot as a senior. Competitive and persistent—that was Art.

I was happy with my new informal gig working out of Art's Midtown office. After my success at Credit Suisse, I had earned a reputation as Mr. Fix-It. Over the winter I felt pretty popular, fielding approaches from big banks and top corporate headhunters. But nothing caught my eye. I realized that what I liked best was building teams, and that's what I wanted to do.

Because both Morgan Stanley and CSFB had dealt with hedge funds, I knew a lot about their structure. But I had never done much investing. I learned how Art looked at deals and made decisions. We were a great combination, bouncing ideas off each other. There was a lot of mutual respect. My schedule was different at Pequot. For the first time in my life, I was working Mondays through Fridays, 9:00 a.m. to 5:00 p.m. I didn't make phone calls or travel to see clients on the weekend. I was surprised at how much I enjoyed this routine.

The more time Art and I spent together, the more our plans solidified. Pequot had about 150 employees, and we decided to grow the firm. I didn't plan to become an asset manager, which requires honing specific skills. Instead I would be the door-opener. I had entrée to clients all over the world. When we met potential investors, I presented the big picture. Art filled in the details. And because I had learned a thing or two about motivating and managing people, I would be the chief team-builder. On June 3, 2005, almost a year after I had left Credit Suisse, we made my role official. The *Wall Street Journal* announced that I would become Pequot's chairman. Art would remain CEO.

At least, that was the plan.

BY THE END of March, the behind-the-scenes rage about Phil Purcell's lackluster leadership at Morgan Stanley boiled over in public. The problems had grown beyond clashing cultures. Many of the Dean Witter people had turned against Phil as well. While the rest of Wall Street charged forward, Purcell—in my opinion, always risk-averse—pulled back. Goldman Sachs's stock price rebounded after the tech bubble burst, while Morgan Stanley's remained stagnant—still less than half its high of $110 in 2000. Business opportunities were missed, morale plummeted, and its greatest asset—the talented people who went up in the elevators every morning—were walking out the door. Eight Morgan Stanley alumni, alarmed by this attrition, sent a private letter to Purcell and the rest of the board. "We believe that the overriding cause of the Firm's poor performance is a failure of leadership by you as the Firm's CEO," they wrote. "It is imperative that the Board act promptly to change the leadership and governance of Morgan Stanley." The signers had all played major roles at the firm. Chairman from 1984 to 1990, Parker Gilbert had taken the firm public in 1986. Bob Scott had succeeded me as president before Purcell forced him out in 2003. Anson Beard had headed the Equities Division. Lewis Bernard was the former administrative and financial officer whom the management committee had once dispatched to mediate between Bob Mulhearn and me in my early days as a sales manager. The Group of Eight, as they were dubbed, didn't control the company—they didn't have enough stock to do that. "We just had a very, very strong attachment to the success of the firm," Lewis later told me. "And we saw that that was being eroded."

In response to the Group of Eight letter, Purcell reorganized the firm. He elevated Zoe Cruz and Steve Crawford as co-presidents to replace Vikram Pandit and Stephan Newhouse. Crawford, who had been the firm's CFO, was a Purcell loyalist, and I didn't think much of him. But I had tremendous respect for Zoe. She was an assertive, committed, intuitive leader. Before I left, I had promoted Zoe to head Global Fixed Income, Commodities, and Foreign Exchange. I tried unsuccessfully to hire her at CSFB.

Pandit's departure, along with that of John Havens, who had headed Institutional Equities, further galvanized the Group of Eight. The previously publicity-shy men released their letter to the *Wall Street Journal*, the *New York Times*, and CNBC. The *Times* ran a front-page story under the headline "Intrigue Engulfs Morgan Stanley; 2 Executives Out." CNBC stationed a reporter outside the Morgan Stanley Building on Broadway, and Parker Gilbert and Bob Scott went on TV. Gilbert embodied the history of the firm. Morgan Stanley had been founded by his father, his stepfather, and his godfather: S. Parker Gilbert Sr., Harold Stanley, and Henry S. Morgan. "We can't stand still and watch this franchise that's been created over a long period of time be run down," Parker told CNBC. The group followed the release of the original letter with more letters, which ran as full-page ads in the *Journal*. Purcell and the board fought back with counter ads. Morgan Stanley's present and past leaders were slugging it out, and the extraordinary spectacle of brawling blue-bloods mesmerized the public.

My phone was blowing up. Reporters were calling me for comments, and Morgan Stanley insiders were keeping me in the loop. They wanted to know what I believed would happen. I knew the Group of Eight had leverage. But did I believe they could force Purcell out? I put the odds at fifty-fifty. Purcell probably suspected I was the one instigating the fight. That's not true. I took the calls and listened, but I didn't stir the pot. I didn't think that was my place. I distanced myself. I didn't want to be seen as pursuing a vendetta against Purcell. That would have made me look small. To this day, I believe sidelining myself was the right thing to do.

Terry Meguid and Joseph Perella, the well-known M&A ace, resigned in mid-April. In May the firm lost a high-profile lawsuit to investor Ronald Perelman. He accused Morgan Stanley of hiding Sunbeam's flagging financial situation when he did a deal with Sunbeam in 1998. Irate that Morgan Stanley failed to turn over the thousands of emails Perelman's lawyers had requested, a Florida judge instructed the jury to assume that Morgan Stanley had intentionally defrauded Perelman. The jury's job was to decide how much Morgan Stanley should pay Perelman in damages. Its decision: $1.45 *billion*.

The stock price continued to drop. By mid-June, about fifty more people had departed, including two groups of traders. Top talent Mayree Clark, who was running the International Individual Investor Group, also left. Those who stayed were too busy speculating about who would leave next to do any work. Even twenty-five-year-old first-year associates at the water cooler were consumed.

Finally, investor pressure on the board got so intense that it drove a wedge between them and Purcell. On Monday, June 13, 2005, Purcell, sixty-one, announced his retirement. He walked away with more than $113 million. According to Patricia Beard's *Blue Blood & Mutiny*, the package included a $42.7 million departure bonus.

Chuck Knight was the board member in charge of finding a new CEO. The former chief executive of St. Louis–based Emerson Electric, he put out a list of people who would *not* replace Purcell: No one in the Group of Eight. No one who had resigned in the past few months like Pandit, Havens, and Perella.

And not John Mack.

I wasn't surprised that Knight specifically said I was out of the running. I never thought I would return to Morgan Stanley. But I knew something else. I was the best person for the job.

————————

ONE THING THAT did shock me: a phone call from Phil Purcell. He invited me to lunch at San Pietro, on East Fifty-Fourth Street. Sitting across the table from me in the paneled dining room, Phil said, "I don't think it's the right thing for the board to do, but they're going to ask you to come back to the firm." Phil shared his opinions about the business and where he thought it should go. I believed that whatever had happened between us was in the past. We had to do the best we could for shareholders and employees. It took guts for Phil to ask me to lunch. I was respectful. I told myself, *Don't gloat.* But the second I walked out of the restaurant, I called Christy. "You'll never believe what Phil just told me," I said. "But we both know the board will never pick me."

A few days after my lunch with Phil, I got another phone call. This time it was from Tom Neff, head of the executive search firm Spencer Stuart. "John, Chuck Knight and Miles Marsh want to talk with you," he said. "Are you interested?" Marsh, who was also on the Morgan Stanley board, ran the Illinois paper products company Fort James Corporation.

"I'll talk to them, but I know they're not fans of mine," I said. "They're not really considering me for the CEO job. They're just checking the box."

"Come to dinner at the Carlyle hotel," Tom said. "We'll keep it private." Famous for its discretion, the art deco hotel at Madison Avenue and Seventy-Sixth Street was once called a "palace of secrets" by the *New York Times*. It was Princess Diana's favorite hotel when she visited Manhattan and where President John F. Kennedy was rumored to entertain Marilyn Monroe. *At least I didn't have to be smuggled in by the Secret Service*, I thought as I crossed the luxurious lobby to the elevator. It made sense for the directors to stay out of the public eye because the media continued to buzz about the intrigue at Morgan Stanley.

Over dinner, I told Miles and Chuck what had gone wrong with Phil and why I had quit in 2001. "We appreciate your honesty, John," they said. Then they offered me the job of CEO.

"The obvious question is, why?" I asked.

Miles and Chuck looked taken aback. This was not the response they expected. "John, I confess I'm a little disappointed," Chuck said. "Why aren't you more excited about our offer?"

"Why should I be excited about coming back, Chuck?" I replied. "When I left, not one of you asked me to stay."

I admit it. I enjoy calling people on the carpet when they deserve it—and they did.

Whoever became CEO would not have an easy job. Eight years after the 1997 merger, Morgan Stanley Dean Witter still wasn't a one-firm firm. Somebody would finally have to integrate Investment Banking and Retail or spin off the latter. The person would have to boost the firm's profitability and share price. The Perelman lawsuit had tarnished Morgan Stanley's reputation, and the bottom line was going to take a massive, billion-dollar-plus hit. Morale had tanked. Did I want to take this on?

I hadn't made up my mind about what I wanted to do. On one hand, taking Morgan Stanley's reins on my own was so tempting. I had so much history there, so many good friends. It was Wall Street's crown jewel. On the other hand, I'd done my time repairing a troubled investment bank at CSFB. And did I really want to work with the same board that had chosen Purcell over me in 2001?

Christy had none of these misgivings. "John," she said, "you've got to go back. Morgan Stanley needs you."

While I was trying to decide, we flew to London for a long-planned trip to see Jenna, who was attending graduate school there. We were eating dinner at one of my favorite Lebanese restaurants in Mayfair, not far from the Dorchester hotel, where we were staying. My cell phone rang. It was Jeff Immelt, who ran General Electric. "John, we need you as CEO of Morgan Stanley," he said. "The firm is very important to GE. We rely on its brainpower and market power. It's not just Morgan Stanley employees who need you. It's clients like us."

"Let's talk when I'm back in New York," I told Jeff.

As we were getting into bed that night, Christy asked me, "What do you think you'll do?"

"Well," I said, "I'd rather take the job and regret it than not take it and wish I had."

"That's your answer, John," Christy said. We flew home the next morning.

On Thursday, June 30, the board held a meeting where they voted unanimously to elect me as the CEO and chairman of Morgan Stanley. With Maria Bartiromo providing running commentary for CNBC, Christy and I walked through the trading room on the sixth floor. It was pure chaos: packed with people waiting for us to arrive, some standing on their desks in order to see. They were hooting, clapping, whistling, chanting, "Mack! Mack! Mack!" I smiled, but I was working hard to hold back a rush of emotion. It was like I was a rock star. Christy and I made our way to the auditorium for the formal announcement of my appointment. When we walked in, the two hundred managing directors stood up and clapped. "We are here to announce the worst-kept secret on Wall Street," Miles Marsh said, introducing me.

Standing behind the mic, I was teary-eyed. I felt like I had been away on a world tour, and now I was returning to my family. I had started at Morgan Stanley less than a month before Christy and I got married. We had grown up here. Quieting the crowd, I swallowed hard and said the first thing that came to mind. "I had no idea I'd be coming back home."

CHAPTER TWENTY

W here's Walid?" I called out. "I want to see Walid."
I had just left the auditorium where I had been named Morgan Stanley's CEO and walked downstairs to the floor below. "Where's Walid's office?" I called out again, this time to a group of startled bankers. They pointed down the hall.

Walid was Walid Chammah, the head of Global Capital Markets at Morgan Stanley. Born in Beirut, Lebanon, he got a master's degree from the Thunderbird School of International Management in Arizona in 1977. He was both a pioneering banker and a brilliant relationship-builder. He had been one of my best hires at Morgan Stanley. When I was heading up CSFB, I tried to recruit Walid, offering him the job as co-head of Investment Banking with Bayo Ogunlesi.

I knew he would be a huge asset in my push to restructure the Investment Banking Division. I put the full-court press on Walid. Wining and dining him like crazy, I reminded him that our relationship went back more than a decade. Using words like "poach" and "wrest," the financial press couldn't get enough of Phil Purcell and me fighting over Walid. Our "battle" made headlines for almost two weeks.

I thought I had won. Walid seemed ready to jump ship and join me. He and Bayo had held planning sessions on the phone. The press reported his "impending" departure. Then, at the last minute, I got word that Walid was staying put at Morgan Stanley. "Score one for Philip J. Purcell," began a *New York Times* article on February 21, 2002. "Mr. Chammah's decision to stay at Morgan Stanley ended a protracted tug of war between the firms. . . ." I wished Walid well in the press, but privately I was disappointed, embarrassed, and, yes, a little angry.

It wasn't surprising that as soon as Walid heard I was coming back to Morgan Stanley, he submitted his resignation to his boss, Zoe Cruz. "It's John's firm," Walid told Zoe, "and I'm not going to be in the way. I don't want to make it complicated for him. Let's face it. I'm a dead man walking. I need to go." Zoe refused to accept his resignation.

Now Walid saw me in the doorway of his office and stood up. Looking at me from behind his glasses, he seemed anxious. I'm sure he assumed that I was coming to tell him to pack his boxes and get out. Instead, I put my arm around his shoulders. "Buddy," I said loudly, so everyone could hear, "I wanted to work with you. I just didn't think I'd have to come back to Morgan Stanley to do it!"

With that, I put to rest any notion that I was out for revenge. You don't rebuild a one-firm firm by setting up a mass firing squad to settle personal grievances from the past. Walid was an irreplaceable talent, and I wanted him at my side as we moved Morgan Stanley into the future.

But from my first day on the job, there were certain individuals I wanted to see gone. Steve Crawford, whom Purcell had named co-president in March, resigned. For his three-month stint, he walked away with $32 million. Purcell had negotiated this appalling payout for his underling with the board.

Before I returned in late June, a board member tipped off the other co-president, Zoe Cruz, that I was about to rejoin Morgan Stanley. She phoned me. "Can I talk to you in person?" she asked.

"I'm up to my eyeballs," I said.

"Then I'll have to do it by phone, John. I'm calling to resign from the firm. You deserve your own team."

I could hear the emotion in her voice.

"You can't do that," I said. "You can't resign from the firm. You're not going anywhere. Let's meet tomorrow morning. I'll come to your apartment at seven."

Supremely talented, tough, decisive, quick, Zoe had backbone and operated from her gut. I admit it: she reminded me of myself. We had both come up through Fixed Income. She had made a lot of money for the firm. I also believed she had a deep allegiance to Morgan Stanley, where she had worked for twenty-three years. To me, that, not opportunism, had motivated her to accept the position of co-president under Purcell. At a moment of crisis in the firm, she stepped forward and took up a post in the watchtower. I wanted her with me.

No question, though, Zoe was a lightning rod at the firm. The Group of Eight and many others saw her as a traitor who had crossed over to Purcell's side. She had even been mentioned as his successor. There were people who considered her combative, divisive, and incapable of dealing with dissent—in other words, not a leader. Gifted veterans of Morgan Stanley like Stephan Newhouse, Vikram Pandit, Joe Perella, John Havens, and Terry Meguid flat-out said they would not return if they had to work with Zoe.

I was not going to let anyone put a gun to my head by telling me who they would or would not work with. I don't give in to ultimatums. It makes a CEO appear powerless and easy to manipulate.

I named Zoe acting president. There was a lot of speculation about the "acting" in her title. I did it to calm things down. Morgan Stanley had been through a traumatic civil war, and the wounds were fresh. Coming from Fixed Income, Zoe often had conflicts with Investment Banking. That was inherent to the job. Seven months later, in February 2006, I named Zoe and Robert Scully, an honest, straightforward, smart veteran investment banker, as co-presidents. I wanted to create balance on the fortieth floor, where I had reinstalled the executive suite. Elevating Zoe generated a lot of media headlines naming her the most powerful woman on Wall Street.

Of course, I hired my designated truth-teller, Tom Nides, as chief administrative officer. It is a huge mistake for those in power to surround themselves with people who tell them only what they want to hear. Tom is genetically programmed to call things as he sees them. Even when he was wrong, he always made me stop and think.

Wei Christianson had joined me at CSFB, where she had done a spectacular job upping the firm's profile and reputation in China. In three years, she hoisted CSFB's business there from seventeenth place to first. After I was fired, she quit immediately in solidarity and went to Citigroup to head its Investment Banking team in China. Again, she killed it. In 2006, I convinced Wei to come back to Morgan Stanley, where our China operation was faltering. We had lost out on the IPO for China's largest bank. "What do we need to be doing differently?" I pressed her.

"People at Morgan Stanley, because they had a fantastic franchise in China all these years, are too comfortable," Wei answered. "They need to get out of their comfort zones and be aggressive. It's a different game than when you started going there, John. Now everybody is competing in China."

I knew China was in the best hands with Wei in charge. I didn't have that kind of ready solution for Retail. Although there had been progress integrating Morgan Stanley and Dean Witter, there was a huge question mark hanging over the future of this underperforming business. Should we keep it or sell it? Many people on the Investment Banking side, along with investors and analysts, were clamoring for the latter. The problem was that the Brokerage Division had never recovered from the puncturing of the tech bubble, and it was dragging down the rest of the firm. We had merged with Dean Witter to provide a steady source of income, and it was doing just the opposite. Zoe began cutting weak brokers—a thousand out of ten thousand—in October 2005.

That was a good start. But I wanted to put someone fresh in charge of Retail, someone who had played no part in the savage battles between Morgan Stanley and Dean Witter or Phil Purcell and the Group of Eight. Another nonnegotiable qualification: a track record running a profitable retail operation. Zoe and I began interviewing candidates.

One stood out: James Gorman.

James, then age forty-seven, is an Australian who grew up in a family of ten children in Melbourne. A lawyer by training, he switched fields and came to the United States to attend Columbia Business School. After twelve years at McKinsey, he went to Merrill Lynch, his McKinsey client, in 1999. There, as head of Retail overseeing sixteen thousand brokers, Gorman worked hard to put more thunder into Merrill's "Thundering Herd." He fired underperformers and drastically reined in expense accounts. Among other impressive changes, James also moved the firm's focus to wealthier individuals. I called his old boss, David Komansky, the ex-CEO at Merrill Lynch, who raved, "Gorman is just terrific, John." The numbers supported Komansky: under James, Merrill's profits in its Private Client unit were nearly four times our profits.

One evening, James and I had a private conversation about the job. He was straightforward. "I want to join the organization," he told me. Surprisingly for someone at his high level, he was willing to report to Zoe, who had limited Retail experience, rather than demanding a direct line to me. This told me a lot about who James was: an all-hands-on-deck, unpretentious guy. It told me something else: with him, I wasn't going to get politicking, ultimatums, and personnel drama.

Impressed, I scheduled a follow-up dinner with Christy, James, and his wife, Penny. "Look, our Retail business is mediocre," I told him. "It will be your call. If you come in and tell me this can't be fixed and we should sell the business and move on, I will do that. If you tell me you can fix it, you'll have one hundred percent of my support."

James accepted the job in mid-August, but his contract at Merrill Lynch kept him from starting until the following February. Theoretically, the first day he could work was on Friday, February 17, 2006, which kicked off the long Presidents Day weekend. Everyone at Morgan Stanley assumed James would not come in until Tuesday, February 21. So his subordinates were jolted when their new boss showed up on Friday at 8:00 a.m. "Why are you here?" they asked. "Don't you want to start on Tuesday?"

"Why would I wait until Tuesday?" he responded. "I'm an employee, and my job has begun." James was sending the troops a strong message about his work ethic and expectations. I liked it.

He wasn't at Morgan Stanley long before he told me he could fix Retail. "The bones of the business are strong," James said. "The financial advisers are doing exactly what the people at Merrill Lynch, UBS, and Wachovia are doing: advising clients on how to manage their wealth." He continued: "The problem is the personnel. We have a lot of poorly performing financial advisers, and they're the ones creating the most legal headaches."

The first thing James did was to change the name from Morgan Stanley Dean Witter to Morgan Stanley. It may seem minor, but it carried tremendous symbolism. "The financial advisers need to understand they work for Morgan Stanley, not for Morgan Stanley Dean Witter," James told me. "With that comes the responsibility to perform at the *level* of Morgan Stanley." *The name change will get the investment bankers' attention*, I thought, nodding. *It will instill pride.*

James displayed his leadership in other ways. Every Monday morning, he unveiled a new initiative. This created anxiety, energy, and tempo. He was turning the burners up full blast on what had been a gently simmering pot. One Monday, he fired two thousand brokers and transferred their clients to high performers. Whenever he came to me and said, "Here's what I'm going to do and here's what the result will look like," I didn't counter with, "What if you did it this way instead?" I had total confidence that he had already gamed out what he thought was the best strategy. It wasn't my job as CEO to second-guess him. My job was to give him the runway he needed to achieve success. I'd say, "Great. You're my man. I back you. Go for it."

Giving James the freedom to execute as he thought best was part of a larger objective. It seemed to me that a culture of "no" had taken root under Phil Purcell. Back then, when people came up with an idea, they described it in a proposal, sent it up the hierarchy, and waited. Months later, the answer worked its way back down the chain of command. Almost inevitably, the answer was negative. I was determined to reinstate a culture of "what are you waiting for?" to stoke people's initiative, not squelch it. I wanted Morgan Stanley to be a place where bold enterprises were hatched and funded once again. A place that fostered optimism and innovation.

That's why I was so energized during a trip to our London headquarters shortly after I became CEO. I had a lengthy open forum with the entire staff there. I wanted *everybody* to walk out of that room motivated to rebuild what we had lost. Afterward, I was scheduled for a fifteen-minute meeting with an investment banker named Georges Makhoul. Born in Lebanon, he coincidentally shared the same name as my grandfather when he arrived at Ellis Island. Georges had moved to the United States for graduate school and then worked at Morgan Stanley Japan before transferring to London.

He and others had been mulling over the pros and cons of expanding into the Middle East. Dubai, a business-friendly emirate that aspired to be a global financial center like Singapore, topped their list. "What's your thinking on this, Georges?" I asked. For the next two hours, he outlined all the reasons that Dubai was the right place for us. Having gained its independence from Great Britain in 1971, it was undergoing rocket-speed modernization with a new generation of business leaders. A major port and transportation hub, Dubai is located on the southern Persian Gulf, making it convenient to North Africa and East Asia. Having a Morgan Stanley office there would telegraph to clients, "We're here. We're in the neighborhood. We're ready to serve you." No longer would they have to fly to London, New York, or Munich to do business.

Remember, this was 2005, and there was a big boom in credit. This benefited emerging markets like Russia, Eastern Europe, Africa, Latin America, and the Middle East. Plus, in the Middle East, oil was commanding $80 a barrel—and rising fast—which meant there was more and more money being spent on infrastructure, on trade, on technology.

I met with Georges on Thursday. He landed in Dubai on Saturday to scout out the situation. The next week he called me. "Look, I think there is a real opportunity, and I think we should go," he said.

"Do it," I said.

"John, I need to tell you something first. Yes, I'm from the Middle East and I speak Arabic, but I've never done business there."

I came right back at Georges. "Buddy," I said, "you built a business in Japan. If you can build a business in Japan, you can build a business anywhere."

By December 2005, we had a license, and we were ready to open our doors. That's how Morgan Stanley became the first American investment bank to establish an office in Dubai.

———————

I STILL NEEDED to rebuild the Morgan Stanley one-firm firm culture. One way was to bring the New York staff and their families together. After 9/11, Morgan Stanley bought the Texaco headquarters in Purchase to have a fallback location outside the city. That's where Retail and Asset Management were now headquartered. The building had beautiful grounds, complete with a pond. It was the ideal spot for a company picnic.

In North Carolina, nothing builds community more than a pig pickin'. It's a beloved fixture at churches, football games, and political rallies. So Christy and I thought it would be fun to hire Bill Ellis, who had been manning a barbecue pit since he opened Bill's Drive-In near Raleigh in 1963. At some point, Bill, a natural entrepreneur, decided he should take his feasts on the road. That's how two semitrucks with "Coast to Coast Catering—Bill Ellis' Wilson N.C. Barbecue" emblazoned on the sides ended up pulling into the Texaco campus parking lot one Saturday in October 2006.

Roasting an entire 80- to 120-pound pig until the meat falls off the bones takes several hours. But it took even longer that day, because the northerners kept lifting the grill hood to peek at the pig, letting out all that heat and good-smelling smoke. What these northerners didn't know is that the rivalry between eastern and western North Carolina barbecue is as fierce as the one between Duke and UNC.

Eastern barbecue, like Bill's, uses the whole hog and a vinegary sauce. Western-style uses just the pork shoulder and a ketchup-based sauce. Bill also barbecued chicken and dished up plenty of sides like slaw, collard greens, and hush puppies that day. I liked Bill's slogan, "Honesty & Hard Work 'The Only Way,'" as much as his victuals.

At the end of October, we hosted a second, even bigger event— a country fair, complete with a Ferris wheel, a carousel, and a petting zoo. Thousands of Morgan Stanley employees and their families attended. The big draw that day was the dunking booth, where a certain CEO sat dressed in swimming trunks while people lined up for a chance to hurl softballs at a target. When they made contact, I hit the water. I never realized how fast you fall until I was the guy in the tank. By the end of the day, I was waterlogged, but we raised a lot of money for charity.

I like to schmooze as much as I like to eat BBQ. But there was a deeper goal to hosting these events. I was floored by how much the culture at the firm had deteriorated. When I started at Morgan Stanley, Frank Petito, Bob Baldwin, and Dick Fisher took pride in how the firm treated its employees. They also held an annual picnic. Playing softball and joking around built camaraderie. It boosts morale when bosses engage with their staff outside the office. Employees take a lot of pride introducing their spouses and kids to the people they work with every day, and vice versa. Morgan Stanley had grown exponentially since then, but I wanted to bring back that sense of family.

IN THE PAST few years, during a period when taking financial risks reaped big rewards, Morgan Stanley had become the most timid investment bank on the Street. Zoe and I believed the firm was missing out. We needed to get our mojo back. My attitude was: we have the brand, we have the capital, let's go for it. I wanted our people to know that I would not hang them out to dry if they were aggressive.

Embracing more risk, we put our capital to work. We bought hedge funds, made bridge loans to private equity companies, and expanded proprietary, or prop, trading. This is when traders buy and sell bonds, derivatives, stocks, and other financial instruments for the firm's benefit, using the firm's money, rather than trading for the benefit of clients. The payoffs can be stupendous.

During this time, mortgage-backed securities were red-hot. The world was on a real estate buying spree thanks to easy loans and soaring home values. A mortgage-backed security is a group of mortgages that are bundled together, sliced into pieces or tranches, converted into bonds, and sold to investors looking for high yields. Wall Street's reward was lucrative fees, and we got in on the action. For the first time, firms, including Morgan Stanley, were buying and selling these mortgage-backed securities to and from each other. We didn't realize that this intertwining of risk held unforeseen consequences. In our hunt for more market share, we also bought companies that originated mortgages here in the United States and in Italy, the United Kingdom, and Russia.

These various bets yielded record profits. In 2006, Morgan Stanley had its best year ever, and our stock price took off. The day I assumed command—June 30, 2005—the share price was fifty dollars. By December 21, 2006, it had climbed to eighty-one dollars.

We got more great news. As general counsel, Gary Lynch had been working hard over the past eighteen months to settle the Sunbeam lawsuit with Ronald Perelman's lawyer. But, talking about the money one afternoon in my office, Gary said, "We are in totally different universes." In March 2007, a Florida state appeals court delighted us by reversing the verdict. Suddenly we were no longer on the hook for $1.58 billion, which is what the penalties now came to with interest.

Another win came in June. Goldman Sachs reported essentially flat earnings over the previous year and Bear Stearns's profits fell 33 percent. By contrast, Morgan Stanley announced a jump of 40 percent in our net income for the quarter.

All this success boosted our confidence. It was good times. We were cruising along in the party boat, and we didn't realize that a dangerous waterfall lay just ahead.

I remember a taxi driver telling me that he had bought a house on Staten Island. He got a second mortgage on that house, took the money, and bought another house. Then he put a second mortgage on that one. Everyone wanted to own a house. And then they wanted to own two or three. Builders were throwing up houses as fast as they could switch on the backhoes. People were getting loans from mortgage companies like Countrywide and New Century Financial. Many subprime mortgage issuers didn't check credit scores or certify income. They made a killing on huge up-front fees, issued the mortgages to borrowers who didn't understand the terms, and moved on.

Listening to the taxi driver describe his budding real estate empire, I didn't connect the dots. But more and more risk and bad debt were being injected into the marketplace. Early in 2007, home values and prices began to fall—and kept falling. We discovered what happens when people walk away from unpayable mortgages: the companies that issued them go bankrupt, and the housing market collapses. But most of us, including top economists, believed the damage was contained. On May 17, 2007, in his first public remarks about the subprime crisis, Federal Reserve chairman Ben Bernanke said he foresaw "no serious broader spillover" into the economy from the rising number of mortgage defaults.

But we all got this wrong, as we discovered that autumn.

NEAL SHEAR JOINED Morgan Stanley in 1982 as a precious metals trader. He rose to oversee Fixed Income and Sales and Trading, reporting to Zoe Cruz. In 2006, Shear took home $35 million because of the stellar performance of his team. But six months later, a complicated trade involving mortgage-backed securities blew up.

In late 2006, Shear's trading group made a $2 billion bet that the market for subprime mortgages would continue to deteriorate in 2007. In other words, they shorted the market. As insurance, Shear's team hedged the original bet—that is, placed a counter bet that the market would go up—by buying $14 billion worth of what we assumed were safe AAA-rated mortgages.

As the market for subprime mortgages kept going down, we were making money on the first trade. But what no one imagined—and no stress test predicted—was that the AAA mortgages would also lose their value. The foreclosure rate on these supposedly safe mortgages turned out to be between 40 and 50 percent, rendering them unsellable. The result was that in late October and November, the value of the hedge began to plunge. What had begun as a short bet became an inadvertent long bet.

The collapse in value was jaw-dropping. On October 31, we expected the loss to be $3.7 billion. By November 30, the loss increased by an additional $4.1 billion. On a single hedged $2 billion bet, which we thought would be bulletproof, we had lost a whopping $7.8 billion. Morgan Stanley ended up at the mercy of counterparties who had bet the AAA mortgages would also decline. And who held that crystal ball? Goldman Sachs, our archrival.

Goldman Sachs aside, mortgage-backed securities and other risky bets took a heavy toll on Wall Street. Merrill Lynch was in trouble, announcing a loss of $7.9 billion. The day before Halloween, its CEO, Stan O'Neal, stepped down. Next, Citigroup announced a $3.1 billion loss, leading to the resignation of its CEO, Chuck Prince.

I wasn't worried about losing my job. The Morgan Stanley board had confidence in me, and I had confidence in Zoe. While I had not named a successor, I believed that Zoe had all the traits to lead Morgan Stanley as CEO.

But over the next couple of weeks, I began to have doubts.

The previous summer, Zoe had come to me. "John, I'm beside myself," she said. "I think we're in good shape overall, but I just discovered that Neal Shear and his team have lost $250 million. I'm so upset because we would have been unique in not having any losses if they had listened to me. In May, I told them to take every bit of risk under the sun off the books. I told them the sky was going to fall."

"You should fire Neal," I said.

Zoe didn't take my advice, which was her right. She was Shear's boss. "I'm sure this experience is seared into Neal's brain," she told me. "He's more valuable to us now than before." But having made the decision to keep him, it was her job to follow up. Every week, she should have demanded, "How much risk have you taken off? Show me the books." Instead, Zoe assumed Neal was following her orders.

On November 7, when we announced the subprime trading loss—then $3.7 billion—Zoe came and sat down in my office. Zoe remembers she said, "You were right, John. I should have fired Neal."

I remember it differently. I recall that she said, "John, I can't understand how Neal allowed these positions to be on the books. How could they do this to me?"

She should have said, "I take responsibility. I will deal with the traders and the risk managers who made these decisions."

I ruminated about Zoe all during the Thanksgiving holiday. Zoe was my friend. She's such a good person. I admired her. None of that mattered. When you're in charge, you're in charge. When you fuck up, you've got to take the pain.

On Thursday, November 29, I attended a board meeting. Then I walked into Zoe's office. I got straight to the point. "I've decided to have a change of leadership," I told her.

Zoe began to laugh. She thought I was joking.

I said it again. "I've decided to have a change of leadership." And then again. "I've decided to have a change of leadership."

Finally, Zoe realized I was serious. She looked shocked, flabbergasted. Zoe left Morgan Stanley within the hour.

As Mack the Knife, I have fired thousands of people. But firing Zoe was by far the most difficult thing I've ever done. The next day, I texted her, "Can I take you for a drink?"

"Maybe someday," she texted back.

"Someday" did not come for several years. Eventually, though, Zoe called me, and we resumed our friendship, which continues to this day. I once asked her, "Why do you still talk to me?"

"I think you made the wrong decision to fire me," she said. "But I never would have gotten to where I rose in the firm without you. You supported me."

THE DAY I fired Zoe, I named two new co-presidents: Walid Chammah and James Gorman. I moved Bob Scully to work with me in the chairman's office to handle Sovereign Fund clients. I removed Neal Shear as the co-head of Sales and Trading. He left Morgan Stanley in early March.

The massive losses exposed structural weakness in our risk management, and I acted immediately to fortify the system. I was already attending more risk meetings. Next, I changed the org chart. Instead of reporting to the person overseeing the Trading Division, the risk managers reported to my new CFO, Colm Kelleher. From County Cork,

Ireland, he had a master's degree in history from Oxford University and a background as a chartered accountant. Colm had joined Morgan Stanley in 1989. My nickname for him was Eeyore, for his tendency to see the worm in every apple. Exactly the trait you want in a CFO.

Soon after the new year, my old golfing and carpool buddy, Ken deRegt, who had headed Fixed Income before leaving Morgan Stanley in 2000, came in to see me. He had several work opportunities and wanted my advice. "Forget about those jobs, Kenny," I said. "We could really use your help here. We'll find things for you to do. Come on back."

"Well, I'm in my fifties," Ken said. "I've got time. I've got energy. I've got some experience. It would be terrific to help you and Morgan Stanley."

I made Ken chief risk officer, reporting directly to me and the board. I knew he had the professional chops as well as the personal finesse to take on this delicate post. I told him, "I don't want you to come in like you're the new sheriff in town. I don't want you saying, 'You people screwed up, and I'm here to clean house.' Talk to people to find out how we can do better."

Four times a year, publicly held companies, including investment firms, have to release their financials. The way it works: First, a press release goes out to Wall Street analysts and the media summarizing the numbers. Then, later in the day, there's a conference call for us to present an overview and answer questions.

These earnings calls were usually pretty enjoyable. I am a natural public speaker, as well as a ham. Not today.

On the morning of December 19, 2007, I was wearing my favorite tie for courage. Jenna had found it in London and given it to me for Christmas. I walked into the boardroom, sat down, and nodded at Colm, who introduced me. What was I thinking as I began to speak? I was thinking, *I fucked up.*

I opened the call with the truth: "The results we announced today are embarrassing for me, for our firm. This was a result of an error in judgment incurred on one desk in our Fixed Income area, and also a failure to manage that risk appropriately. Make no mistake, we've held people accountable. We're moving aggressively to make necessary changes."

I continued: "I want to be absolutely clear: As head of this firm, I take responsibility for performance." For the first time in its seventy-two-year history, Morgan Stanley had suffered a quarterly loss. We were taking a $9.4 billion write-down for the year. It was a crushing number. And it happened with me in charge.

Ironically, 2007 had been a banner year. Investment Banking, Equity, Sales and Trading, and Asset Management had all delivered record profits.

I also used the call to announce that China's sovereign wealth fund, the China Investment Corporation (CIC), had agreed to buy a 9.9 percent stake in Morgan Stanley for $5.6 billion. Once again, Wei had been a superstar, bringing the Chinese to the negotiating table.

At the end of every earnings call, I took questions from the analysts who covered Morgan Stanley. "Help us understand how this could happen, that you could take this large of a loss. I mean, I would imagine that you guys have position limits and risk limits," said William Tanona of Goldman Sachs.

Deutsche Bank's Mike Mayo asked whether we would be changing our risk profile. "I think we've been sprinting, and we're going to be jogging right now for a while," I told him. "But we will still be in the market taking risk."

Because I am a firm believer in pay for performance, I told the board I would not accept a bonus for 2007. In doing this, I wanted to make clear to shareholders and employees the deep pain I felt about the $9.4 billion write-down. CEOs can say they take responsibility, but to give up millions of dollars—that says they're serious.

It had been an extraordinarily tough few months. But as our family sat down to a Lebanese feast on Christmas Eve, I felt that Morgan Stanley had weathered a once-in-a-century storm. Raising my wineglass, I thought, *To calmer seas ahead.*

CHAPTER TWENTY-ONE

F riday, September 12, 2008. Just before 5:00 p.m., my executive
  assistant poked her head into my office, where I was reviewing
the week's numbers with Colm. Rain slapped against the windows on
the fortieth floor. "Tim Geithner's office just called," she said. "They
want you at the New York Fed by six o'clock for an emergency meeting." Geithner was the New York Federal Reserve president. Ten minutes later, Colm and I were in the back seat of my silver Audi. "We
need to get to 33 Liberty Street now," I told Joe, my driver.

Going to the New York Federal Reserve wasn't unusual for me.
All the Wall Street CEOs had attended a black-tie dinner there in July
to welcome the new Treasury secretary, Hank Paulson. I knew Hank,
the former CEO of Goldman Sachs, from my early trips to China.
And Geithner regularly invited small groups of us to lunch to find out
what was happening on the Street.

But this was different. Ominous. When you're summoned to the
New York Fed with an hour's notice, it's not because they can't wait
to share good news.

"What do you suppose this is about?" Colm asked me, looking up from his BlackBerry.

"It's got to be Lehman," I said.

The previous weekend, over Labor Day, the Treasury Department had taken over mortgage behemoths Fannie Mae and Freddie Mac. We knew Lehman Brothers could be next. Wall Street's fourth-largest investment bank, it was teetering toward insolvency. In recent months, I had talked to Dick Fuld, its CEO, about a potential merger a few times.

I felt bad for Dick. I liked him. Tough and abrasive, he was a fierce competitor who earned his nickname, the Gorilla. In 2006, Lehman posted record profits. Its stock price topped $86 per share in February 2007. But when I checked the closing numbers just before we got into the car, the share price had plunged to $3.65.

In March, Bear Stearns, the country's fifth-largest investment bank, ran out of money. JPMorgan Chase immediately swooped in. It gobbled up Bear for a pittance, getting a big financial assist from the US government.

Bear Stearns's sudden death in March woke us up. Over the past six months, Colm had diligently sold off assets and put that money in the bank. We had lowered our debt and increased our liquidity, building a balance sheet that would keep us safe in an increasingly agitated market. By that afternoon, we had stockpiled a bulging war chest: $131 billion in cash.

Our main worry at that moment was the weather. Working furiously, the windshield wipers couldn't keep up. Friday rush hour is bad enough, but New York City traffic becomes paralyzed when it rains. It's like no one remembers how to drive. To get downtown from Morgan Stanley on Broadway, between Forty-Seventh and Forty-Eighth Streets, usually took less than thirty minutes. Now it was 5:35 p.m. The West Side Highway, which runs parallel to the Hudson River, was a parking lot. Liberty Street was still almost five miles away. We didn't have a minute to spare. Geithner was the third-most-powerful person in American finance, after Paulson and Ben Bernanke. No one makes the New York Fed chief wait.

"Hey, boss, that bike lane over there—does that go all the way to the Battery?" Joe, an ex-cop, asked me in his thick Bronx accent.

"Yeah, it does."

The next thing I knew, he had maneuvered the car into the bike lane, gunned the engine, and sped downtown as if the world were ending.

We pulled up under the portico inside the Fed garage at 5:55 p.m. Reporters and TV camera crews were lined up. I don't know who leaked that Geithner had called an emergency meeting, but in the forty years I spent on Wall Street, I learned there are no secrets. When Colm and I got out of the car, the reporters hammered us, shouting, "Why are you here? What's going to happen?"

I put my game face on. I didn't know what was going to happen, but in that instant, I wasn't concerned. I knew that Morgan Stanley had battened down the hatches.

As I walked into the wood-paneled conference room on the first floor of the imposing stone Fed building, I saw all my contemporaries. They included Lloyd Blankfein of Goldman Sachs; Jamie Dimon of JPMorgan Chase; Morgan Stanley alum Vikram Pandit, who had taken over at Citigroup; Brady Dougan, my successor at CSFB; and John Thain, who had recently been brought in to take the helm at Merrill Lynch.

I scanned the room. One CEO who wasn't there: Dick Fuld.

Like me, the CEOs had all brought their CFOs. Typical of Goldman Sachs, they had tacked on a third person: Gary Cohn, their president and COO.

In classic hurry-up-and-wait fashion, we had all raced to get there and now we stood around as the minutes ticked by. Around 6:45 p.m.,

Geithner walked in. That, I expected. What surprised me was that Paulson and Christopher Cox followed. Cox was the chairman of the Securities and Exchange Commission. The fact that Paulson had flown up from Washington, DC, to talk to us in person made me realize how grave the situation was.

Geithner told us the markets were in big trouble. Then he moved on to specifics. Here are the rough numbers for Lehman. Come up with a rescue package. If not, the results will be catastrophic. "There is no political will in Washington for a bailout," he said.

Tim had my attention, but the truth is, I thought ultimately the US government would step in. The regulators had helped Dimon buy Bear Stearns, and they had rescued Fannie Mae and Freddie Mac. I'm a free-market guy, but I believed the government's role was to limit damage to the system.

Paulson spoke next. After he thanked us for coming, Hank cut to the chase: Lehman is in trouble, he reiterated. We need you to find a solution.

I noticed Hank did not say help *us* find a solution. I flashed a look at Colm.

Hank went on: If you don't, Lehman is not opening for business on Monday. And the fallout for everyone in this room will be dire.

On the Street, we lived to pick off business from one another. When I managed Fixed Income, I roamed the trading floor shouting, "There's blood in the water! Let's make some money!" But I wanted to beat our competitors. I did not want to watch them die. I was ready to do what I could to help Lehman.

Hank, talking to us in a language we all understood, was direct. He used the threat I often employed to light a fire under people: I'll remember who's helpful and who's not.

"Come back in the morning," Tim told us. "And be prepared to do something."

As soon as the meeting broke up, around 8:30 p.m., I called James Gorman and Walid Chammah. "We're supposed to come up with a way to save Lehman," I said. "Paulson and Geithner gave us their balance sheet. I'll show it to you when Colm and I get back to the office. They want us at the New York Fed tomorrow at nine a.m. It's going to be a long weekend."

Thanks to my mother, Alice, I knew that everyone thinks better after a good meal. "I'm calling San Pietro," I told Joe and Colm as we headed to Midtown. "We need to pick up dinner for the team."

As we idled outside the restaurant waiting for the order, I remembered the Saturday morning just two months earlier, in July, when Dick Fuld had come to our house in Rye. He had called me several times suggesting there might be ways to combine our firms. I didn't know what he envisioned, but I was willing to hear him out. It never hurts to take a meeting. You always learn something. Walid, a sharp strategist, thought there was potential. He believed that if we merged, we could build a new, more powerful IT system that would give us a technological edge.

At 10:00 a.m. on July 12, the two teams sat down in our living room. Our side included Walid and his talented deputy, Cordell "Cory" Spencer, and Paul Taubman, who now headed Investment Banking. I expected Dick to start the conversation with "We think you guys should buy us, and this is the way it should look." Instead he opened the meeting by saying, "I've been talking to John a lot, and he says you guys may have a bunch of thoughts." My team shifted uncomfortably on the couch. *Who called this meeting?* we all thought.

An awkward five minutes ticked by. I resisted stating the obvious: *Wait a minute, Dick, you're the one in deep shit, and you're the one who wants to talk to us about how we can save you?* I would never humiliate a person I had invited into Christy's and my house. To fill the silence, I went around to each member of my team and asked, "What do you think?" They came out with a few generic niceties about Lehman's strengths.

In response, Dick brightened. "I understand you guys really admire my company and think there might be ways we could work together," he said. "Well, what do you have in mind?"

We never got around to answering the central question: Should we combine firms? Instead we came away firmly convinced that Dick was in denial. He still viewed Lehman as a plum catch.

Just two days before the meeting at the Fed, Dick had called me. Moody's Investors Service had just issued a press release announcing that it was considering lowering Lehman's rating. We had arranged for our two senior management teams to meet that night at Walid's apartment without us. When we had met in July, Lehman's stock was selling at forty dollars a share. Now it was below ten dollars. I talked to Walid about whether this was the time to do a deal with Lehman. But after going over the numbers, Walid told Dick's people there was no hope of a deal. "I could see their faces dropping," he reported back to me.

Now, here we were in my office just two nights later, eating pasta and talking about whether Lehman would implode and how to limit our exposure to the firm.

———

ON GEITHNER'S ORDERS, I assembled my A-team to go to the New York Fed on Saturday. In my car, I took Colm, Gary Lynch, and Tom Wipf, an expert in financing. I told Tom Nides to join us at the New York Fed. To get Paul Taubman away from a member-guest tournament at the Golf Club of Purchase, I left him eighteen messages saying, "You've got to get your ass down to the New York Fed."

When we arrived at 8:00 a.m., an hour early, the place was in chaos—a free-for-all. Here were the country's top financial leaders and their staffers, all of them elbowing one another to grab a chair and an outlet so they could keep their laptops and cell phones charged. I opened a door to a gorgeous, empty conference room on the first floor. "*This* is where Morgan Stanley sits," I announced with a sweep of my arm.

Everybody focused on Lehman's balance sheet. The question was, could the financial industry come together and commit enough capital to do an orderly wind-down with Lehman, as opposed to them having to declare bankruptcy? We broke into working groups. Morgan Stanley's assignment: coordinate with Citigroup and Merrill Lynch to evaluate Lehman's liquidity issues. Every hour and a half, Geithner came into the room like a high school teacher encouraging group participation. "So, what are we doing?" he asked. "What will it take? What have you got for me?"

We all just stared at him like, *And what do you have for us, pal?*

As the day went on, one thing became abundantly clear: the more we looked into Lehman, the more we recognized they were in much worse shape than anyone had envisioned. And the longer I was at the Fed, the more I sensed that the tectonic plates undergirding the financial landscape were shifting. It was known as "the Lehman weekend," but Lehman wasn't the only business in trouble. Out of sight, the regulators were dealing with the world's largest insurance company, American International Group Inc. (AIG). It operated in 130 countries, employed 115,000 people, and boasted a $1 trillion balance sheet. Disastrously, it had sold insurance for mortgage-backed securities against the possibility of a housing crash, and those calls were coming due. It, too, was running out of money. We were told that there was a private solution being formulated for AIG and that JPMorgan Chase would probably finance it.

With Wall Street in such flux, I decided there was no harm in speaking with Merrill Lynch. It was carrying a lot of toxic assets on its books, but it was a world-famous franchise founded in 1914, well ahead of Morgan Stanley. If Lehman went off the cliff, Merrill was right behind it. So on Saturday afternoon, I suggested to Merrill's CEO, John Thain, "Maybe we should talk."

That evening, my team and I met with Thain and his team at Walid's apartment on the Upper East Side. After a productive two-hour discussion, I said I would talk to my board on Monday, and we could start due diligence the day after. We would have gladly taken Merrill's Wealth Management business. It would have been a genius move.

Surprising me, Thain said he needed a decision immediately. "Before Asia opens," he told us. In other words, by Sunday night.

"That's not possible," I said. It was too dangerous, because his company's balance sheet was so unquantifiable. I realized then that Merrill Lynch was under indescribable pressure to make a deal. Because we didn't think we had a gun to our heads, I didn't have to make those kinds of desperate decisions. I was grateful not to be in that situation.

Little did I know that in the coming week, I would be tested in ways I could not imagine.

Seven of us gathered for a late dinner that Saturday night on the patio at San Pietro to unpack the meeting with Thain for those who hadn't attended. That weekend, we thought we were survivors, and we would act as a savior to other firms. Hank and Geithner believed we would be helping them solve the problems Lehman and Merrill faced. Bank of America would buy Merrill Lynch before the end of the weekend.

On Sunday morning, we were back at the Fed at 8:00. As we sipped bad coffee, the regulators told us that British-based investment bank Barclays had reached an agreement to buy Lehman Brothers.

But the firm, now run by my nemesis Bob Diamond, wanted only the good assets—that is, the non–real estate assets. To get the deal over the finish line, Paulson and Geithner needed the rest of us—the thirteen big banks present—to pony up $33 billion. This money would be used to take Lehman's toxic assets off its balance sheet. We were left to figure out how much cash each firm would chip in.

We were arguing over how many billions we could afford. For a while, there was a discussion about every firm kicking in $3 billion, but not all hands went up. It was clear that there were a lot of reservations in the room. Then, just before 1:00 p.m., Hank walked in. One look at him and I knew—he was bringing bad news. "The British screwed us," he said. The Financial Services Authority (FSA), the regulatory body in the United Kingdom, refused to approve the deal with Barclays on such short notice. It looked like Lehman had come to the end of the runway.

My phone rang. It was Dick Fuld. "There's nothing I can do, Dick, I'm sorry," was all I could say.

Before we left the Fed that afternoon, Geithner pulled Colm and Goldman Sachs's CFO aside. "What do you need? Do you have enough money to last through next weekend?" he asked.

"John, I thought he was making a joke," Colm told me when he recounted the conversation to me afterward. "I mean, we have $131 billion of liquidity. In all seriousness, John, I think we're pretty well set. We have triple the amount of money we would normally have on hand. I feel pretty good about it."

Around 10:00 Sunday night, I got a call. The Federal Reserve wanted Morgan Stanley to represent it in an agreement it was negotiating with AIG. There had been a shift. The government was considering a bailout for the insurance giant. Because AIG was involved in everything from pensions to life and home insurance to annuities, its failure would destroy the personal finances of millions of ordinary people. Paulson and President George W. Bush could not allow that to happen.

Dick Fuld and his employees met a sadder fate. I learned before I went to bed that at 1:45 a.m. on Monday, September 15, Lehman filed for Chapter 11—the biggest bankruptcy in US history. At 745 Seventh Avenue, a few blocks up from Times Square and around the corner from Morgan Stanley, employees were streaming out of Lehman Brothers, carrying cardboard boxes of their possessions into the darkened streets.

I set my alarm for 5:30 a.m. so I could get to the office early. Then I closed my eyes and slept.

CHAPTER TWENTY-TWO

On Monday, September 15, the world woke up to terrifying headlines. The *Wall Street Journal* ran with "Crisis on Wall Street as Lehman Totters, Merrill Is Sold, AIG Seeks to Raise Cash." The lead story on the front page began: "The American financial system was shaken to its core on Sunday."

My job was to fill in my managing directors on what had happened over the weekend. And more importantly, what the upheaval meant for us. By the time I took up my position behind the podium, stock futures in the United States and bank stocks in Europe were slipping. I looked out at a crowd of anxious faces waiting to hear what I had to say. "I am energized, and you ought to be energized, too. I wish I could come in here and say . . . this is a great opportunity, kick back, we're going to do great, all of the competitors have basically been eliminated.

"I'm not going to say that," I said. I paused and looked around. I hadn't rehearsed. I always think it's best to speak from the heart.

"What I want to say is: kick it up," I continued. "Work harder. Think about what has happened this year. And what has happened is that all of a sudden, three of our competitors are no longer in business. I understand that all of you, and not just all of you here but I think in the industry, are shaken. You should be shaken. But that doesn't mean that we crawl back in and we shake. . . . We're here to do business, to serve our clients, to take market share. . . . I think that once this turmoil abates, and it will settle down, the opportunities going forward are unbelievable."

By the time I finished, people looked calmer.

But something eerie was happening. On an ordinary Monday, whether the markets were up or down, the phones would be ringing nonstop. The air would be charged with the electricity that working money gives off. Today, the financing room was silent. Scarily silent. People sat at their desks with nothing to do, frightened. Fear of what might happen next had frozen the pipeline of borrowing and lending that usually flowed back and forth between investment and commercial banks. We set up a cash room on the third floor with about a dozen trading and finance folks to monitor exactly how much money we had coming in and going out. I put Tom Wipf, an even-keeled mountain of a man who had been working in corporate finance since 1977, in charge.

Almost immediately, we began to see massive withdrawals. Hedge funds were moving much quicker than any of us had anticipated. Once they couldn't get their money out of Lehman, they stopped behaving in a rational way. The animal spirits took over. They were thinking, *I already have to tell my boss I've got money stuck in Lehman. I have another problem if I even* think *Morgan Stanley has an issue. So if I can get my money out of Morgan Stanley, I'm doing that. If I can get my money out of Merrill Lynch, I'm doing it. If I can get my money out of Goldman Sachs, I'm doing that. I'm putting everything I've got into US Treasuries.*

On Monday night, Wipf and his staff tallied up the money with our treasurer, David Wong. Over the decades, I had trained people to get bad news upstairs to me as quickly as possible. This is a John Mack commandment. Good news travels all by itself. I wanted to know the bad news. The worse it was, the less I would allow myself to react because I needed to keep that flow coming. I never wanted to scare people or make them hesitant to tell me the truth. So when Colm came into my office and announced, "John, we're down $10 billion," I said "Okay," as though he'd just announced we had lost $10.

The cash we had painstakingly stockpiled that we thought would last for months was vanishing. Although we didn't have lines of desperate depositors demanding their money at Morgan Stanley offices around the world, it was nonetheless a run on our bank like the one in *It's a Wonderful Life*. The only difference was that the numbers were bigger, and we were dealing with hedge funds. But the concept is the same. If Mrs. Jones and all her neighbors withdraw their money one after the other, then you're screwed. You don't have the money to give them.

Colm and I kept only one other person in the loop: Gary Lynch. As our chief lawyer, he needed to be ready in case the unthinkable occurred: closing our doors and declaring bankruptcy.

On Monday, the stock market also had a hellacious day. It plunged 504 points in the worst one-day point drop since the day the market reopened after 9/11. We had started 2008 with a share price of $50.95. On Friday afternoon, when Colm and I were racing to the New York Fed, our stock closed at $37.23 per share. Now it had fallen to $32.19.

On Tuesday, September 16, the *Financial Times* captured what we had experienced the previous day: "Banking's Black Monday Day of Reckoning on Wall Street." The lead story in that day's *Wall Street Journal* began: "The convulsions in the U.S. financial system sent markets across the globe tumbling. . . ."

When I got to work at 7:00 a.m. that day, Colm and I happened to get on the same elevator up to the fortieth floor. His face looked gray. "Colm, make sure we're both smiling when we exit the elevator," I told him. "People can't know we're worried."

Putting my best face on in a bad situation was baked into my DNA from the time I was eleven years old. Growing up, I hero-worshipped my half brother George, who had been a tail gunner on a B-17 Flying Fortress bomber over Germany in World War II. Afterward, he returned home to Mooresville and worked at Dad's warehouse. Then, out of the blue, George went into the hospital. Nobody told me what was happening. When I saw him in an open casket in our living room, I was shocked. George had died of leukemia. He was thirty-four years old.

I remember standing in the hallway outside my parents' bedroom, watching my father on his knees praying. I saw the grief in his tired eyes. Our house was weighed down with his sadness. After George's death, I decided I would never do anything to add to my father's burden. I was going to be upbeat, uncomplaining, cheerful at home and in the warehouse. I, too, was grieving. But I wasn't going to show it. This ability to mask sorrow and fear became part of my character.

It wasn't just our employees we had to buck up. With Lehman having unraveled and Merrill Lynch taken over by Bank of America, all eyes were on Morgan Stanley and Goldman Sachs, the Street's last two independent investment firms. Investors saw us as the next dominoes to fall. We knew this death sentence was wrong. Our numbers were good. Analysts had predicted we would have net revenues of $6.2 billion, and we were coming in at $8 billion. We had beaten the Street's expectations—by a lot. To reassure the markets that Morgan Stanley was standing solid, we decided to move up our earnings call with analysts from Wednesday to Tuesday afternoon. Deutsche Bank analyst Mike Mayo asked, "I think I know the answer to this, but why did you report early tonight, and what did you want to highlight the most?"

Colm answered: "I wanted to highlight the strength and robustness of Morgan Stanley. I want to have a building block in a bridge to rebuilding confidence in this market where things are frankly getting out of hand and ridiculous rumors are being repeated, some of which if I wrote down today and reread tomorrow I would probably think I was dreaming. That is exactly why we've reported, Mike, because I think it's very important to get some sanity back into the market."

Good news usually gooses a stock price. Not this time. Overnight, our stock had gone from $28.70 at the close to open at $22.83. We were under attack from short sellers. Investors traditionally buy stocks and make money when the stocks they're holding rise in value. Short selling is the opposite. It is a sophisticated investment strategy of borrowing stock with a plan to sell it and then rebuy it at a lower price, making money on the difference. "Shares of Big Brokerages in Free Fall," read the *New York Times*' "Dealbook" headline at noon on Wednesday, September 17. "Morgan Stanley's decision to report its third quarter results a day early doesn't seem to have calmed Wall Street's fears about the viability of its business model," it reported.

I used to check the stock price once a day, after the market closed at 4:00 p.m. Now I was glancing at every Bloomberg terminal I passed, like a heart attack victim glued to the monitors in the ICU. The number of our shares being traded was nine times what it was on an ordinary day. This was the abusive shorts in action. They were driving our stock down. Investors and employees, including me, were watching our wealth evaporate before our eyes. Nonstop coverage on CNBC and other cable channels was adding to the end-times atmosphere. At one point that day, the stock price dipped to $16.08. Christy and I had 90 percent of our wealth in Morgan Stanley stock. But losing that wasn't the worst pain. Far from it. These short sellers were destroying a storied franchise, built over almost three-quarters of a century of hard work and integrity. This wasn't the first time I had complained that hedge funds were short-selling Morgan Stanley stock. I had been pointing out the problem for months.

The SEC was doing nothing to stop the madness. I called the SEC chairman, Chris Cox. "Mr. Chairman, you need to step up and ban the short sellers," I told him. Cox's response was that short selling was legal and that he couldn't interfere. Moreover, he informed me, academic studies had demonstrated that limiting short selling did not stop panic in the markets.

"This is not an academic study," I exploded. "This is real time!"

Frustrated with Cox, I called Hank Paulson; the White House; New York's two US senators, Charles Schumer and Hillary Clinton; and Goldman Sachs's CEO, Lloyd Blankfein—all in an effort to get traction on a shorts ban.

As the panic mushroomed and clients lost confidence in Morgan Stanley, they tried to take additional money from us, saying things along the lines of, "Just send us an extra $5 million, because we're worried about your credit." I was determined that we pay what we owed, but not a penny more. While the cash room protected what we had, it was my job to figure out how to replenish our coffers. My message to Wipf was "You guys stall, and I'll think of something."

On the flip side, people stopped paying us. Say you're working in some back office, and you owe Morgan Stanley $100 million. You look at the news, which predicts "Morgan Stanley is going out of business." You're like, *My boss will be happy if I don't send this money.* "Go out and aggressively chase down the people who haven't paid us," I told the cash room guys. Wipf gave me a list of the companies that were stiffing us. I dialed the CEOs and demanded the money. Ordinarily I called on clients to help our bankers get business. Now I was Mack the Bill Collector.

I sent out a firm-wide memo to employees explaining what I was seeing and the steps we were taking to combat it. I made it a point to tell my employees as much as I possibly could, omitting only what was confidential. "What's happening out there?" I wrote. "It's very clear to me—we're in the midst of a market controlled by fear and rumors. . . . We have talked to Secretary Paulson and the Treasury. We also are communicating aggressively with our long-term shareholders, our counterparties, and our clients. I would encourage all of you to communicate with your clients as well—and make sure they know about our strong performance and strong capital position."

Nothing made a difference. Our stock closed that day at $21.75.

We were battling it out on another front. Unlike a commercial bank like JPMorgan Chase, we weren't sitting on a vast pool of deposits. Instead, we borrowed money on a short-term basis from other institutions to fund our day-to-day operations through traditional debt and short-term money markets. As longer-term debt markets began to close, we relied more on shorter-term borrowings like repurchase agreements. The market's view of our credit was reflected in the CDS, or credit default swap, market, a derivative product that tracked the cost of insuring our debt by the "spread" reflected in basis points (1/100th of 1 percent). For example, in January 2008, our rate was 228 basis points. But now the cost had soared to a staggering and unsustainable 866 basis points. At one point, we got a call from JPMorgan Chase. They threatened to stop trading with us altogether unless we signed an agreement and deposited $10 billion as a guarantee. They said, "If this isn't signed tonight, we're not going to trade with you tomorrow morning." Gary got on the call and said, "It's six thirty at night. That means it's eleven thirty p.m. in London" (this kind of transaction was done out of London). We had no choice. We had to deposit the money.

The market was telling us in blunt terms that our model—an independent investment bank—could not survive. I was looking for a line of defense. I talked to *anyone* who might have a good idea. I knew I didn't understand every detail, so I surrounded myself with people who did. In addition to the usual suspects, there was a stream of other people coming in and out of my office. Board members Roy Bostock, who was chairman of Yahoo!, and Erskine Bowles, who had been White House chief of staff and head of the Small Business Administration under President Bill Clinton, were there. The head of the Financial Institutions Group, Ruth Porat, joined us, along with Donald Moore, a Morgan Stanley veteran, who flew in from London. To some, it probably looked like a three-ring circus, complete with high-wire acts and fire-eating jugglers. But you can never predict who's going to have the breakthrough idea.

Friends and family checked in to offer their support. Among them, Tom Bell and Coach K, who gave me an impassioned halftime pep talk. "Now is the time to turn this into a win, John!" he encouraged me. Wei Christianson often phoned me from her office in Beijing. Her calls always calmed me down. It was a relief to talk about what was happening on a different continent. Then, on Wednesday, she called from Aspen, Colorado, where she was attending the annual investors' conference given by Teddy Forstmann, a private equity trailblazer. On top of the situation as always, Wei told me Gao Xiqing was with her at the conference. Gao was the president of CIC, the China Investment Corporation, which had invested $5.6 billion last December. Wei and I discussed the need to bring CIC to New York, given their need to protect their 9.9 percent ownership. It would also help them understand the volatile market situation.

I knew Gao well: we were both on the board at Duke University. Wei said that she and Gao would fly from Aspen to New York on Friday night.

Although I was heartened by the possibility of a deal with CIC, we didn't have the luxury of waiting around. My team and I called everyone we could think of. We contacted sovereign funds in the

Middle East and Asia, foreign banks, including HSBC Holdings of the United Kingdom and Banco Santander of Spain, as well as Canadian pension funds. We reached out to the deep-pocketed Warren Buffett. I was on the phone with Vikram Pandit about doing a deal with Citigroup. I also talked extensively with fellow North Carolinian Bob Steel of Wachovia. I told James to call the CEO of Wells Fargo, John Stumpf. He tracked him down at his mother's place in Florida.

Everyone was floating ideas. All of them were characterized by two words: life raft.

And still, more money was leaving the building than coming in. On Wednesday evening, Colm, who put on thirty-five pounds that fall, walked into my office. "John," he said, "I feel physically sick. I'm tasting bile in my throat. The fact is, we'll be out of money by Friday." More than $50 billion had walked out the door that day as hedge fund clients withdrew their funds.

I was dumbstruck. "Could you take another look, Colm?" I asked, my stomach roiling. "See if Wipf and the financing desk can dig something up."

About thirty minutes later, Colm returned. "I think we found enough to get us to the beginning of next week."

People were sleeping on couches and under their desks at Morgan Stanley. An ambitious first-year analyst bunking in under a desk—a rite of passage. But having the firm's co-presidents and its CFO crashing on their office sofas night after night? Unheard-of. Some people stayed because they needed to talk to bankers in different time zones. Anxiety kept others rooted in place. Even though they were just wringing their hands, with little to do in the hours after midnight, few could bring themselves to leave. Gary Lynch stayed at the office until 4:00 a.m., went home to catch an hour or so of sleep, took a shower, put on fresh clothes, and arrived back at 7:00 a.m.

Tom Wipf and his cadre in the cash room were like vampires—never seeing daylight. They came in at 6:00 in the morning and wrapped up at midnight. Colm wasn't the only person stress-eating. What the cash-room managers lost in sleep they made up for in calories. Takeout guys were doing a brisk business delivering cheesy egg and bacon sandwiches, double pepperoni pizzas, and meatball subs. Dinner was a late-night steak and a beer. They looked like shit, and I was worried they would keel over from the stress and their artery-clogging diet. I made an executive decision. "Let them order as much as they want," I instructed their administrative assistants. "But from now on, the only food I want delivered to the cash room is tuna-fish sandwiches and salads. If they have a problem, tell them to take it up with me." I dropped by every few days to eat with them—always a salad.

Thursday's chilling *Wall Street Journal* headlines: "Mounting Fears Shake World Markets as Banking Giants Rush to Raise Capital" and "Worst Crisis Since '30s, with No End Yet in Sight." One of the articles opened with "The financial crisis that began thirteen months ago has entered a new, far more serious stage." With news stories like these, the natural inclination is to hunker down in your office with your smartest advisers. But a bunker mentality won't work. A leader has to project confidence. I had to instill the belief that Morgan Stanley was going to survive this calamity. Every morning, I walked the halls, greeting people. In the afternoons, I sat down with traders to drink a cup of coffee, BS about the Yankees, and answer questions about what was happening. They thought, *If John Mack can be laughing and carrying on like this, things can't be that bad.*

As a joke, I bought a blood pressure machine so people could check their numbers. But that backfired. Tom Nides ended up in the emergency room, alarmed he was having a heart attack. The diagnosis: a panic attack. And for one of my top executives, the stress was simply overwhelming. He got up from his desk one afternoon, walked out, and never returned.

Employees wandered the halls stunned. They were terrified that they were going to lose their jobs and that their Morgan Stanley stock was now worth next to nothing. It hit a low of $11.70 on Thursday, September 18. That afternoon, I held an open-forum broadcast to six hundred–plus offices in thirty-five countries. Standing on the trading floor, I addressed what was foremost on people's minds: Should they sell their deteriorating stock? "I know some of you are very scared," I said. "Well, maybe all of us are very scared. You want to sell stock? Sell your stock. I'm not going to look at [who sold and who didn't], and I don't care.

"I'm not selling," I added. "But I really care much more about your getting peace of mind. So if you want to sell, sell. Do it." What I was saying applied equally to the IT people in the basement and to my top officers on the fortieth floor. If the latter sold, they would have to report the sale to the SEC—information the media would pounce on. It would be reported as "top executives have lost faith in Morgan Stanley." That didn't matter to me. I wanted them to know I would not hold a grudge. There would be no retribution, whatever happened. My message: We need you to be here mentally and physically to help us get through this. We need you to give us everything you've got.

I took some questions, and then I realized that I needed to get off the floor. If I stayed ten more seconds, I was going to break down. I could sense it. So I smiled and ended the broadcast. This happened each time I did a town hall. I'd be on the verge of cracking and finish just in time.

Around 3:00 p.m., Charlie Gasparino announced on CNBC that sources were telling him the feds had "some sort of RTC-like plan" to "get some or all of the toxic waste off the balance sheets of the banks and brokerages." The RTC was the Resolution Trust Corporation, a George H. W. Bush–era entity created in 1989 to sell the failed savings banks and their assets. This helped to resolve the savings-and-loan scandal of the 1980s, when the S&Ls used deposits to speculate on real estate. After those investments went bust, they ended up costing customers and the government billions of dollars. In other words, Gasparino was saying that now the government was going to take on the billions of subprime mortgages and other bad loans that were paralyzing the economy. This became known as the Troubled Asset Relief Program, or TARP. In a market rally off the news, our stock bumped up, closing at $22.55.

Tom Nides walked into my office with more good news: the SEC had decided to issue a temporary ban on short selling. Chris Cox made it official the next morning. "The emergency order . . . will restore equilibrium to markets," he said. "Equilibrium" sounded good to me. Between the TARP proposal and Cox's announcement, the market calmed. But I knew Morgan Stanley was still fighting for its life. We needed an investor to step up and take a big stake in the firm. And it needed to happen this weekend.

Teams from Wachovia and Morgan Stanley had been holed up together since Wednesday running the numbers and starting due diligence for a possible merger. But by Friday afternoon, I suspected that wasn't going to happen. This left us desperate for a deal with CIC. Wei and Gao were flying in from Aspen that night. I had a concern, though. When we had negotiated with CIC a year earlier for the 9.9 percent stake, the process had been interminable. Morgan Stanley sat at one end of a long conference table, and the Chinese sat at the other end. Over the ensuing days, our two teams discussed, argued, and cajoled. Finally, we reached a deal. Let's characterize it this way: each side eventually came to the middle of the table. The Chinese lived to negotiate. It was fun for both sides. But now we didn't have the luxury of time. We had to get to the middle of the table immediately.

Before they arrived, Wei called to tell me that Gao was suffering from excruciating back pain. We set up a workspace for the CIC team in the conference room next to my office. In addition to ordering dinner for them, I had a couch wheeled in for Gao to rest on. I also arranged for my physical therapist and friend Peggy Brill to come over to Morgan Stanley and help him.

I knew Gao's back pain wasn't the only thing bothering him. The Chinese were angry. On December 19, 2007, when we announced the CIC's $5.6 billion infusion, our share price was $50.08. Today it was $27.21—meaning their investment had lost almost half its value. Gao told us that CIC wanted to increase their investment in Morgan Stanley from 9.9 percent to 49 percent. But the amount they were willing to pay for the additional 39.1 percent of the firm was insultingly low: $5 billion. It was an intolerable squeeze play. In any other circumstance, we would have told them off. Not tonight. We agreed to let them look at our books. Later, we were told by the CIC that they had been following the counsel of Deutsche Bank, which they had hired to advise them.

Saturday morning I was up early reading the *Wall Street Journal* at our kitchen table when my phone rang. Tim Geithner was on the line. He was ordering me to call Jamie Dimon. I had spoken with the JPMorgan Chase CEO on Thursday, after he phoned both Colm and James. "He asked if there was anything he could do to help," Colm told me. Like every smart businessperson, Jamie was poking around for intel. I would have done the same thing if our situations were reversed. I got him on the phone. "Jamie," I told him, "if you want to be helpful, you talk to me. I don't want you going around me."

Now I dutifully did as Geithner said. I called Jamie a second time. It was a short conversation. Although Geithner thought it was a good idea to reunite the original House of Morgan, I thought there was too much duplication between our firms. Jamie sounded as unenthusiastic about a merger as I was.

The frequent conversations I had with Lloyd Blankfein, the CEO of Goldman Sachs, were different. Suddenly we were comrades in arms. Our firms were sworn enemies—the Hatfields and the McCoys. But as the last two investment banks still standing on the Street, we faced the same mortal threat. Lloyd kept telling me, "John, you gotta hold on, because I'm twenty seconds behind you."

———

FRIDAY AFTERNOON, SEPTEMBER 19, Colm was grabbing lunch at a nearby sushi restaurant called Blue Fin with James, Walid, and Tom Nides when he got a call. It was Jonathan Kindred, the president of Morgan Stanley Japan. "Mitsubishi wants to invest in Morgan Stanley," he told Colm. "Can you put a deal team on?"

Mitsubishi UFJ Financial Group (MUFG) was the largest bank in Japan. But there was a catch. If the Chinese were slow at the negotiating table, the Japanese were glacial. Colm thought it was a nonstarter. "I'm stretched to the teeth," he told Jonathan. "I haven't got people to give you." Kindred insisted, "They're serious, they're serious." So Colm grudgingly put together a team.

Like Colm, most of us were skeptical that the Japanese could possibly get to a decision on our timetable. And because the call wasn't CEO to CEO, we suspected that midlevel bankers reading the US news were just trying to find out the state of play. The sentiment around my office was, they're just leading us on.

Only James Gorman was optimistic. He explained his thinking: "At Merrill Lynch, I set up a joint venture with them. I found them extremely smart, extremely disciplined, very thoughtful, very intentional. They don't make phone calls like the one they made to Jon Kindred on a whim."

James went on: "They didn't just wake up like some random sovereign fund that decides to buy Morgan Stanley. These guys don't do that. They are consummate pros. Yes, they're very slow-moving, but the decision to call us probably came out of years of work. I bet they have two hundred people working on it."

"James, I hope to hell you're right," I said.

As we tried to figure out what was happening 6,700 miles away in Tokyo, we also had to figure out what was happening literally next door, where Wei was keeping tabs on the CIC team. "John, those Deutsche Bank bankers are nasty," she said. "They're telling the Chinese to put up virtually no money and to demand control of the company. There's a huge gap in our valuations. But we're making progress. Gao has to talk to the head of CIC, Lou Jiwei. Then Lou Jiwei has to get the green light from other ministries and the senior leadership of China."

On Saturday afternoon, I got a call from Hank Paulson. I welcomed his frequent check-ins. Hank was like the best coach. He never sounded panicked, and he was always encouraging. He'd say, "How are you doing? What's going on? What are your ideas? What are your options?" At the end of every call, he would always repeat: "We're going to get through this. We need independent investment banks. I'm working on it."

I heard a different tone in his voice now. "John, the markets are fragile," he told me. "We cannot have Monday morning open without a solution to your firm. You have to find a partner."

"Hank, you've been my biggest supporter," I said. "You've been helping us the whole time. Now you're breaking away. I just can't believe, given everything you've said during the week, this is happening."

"Look, John, it's not about Morgan Stanley," he responded. "It's about financial meltdown on a global basis. You need to find a partner."

"Well, I believe the Japanese are going to invest with us," I said. "That's my partner."

"You and I both know they will never make a decision that quickly," Hank said. It was clear from his tone that he thought I was not being rational.

After we hung up, I had to pull myself together. Hank had been keeping me pumped up. He had been my ally, the man who kept me going. I sat alone in my office with the door closed, trying to remind myself, *Don't worry about what's happening around you. Focus on what you're trying to accomplish.*

Paul Taubman had been on the phone to our team in Tokyo, where it was 3:00 a.m. "You've got to call and get the Mitsubishi bankers out of bed," he implored them. "Then you've got to get them to wake up their top executives." Demanding that subordinates telephone their superiors and roust them from their slumber was an unheard-of breach of etiquette in Japan. "Ask them: 'Are you willing to miss the opportunity of a career because you're scared to call your boss in the middle of the night?'"

Paul continued: "The message has to be: 'You have like a day and a half. If you're serious, you need to move your schedule completely.'"

I knew that when the market opened on Monday, if we didn't announce that we had hooked a big investor we were going to get pummeled. In turn, people would refuse to trade with us. It would be the beginning of the end. Given the growing possibility that Morgan Stanley might not make it, my board had flown in from around the world for an emergency meeting, where Colm explained that we could be out of money by Wednesday. The board then hired outside advisers to protect the members in case there were lawsuits if we declared bankruptcy.

I couldn't believe what was happening. *The great Morgan Stanley is sitting here on Saturday night with no options,* I thought. *The cash is leaving by the day. We're down to hours at most.* I had a terrible head cold, and I knew from experience that everything looks better after a good night's sleep. There's no way things could look any worse. The best thing was to go home.

When I got there, Christy met me at the door. "I think I'm going to lose the firm, Chris," I blurted out.

"What?" Christy said, stunned. I hadn't told her how bad things were.

I hadn't admitted it to myself until that moment, either.

I was so intent on projecting normalcy that one night I even left the office to attend an employee's fiftieth birthday party. Henri, who had worked in Morgan Stanley's mailroom for decades, had been planning this celebration all year. He was alone in the world. His parents and siblings had died, and we were his family. People told me that he kept asking, "Do you think Mr. Mack will come?" Everyone warned him that I would probably be too busy because of the crisis. But I didn't care what wildfire was raging on the fortieth floor. I walked over to Bobby Van's Steakhouse, shook everyone's hand, and toasted Henri. "To the person who keeps Morgan Stanley running!" I said. And then I headed back to the office.

Now, in the foyer of our home, my eyes filled with tears. Leaving Christy standing there, I paced around. After a few minutes, I went back to the foyer and hugged her. Taking a deep breath, I said, "I'm so scared. But I'd rather be doing this than reading a book on the beach in North Carolina."

CHAPTER TWENTY-THREE

Sunday afternoon we were living minute to minute. The Mitsubishi bankers had responded to the middle-of-the-night wake-up calls and had been working since the wee hours Sunday, their time. They sent a letter saying they were going to attempt a deal. But Nobuo Kuroyanagi, Mitsubishi UFJ Financial Group's CEO, first insisted on a conference call with me. He wanted to walk me through the term sheet.

There was a delay, however. Nobuo needed to drive from his home outside Tokyo to the office because he wanted his interpreters sitting right next to him, rather than on the phone. This pushed the call back a couple of hours, to 5:00 p.m. on Sunday in New York—6:00 a.m. on Monday in Tokyo. Even though I had told Hank that Mitsubishi was our partner, most of us thought the chances of the deal succeeding were fifty-fifty. Even with the CIC team still negotiating next door, Morgan Stanley's survival looked unlikely.

Midafternoon, a bunch of us were sitting around my office. We had the New York Giants–Cincinnati Bengals football game on TV in the background. But no one was paying any attention. We were on death row, waiting to hear if the judge would stay the execution. My assistant, Stacie, opened the door. "Secretary Paulson is on the line," she said.

When I picked up, Hank said, "John, I'm here with Ben Bernanke and Tim Geithner."

"I'd like to put you on speaker so my general counsel can hear," I said.

The room was silent. Frozen. Everyone was listening.

Hank began, "We cannot have chaos on Monday morning. We need you to do something with your firm."

Bernanke then spoke. "John, we see things you don't see. This is much bigger than any one firm. This is about a global crisis. We have to have a solution, and we need a solution for your firm."

Geithner spoke next. He was calm but steely. "We have a systemic problem," he said. "Every bank is in peril. For the sake of the country, we need to eliminate risks. The way to do that is to combine banks and institutions." They were trying to take a problem off their plate.

"You need to call Jamie and get a deal done," Geithner said.

"Tim, out of respect for you, I already called Jamie," I said. "He's not interested."

"You should call him again. He'll buy Morgan Stanley."

"Yeah, he'll buy the firm for a dollar," I said. "Let me ask you a question, the three of you. I have forty-five thousand employees. In New York City, between AIG, Lehman Brothers, Bear Stearns, and Merrill Lynch, probably forty thousand jobs have already been lost. From a public policy point of view, does this make sense?"

"It's not about public policy," Geithner said. "It's about stability. That's what we're focused on. We want you to do something with your firm."

"Look, I have the utmost respect for the three of you," I replied. "What you do for this country makes you patriots. But I have forty-five thousand employees. I won't do it. I'll take the firm down."

I pushed the off button on the phone. The conversation was over.

The crowded room was still. Nobody moved. Nobody spoke. I could feel everyone's eyes on me.

When I hung up, I hadn't been trying to be an ass. The regulators were doing their job, and they were doing it well. And I was doing my job, which was to protect the firm and its employees. I was thinking about the human impact of Morgan Stanley going down.

To me, giving away the firm to JPMorgan or declaring bankruptcy were the same thing. The way I saw it, either way I was signing Morgan Stanley's death warrant. The firm I loved would no longer exist. It would be a ghost.

I could tell that my pushback bucked up everyone in the room. I could see it in their postures and on their faces. Everyone leaned forward. They no longer looked terrified; they looked expectant. The atmosphere had shifted. Suddenly we weren't waiting for the executioner. I could tell that we all had more courage. We were rejecting Plan A—selling out to Jamie—and we had no idea if Plan B would work. But it was like, Fuck it—we are retaking control of our destiny. There was a sense that we might just get through this after all.

Thirty minutes later, I was on the life-or-death call with Nobuo. Paul Taubman and his deputy, Ji-Yeun Lee, were the only people with me. The door was shut. It takes enormous concentration to negotiate through translators. I spoke, waited thirty seconds for the translator. Then Nobuo talked, and I got the translation at my end. In the middle of this, Stacie knocked and came in. "Tim Geithner's on the phone. He wants to talk to you," she said.

"Tell Tim I'll call him back. I'm on the phone with the Japanese."

I returned to the conversation with Nobuo. I talked. I waited. I listened. We went back and forth. Stacie came in again. This time she said, "Secretary Paulson is on the phone. He wants to talk to you."

"Tell him I'll call him back. I'm on the phone with the Japanese."

Three minutes went by. Stacie was back. "Tim Geithner is on the phone, John. He is very insistent. He's demanding to talk to you *now*."

I looked at Stacie. I was in the middle of probably the most important conversation of my entire career. I was trying to negotiate a deal worth billions that just might save Morgan Stanley. I was not hanging up with the CEO of Mitsubishi to be instructed to call Jamie Dimon again.

I covered the receiver. "Tell Tim to get fucked."

———

AT THE END of our call, I believed that Nobuo and I had reached a tentative agreement that Mitsubishi would buy up to 20 percent of the firm for as much as $8.5 billion. We expected a signed letter of intent to follow almost immediately.

But my work was not done. Gao and his team were still next door. I knew as CEO that I was the one who had to deliver the news. I went to the conference room and told them that we had just reached a deal with Mitsubishi. Irate, they packed up and left for the airport.

Just before 9:30 Sunday night, the New York Fed called to tell us that it had granted our request to become a bank holding company, along with Goldman Sachs. The day before, Gary Lynch had filled out the application—a stack of papers two feet thick. We were no longer a lightly regulated investment firm under the supervision of the SEC. Now we had a different regulator: the Federal Reserve would exert far more control over us. In return, we had permanent access to the Fed lending window.

This was good news, but by itself it wasn't enough. Things were still hanging by a thread until the Japanese faxed over the signed letter of intent. As we waited, midnight turned into 2:00 in the morning, then 3:00 in the morning, 4:00 in the morning. We hovered by the fax machine, willing it to spit out the document that would save us. Finally, the term agreement arrived in the dawn hours on Monday.

COLM LATER TOLD me that my hanging up on Paulson, Bernanke, and Geithner was the defining moment for Morgan Stanley. "No other CEO had the brains and possibly the recklessness to tell them to get stuffed. Other CEOs would have folded. Anyone standing up to those three was running a huge personal risk. You so believed you were doing the right thing."

When I think back on that Sunday afternoon, I agree with Colm. I think almost any other CEO would have said, Look, I don't agree with you. I think you're misreading the situation. But you are the three most important people in the United States' economy, and I'm going to do what you're telling me to do.

It amazes me that I didn't hesitate before I told them no. I didn't think about it. I spoke from my gut. I was all in. I would never "give" the firm away. Never.

At 12:22 on Monday morning, September 22, James Gorman sent me an email: "I don't blow smoke, but you really did a great job this week," he wrote. "When you stood down Bernanke, Paulson, and Geithner, that may have been the most valuable ten minutes of your career. Frankly it was a thrill for me to see it. You were right . . . this whole thing made no sense. . . . And you stuck to your guns. Thanks."

This meant a lot to me. James had been a strikingly calm, stalwart presence. When other people were agonizing that we were running out of cash, James was focused on how we could raise more money. It was a real-life example of the principle—never be part of the problem, always be part of the solution.

When James and I later talked over what had happened that night, he was insightful. "You had an instinctual reaction that it was too early to capitulate. I don't think you actually knew how you would get out of the box. You just knew it was too early to declare defeat."

Today, on the wall in my home office in Manhattan, I have a framed copy of James's email with a note he handwrote at the bottom: "John, I learnt more in these 10 minutes than in any 12 month period of my career. It is a story I will never stop telling. Thank you. James."

CHAPTER TWENTY-FOUR

We took a deep breath. Then we were right back at it.

Despite our new access to the Fed window as a bank holding company and the letter of intent from Mitsubishi, market confidence in Morgan Stanley did not rise. Our stock price stayed flat on Monday, September 22, closing at $27.09, before falling to $24.79 on Wednesday, September 24.

That's the day I departed for Asia. I knew Morgan Stanley's survival depended on my convincing Mitsubishi to go forward with the deal. Although they had signed a term agreement and were now examining our books line by line, there was no guarantee they would deliver. But Tokyo was not my first stop. That was Beijing. I had to go there to meet with Gao and his boss, Lou Jiwei, chairman of the CIC board.

I dreaded it.

Ordinarily, when I flew on the Morgan Stanley jet, I played endless rounds of gin rummy with Ria Mills. On this trip, I just shook my head no when she got out the deck of cards. I sat quietly, staring out the window at the cloud formations. Until we were in the air, it didn't hit me how wrung-out I was. During the past nine days it had felt as if we had been clinging to a sheer rock face by our fingernails, and I had had to make decision after decision to keep us from falling. Even now, some of my team urged me to stay at my desk in New York. "You've got to be kidding! It's still touch-and-go!" they warned me. "We can't have you out of pocket."

Wei disagreed. She insisted I come to Beijing. "Your old friends in China are very upset with you, John," she told me. "You need to do damage control in person. You cannot wait." I was aware that Morgan Stanley was one of CIC's first investments and that the stock had gone to shit. Their lowball offer of $5 billion for an additional 39 percent of Morgan Stanley was an attempt to adjust the original $5.6 billion they had invested in December 2007. There was a big public outcry in China that they had wildly overpaid for an investment that wasn't in the country's self-interest.

In pursuing the second, unsuccessful, deal with Morgan Stanley, Lou had put his personal reputation at stake. When he and Gao found out that we had been simultaneously negotiating with the Japanese, they felt betrayed. Because of this shame for the Chinese, both Lou and Gao were under extreme pressure. "Their careers are at stake," Wei said. There could also be crippling ramifications for Morgan Stanley. To punish us, China might blacklist the firm from doing business there, something that had happened to other investment banks when deals went sour. CIC remained a major investor in Morgan Stanley. Even though the second deal didn't come off, they still owned 10 percent of the firm. I had to do everything I could to make amends.

In the meeting with Gao and Lou, I was calm and direct. I explained step-by-step how the deal came together with Mitsubishi. Lou was emotional. I listened attentively; I didn't get defensive. I just sat there and took it. When the meeting ended, I didn't know if I had succeeded in repairing the rupture. Then I headed to the airport, feeling pretty beat down.

While I was away, another gigantic US financial institution crumbled. On September 25, the US Office of Thrift Supervision seized control of Washington Mutual, the nation's largest savings-and-loan association, which had opened its doors in 1889, the same year Benjamin Harrison was sworn in as the twenty-third US president. With more than forty-three thousand employees and 2,200-plus branch offices in fifteen states, WaMu was the biggest bank failure in American history. The news sent investors' anxiety soaring, which was reflected in the stock market's gyrations.

Given this carnage on Wall Street, I was surprised at how pleasantly my meeting in Tokyo began. I had gotten a good night's sleep and a workout in the hotel gym before the meeting. I felt pretty calm, considering the gravity of this situation. Nobuyuki Hirano, a Mitsubishi managing director, was spearheading the deal. He and his team hosted me and my team on the ground at an elaborate lunch in the corporate headquarters. I allowed myself to hope, *Maybe the deal will actually go through.*

Then Hirano asked to speak to me alone. *Here it comes*, I thought. *They're pulling out.*

"Mr. Mack, since we first began talking, your stock has traded in a wide range," he said. "We need to make some adjustments." He explained Mitsubishi's new terms.

"I don't want to make a decision on the fly, Hirano San," I said. "Let me get back to New York. We want to do something with you, and I need time to consider the changes." I was making an effort not to sound desperate. But that's how I felt.

Back in New York, I walked my senior team through the revised offer. "John, if we agree to the price that they want but we change the maturity date and tweak the deal here," Paul said, "it would be better for us and not quite as favorable to them. They wouldn't get all they want, but they might agree to it."

I phoned Mitsubishi. "I'll do the deal you want, Hirano San," I said, "but would you consider these small changes?"

"Mr. Mack, out of respect for you," he said when he called me back the next morning, "we would like you to choose either the deal that we proposed or the revised deal that you suggested."

I was so moved by Mitsubishi's graciousness. When I told our management committee about Hirano's offer, I said, "I don't think we would have behaved as generously. We would have taken the last penny off the table. What does that say about us?"

We went with the better terms for Morgan Stanley. On Monday, September 29, the two companies announced our definitive agreement, subject to regulatory approval. Mitsubishi would invest $9 billion for a 21 percent stake in Morgan Stanley. They agreed to pay $29 a share on average, a premium over the previous Friday's share price of $24.75. But sinkholes continued to open up all over the global economic landscape. Our announcement occurred on the same day the Dow lost a record-breaking 777 points. This historic stock market crash was triggered by Congress's rejection of Hank Paulson's $700 billion bailout plan. That day, Morgan Stanley's share price dipped to $20.99. No one believed that Mitsubishi would come through for us.

Although on Friday, October 3, Congress reversed course and passed the bailout, the next week was Armageddon for Morgan Stanley's stock. None of us could process the new lows we were hitting. On Tuesday, October 7, the share price fell to $14.13. We braced for worse, because at the stroke of midnight on Wednesday, October 8, the short-selling ban expired. That same day, our cash balances hit the lowest point *ever*. All this occurred as we sat by helplessly, waiting for the regulators to sign off on the Mitsubishi–Morgan Stanley deal. Nothing could budge without their approval.

Continuing their honorable behavior, Mitsubishi released a statement that day contradicting the ceaseless speculation that the deal was dead on arrival. "We have been made aware of rumors to the effect that MUFG is seeking not to close on our proposed investment in, and strategic alliance with, Morgan Stanley. Our normal policy is not to comment on rumors," the statement said. "Nevertheless, we wish to state that there is no basis for any such rumors." I was so grateful. Nonetheless, the world believed that Mitsubishi would pull out, and we would go bankrupt.

"It is clearly a panic, and it's a panic around the world," I told my dazed employees at Morgan Stanley's Canary Wharf offices. I had flown to London to rally them and to meet with bankers from Mitsubishi. During trading that day—Friday, October 10—just at the time the Mitsubishi team was performing the final due diligence on the firm, our stock price hit a low of $6.71. At the final bell, it remained in the single digits, at $9.68.

While I was in London, Walid was trying to hold things together in New York. On Friday, demonstrating true leadership, he started on the fortieth floor and gave the same speech to employees on every single floor. "We are not going to let the firm go down," he told them as he stood on desk after desk. "Morgan Stanley has been around for seventy-three years. We'll be around for another seventy-three years. This firm will open for business on Monday, and nobody is going to carry their things out in a box."

I was calling Walid every fifteen minutes. "Have you heard from Mitsubishi?" I asked. "Do you think they'll want to renegotiate? Are they pulling out?"

"I've heard nothing," he said. "John, it's a morgue here. You walk onto the trading floors, you could drop a pin and you would hear it. Not a single phone ringing. I told everyone I would see them all here on Monday morning at their desks.

"Are we going to open on Monday, John?"

I wasn't sure.

I WAS FLYING directly from London to Washington, DC. The World Bank was holding an emergency meeting on Saturday, October 11, for foreign leaders to discuss the financial crisis, and Hank Paulson wanted me there. Walid had planned to join me in Washington. "Why don't you stay in New York tonight," I told him. "In case something happens."

On Saturday afternoon, Walid, having heard nothing from Mitsubishi, was standing in line to board the DC shuttle out of LaGuardia Airport when his cell phone rang. It was a banker working with Mitsubishi. "We need to talk to you, Mr. Chammah," he said.

"I'm getting on the jet with every banker in the world, heading to Washington," Walid told him. "Hold on, I can't talk. Let me step out of the Jetway."

"The $9 billion is still here," the banker said, "but can we give it to you as a loan instead of equity?"

"No," Walid responded. "A loan doesn't help us. We need equity, but we can certainly make modifications."

Walid raced back to the office, where Paul Taubman and Ji-Yeun Lee were already working. Robert Kindler, a superb lawyer turned Morgan Stanley banker, flew back from Cape Cod to join them. By Sunday they had made the necessary changes to the agreement to keep Mitsubishi with us.

The regulators had finally signed off. We could close the deal on Monday, October 13. But there was a problem. October 13 was a bank holiday—both in Japan, where it was Health and Sports Day, and in the United States, where it was Columbus Day (now Indigenous Peoples' Day). This meant that Mitsubishi could not wire us the $9 billion. The New York Stock Exchange, on the other hand, *was* open. We could not risk having another day like Friday. We couldn't survive our stock price being battered, possibly all the way down to zero. We had to get that money in hand before the markets opened.

The investment team came up with an unorthodox solution. Would Mitsubishi write Morgan Stanley a check for $9 billion?

"It doesn't even have to be a certified check," Kindler said.

To our astonishment, the Japanese agreed. Around 6:30 a.m., Rob walked to the law firm Wachtell, Lipton. Still wearing his khakis and sandals from Cape Cod, he had worked around the clock, not even leaving the office to grab a change of clothes. He expected to pick up the check from a courier sent by Mitsubishi. Instead he was greeted by an entourage of Japanese bankers in suits and a camera crew. Flustered, Rob assured them that he was indeed a vice chairman of Morgan Stanley. "John Mack would have been here if he possibly could have," he told them.

At 7:53 a.m. in Washington, my BlackBerry pinged. It was an email from Rob. The subject line: "We Have the Check!!!!!!" And the body of the email: "It's Closed!!!!!!!!"

That email made me happier than any email in my whole life. Now I could exhale. This was a Hail Mary pass that landed in the receiver's hands in the end zone in the last seconds of the Super Bowl.

Good thing I didn't know what they were doing back at Morgan Stanley headquarters. Gary Lynch later confessed that the punch-drunk bankers and lawyers ran around the office laughing and yelling like little kids after too much sugar: "Where did the check go? What happened to the check? Did I give you the check? No, I gave *you* the check!" Even these hardened Wall Streeters who routinely dealt with billions couldn't believe that they were holding a $9,000,000,000.00 check. The market also signaled its relief. Morgan Stanley shares nearly doubled on Monday, closing at $18.10.

On Wednesday, I held an open forum about our deal with Mitsubishi. A Morgan Stanley manager asked me to describe my "personal experience" over the past five weeks.

"In the heat of battle," I told her, "I was absolutely, totally engaged and focused. We've experienced something that I hope we never have to experience again. . . . Don't lose the moment. Let's continue it. Stay focused. Don't compromise. Be an owner. I want to be in battle mode until the day I die. You should stay in battle mode, too."

As awful as the past five weeks had been, they had also been exhilarating. I felt fully alive. Crazy, I know. But I loved the stress. I loved being in charge. I loved the action. But my intensity would not have gotten us through the ordeal if we hadn't had a willing partner on the other side. Mitsubishi demonstrated exceptional good faith repeatedly during our negotiations. The relationship between the two banks dates back to the 1970s, when David Phillips signed Mitsubishi up as a client. During that period, we started the training program to bring promising young employees from Japanese banks to Morgan Stanley's headquarters for a year.

Who knew then that fortune was smiling on us? One of those trainees—from September 1983 to August 1984—was Nobuyuki Hirano. He was so committed to getting the deal done, he slept with his cell phone by his ear on a tatami mat in the Mitsubishi offices in Tokyo during that frenzied weekend leading up to the term agreement. Our culture, with its emphasis on integrity and loyalty to clients, had left a lasting impression on Hirano and his colleagues. When Mitsubishi president Katsunori Nagayasu visited our trading floor, everyone at Morgan Stanley gave him a standing ovation. In his speech, he said, "Trust. Trust is the key to our alliance."

To that, I would only add, we got lucky with Mitsubishi. Very, very lucky.

CHAPTER TWENTY-FIVE

J ust before 8:00 a.m., Rob Kindler had gotten the check from Mitsubishi. At 3:00 p.m., Hank Paulson was demanding my presence at the US Treasury Building in Washington, DC. Hank promised good news.

This meeting was kind of a reprise of the Lehman weekend a month earlier. Paulson, Bernanke, and Geithner were there, along with two new faces: Sheila Bair, the head of the Federal Deposit Insurance Corporation (FDIC), and John Dugan, the comptroller of the currency. Seated in alphabetical order according to the name of our institution were my fellow CEOs Vikram Pandit, Lloyd Blankfein, John Thain, and Jamie Dimon. Joining us were Thain's new boss, Ken Lewis, from Bank of America, plus the top executives from Bank of New York Mellon, State Street Corporation, and Wells Fargo.

To rescue the American economy, Hank told us, it was critical to stabilize the US financial system and restore the flow of credit. As part of TARP, our banks would receive a massive injection of capital, whether we wanted it or not. Every bank present was expected to accept the money because the Federal Reserve didn't want it to look like some banks were more troubled than others—even though it was obvious that BofA, Citi, and Morgan Stanley were struggling far more than, say, JPMorgan.

Each CEO was given a piece of paper that outlined the individual bank's terms. The amount we were being given depended not on our bank's health but its size: $25 billion for Citigroup, Wells Fargo, and JPMorgan; $15 billion for Bank of America; $3 billion for Bank of New York Mellon; and $2 billion for State Street Corporation. Merrill Lynch, Goldman Sachs, and Morgan Stanley were each getting $10 billion. In exchange, we were all to give preferred stock shares to the Treasury.

Some recipients who didn't need the TARP money, like Jamie Dimon, were statesmanlike, saying, in effect, It's right for the system, so I'll go along with it. On the other hand, Dick Kovacevich, the chairman of Wells Fargo, was furious. Flying in from the bank's San Francisco headquarters, he resented being lumped in with "the New York gang," as he called us, who couldn't run our balance sheets. "I'm not one of you New York guys who makes all these loans," he grumbled. "My bank is in good shape. I don't know why I'm here."

"You're here because your regulator wanted you here," Paulson said. "Now just listen."

For me, taking the money was a nondecision. I knew that if I didn't and something blew up, I'd be out of business. I reached across the conference table, picked up the term sheet, signed it, and slid it back over. "Aren't you going to go back to your board and ask for permission?" Thain asked, staring at me in disbelief.

I looked at him. *Are you kidding me?*

"I've got my board on twenty-four-hour call," I said. "Of course my board will approve it. And if they don't, maybe I'll get lucky and they'll fire me."

WITH THE MONEY, we stepped back from the brink. But even the TARP infusion, becoming a bank holding company, and the Mitsubishi check could not erase how harrowing the last five weeks had been. Boom and bust—that is the rhythm of Wall Street. But this was different. It was an existential threat to the financial system and the global economy—something that had not happened since the Great Depression of the 1930s.

During the 2008 crisis, each multibillion-dollar withdrawal from Morgan Stanley, each afternoon attack by short sellers, each new low that our share price hit felt like life or death. I had to pause and remind myself that while that's how these things *felt* in the moment, whatever happened was not *actually* going to kill me. Yes, if Morgan Stanley had gone under, my reputation would have been destroyed. I might have faced a host of lawsuits from angry shareholders. Certainly, tens of thousands of people would have lost their jobs. And I would never again work on Wall Street. But career death is not the same as real death. I would not lose the things that really mattered: my marriage to Christy, having kids who were happy and healthy, spending time with our friends.

I did get punished, though. My sense that we knew what we were doing took a body blow. I was humbled. Because I had made mistakes, I again refused a bonus. I went three years in a row without a bonus. Walid and James went without bonuses in 2008 as well. We also cut bonuses for those on the operating committee by 75 percent and installed a clawback provision that allowed us to penalize excessive risk-taking. We tied some compensation to multiyear performance.

I knew back in 2007 that there was too much risk, too much leverage, and, let's be honest, too much greed in the market. That summer I called up Tim Geithner to talk about it. "It's out of control," I told him. "I can say no to one leveraged buyout, and I can say no to two. The second one will be a little harder, because a story about it will appear in the *Wall Street Journal* that we're not competitive. My employees will read it, and they won't like it. Clients will also see it. Some will say, 'John Mack is really smart'; more will say, 'Mack is really dumb to pass it up.' You need to step in and stop the craziness. You've got to calm us down."

"You won't like this answer, John," Geithner replied. "But you're the second CEO who has called me with the same issue."

I am not blaming the regulators. I want to be clear on that. I take responsibility. I was too aggressive. I took on too much leverage. When I was called to testify before the House Financial Services Committee in Washington, DC, on February 11, 2009, I knew what I needed to do. The next day's *New York Post* ran the front-page headline "Bankers on the Hot Seat." The tabloid graded each bank CEO who testified. Jamie Dimon got a B. John Stumpf of Wells Fargo got a C. Vikram Pandit and Lloyd Blankfein both got Ds. I got the only A. Do you know why? Because I apologized. Leaning into the microphone, I told the assembled congresspeople, "We are sorry for it." The *Post* got the "hot seat" part right. People across the country were enraged and wanted answers. My fellow CEOs and I were summoned to Capitol Hill multiple times over the next eighteen months. When I look at news photos from that period, I can see just how tense I was. The atmosphere on Capitol Hill was no more relaxed in January 2010, when I testified before Congress's Financial Crisis Inquiry Commission. Seated next to Jamie Dimon, I said, "We did eat our own cooking, and we choked on it."

In some ways, what saved Morgan Stanley was our first-ever quarterly loss in December 2007. God, I hated announcing those numbers. But that humiliation made me slow down. We got the capital from CIC, we sold assets, we stockpiled cash, and we pulled in our horns.

The hero of the day was Hank Paulson. Number one, as an ex–Wall Street CEO, he understood the business. Number two, he had President Bush's ear. Paulson, Bernanke, and Geithner flooded the market with liquidity and supported the banks. These were courageous moves. They saved the banking system and created a safety net so that the market didn't totally crash and bring down the world economy. They performed a real service to the country.

Things did not settle down immediately after we took the TARP funding. In the last quarter of 2008, we posted a $2.36 billion loss. Our stock bounced around in the low to mid-teens for the rest of the year. "Every time we're seeing the shoreline, we keep getting blown back out," Colm told the *New York Times*. "This is not about us or our positions. It's about the environment." By the spring of 2009, though, the wind had calmed down a bit, and our share price rose. Morgan Stanley was able to pay back our TARP $10 billion with an annualized 20 percent return to taxpayers that June.

By contrast, Citigroup required an additional $20 billion from the government. Citi's ongoing need for capital gave us an opening to pounce on an opportune deal. In 2006, when James Gorman joined the firm, he told me he could fix our Retail operation "to a certain level." But he made it clear that after that, for Morgan Stanley to become a real player, we had to scale up. I said to James, "You tell me to buy a retail brokerage, and we will." In January we negotiated to merge our wealth management group with the Citigroup Smith Barney wealth management business. We paid $2.7 billion to Citi to ensure we had 51 percent of the combined business. The joint venture gave us more than eighteen thousand brokers in a thousand offices and $1.7 trillion in assets. We were now the nation's dominant force in wealth management.

With this, Morgan Stanley achieved the goal that Dick Fisher and I had shared when we first pursued the merger with Dean Witter in the 1990s. Expanding our wealth management business meant an increased source of steady revenue. This would help us through the future hard times that 2008 had taught us were inevitable. Buying Smith Barney confirmed the wisdom of the merger with Dean Witter, even though it brought me personal heartbreak. The culture clash obscured just how forward-thinking and creative the deal was. I'm telling you: Morgan Stanley wouldn't have survived 2008 if Phil and I hadn't done that merger in 1997.

Christy pointed out how my career had come full circle. I had moved to New York in 1968 to work at Smith Barney. My dream was to open a retail office somewhere in the South. Now Smith Barney was part of the Morgan Stanley family.

ON NOVEMBER 17, 2008, I turned sixty-four. As I blew out the candles on my birthday cake, I knew it was time for me to start thinking about stepping down. I told myself, *You've had a great career. You got through the crisis. You're a hero to Morgan Stanley. You're respected on Wall Street. Why do you keep playing the cards? Because with the next screwup, you might not get out so easily.*

Choosing a successor is a lot like drawing up a last will and testament. It is an existential acknowledgment that you will not always be present. Selecting the person to replace you is one of the most monumental decisions a leader can make. If you choose poorly, your legacy will be tarnished and your company damaged. Before his death in 2020, General Electric legend Jack Welch told financial writer and former investment banker William Cohan, "[When] you pick a CEO, you're picking the fate of the company."

I knew that either of my two co-presidents would make an outstanding CEO and steward of Morgan Stanley. Each had his specific strengths, but both were extraordinarily talented executives and worthy of the crown. One was Walid Chammah. He was the quintessential international investment banker, always impeccably dressed and holding a cigar. He lived on planes and was at home in any capital in the world. Walid had deep roots on Morgan Stanley's institutional side. I had sent him to London to oversee our European and Middle Eastern operations as chairman and chief executive of Morgan Stanley's non-US business.

Walid had been a loyal lieutenant. He sometimes disagreed with me, but the second I made a decision, he walked out of my office and supported me 100 percent. I could see that he had also grown in the co-president job. During the financial crisis, Walid had an unerring sense of what would be in the firm's best interests when he dealt with potential partners. On October 10, he filled my shoes when I was in London and our stock price plunged to $6.71. I saw how well Walid performed under pressure. But he was reluctant to take the CEO job. Walid and his Austrian-born wife, Karin, loved their life in England.

My other choice was James Gorman. With less than three years at the firm, James was obviously far from being a Morgan Stanley lifer. He had never worked on a trading floor. He had never underwritten a deal. He had never done an IPO. And yes, I saw the irony in James's background as a McKinsey consultant, like Phil Purcell. Also like Phil, James came out of Retail, he was very analytical, and he was not a natural hall-walker.

But I had gotten to know James well. We had a standing breakfast meeting every week at Morgan Stanley's Retail offices in Purchase. Early on, when he came into our Manhattan headquarters, I could see James straining to get on top of what traders and investment bankers were doing. "Relax," I told him. "You don't need to push too hard. You're doing a great job." That was the only time I had to say that. He quickly fit into what could be an insular and unfriendly culture. He had done a fantastic job integrating Dean Witter and growing the Retail business. During the crucible of the financial crisis, James was the only one of us who thought Mitsubishi would come through. A few months later, he spearheaded the acquisition of Smith Barney from Citigroup and served as chairman of the joint venture. I saw that he had a clear grasp on what the firm needed to do organizationally. And he was white-hot smart. James was a known quantity. But precisely because he did not have relationships going back decades, he had a freer hand to take the firm in whatever direction he thought was necessary.

In September 2009, just after Labor Day, I invited James for dinner at a Lebanese restaurant, Ilili, near the Flatiron Building. "James, I'm recommending to the board that they name you Morgan Stanley's next CEO," I said. I had already told Walid I was recommending him as chairman of Morgan Stanley International. When the board met a few days later, they unanimously supported my choices.

At 8:00 a.m. on Friday, September 11, James, Walid, and I presided over an open forum meeting. I announced that as of January 1, 2010, James would become Morgan Stanley's CEO. "As chairman, I won't be going to a lot of management meetings. I'll be spending a lot of time with clients," I said. The three of us sat together on the dais in the sixth-floor auditorium. I remembered being in the same room four years earlier when Miles Marsh had announced that I was the new chairman and CEO of Morgan Stanley. Christy had been in the front row that day. Now, as I looked out, there she was, my partner in life. Walid talked about my leadership during the financial crisis. The sustained applause got me really choked up.

James used his remarks to reassure the Investment Banking side. "We are not about to become a wealth management firm," he said. "The heart, the DNA, the fabric of this place has always been the institutional securities business and, frankly, should always be the institutional securities business."

Then his speech became more personal. James said that he and his wife, Penny, were touched that Christy had sent them each a hand-written note of congratulations. He also told a story about the period after he had accepted the job at Morgan Stanley but before he started working. "My mother was in the hospital in the UK. . . . She had heart issues. She was about eighty. There was some suggestion that she was going to die there. John heard about this.

"He called me up at home and said, 'I heard about your mother. Why don't we send the plane over, pick her up, bring her to New York–Presbyterian, and let her see the top heart doctor who operated on Bill Clinton?'

"Who does that? . . . Who thinks in such grand terms to fly the plane to pick up the eighty-year-old mother of someone who hasn't even started working here? John thought if the doctor was good enough for Clinton, he must be good enough for Mrs. Gorman from Melbourne. It's rare."

I had forgotten the whole incident, but it meant a lot that James remembered it. It told me that he valued the culture we had built at Morgan Stanley—a culture where we looked out for each other—and that set us apart.

I knew that I was leaving the firm in good hands.

ONE MORE LESSON

s I finished this book, I received news that threw a major curve into my life, and I feel it right to share it with you. A doctor informed Christy and me that I have mild cognitive impairment (MCI), which is most likely the first leg on the Alzheimer's disease track. My family and friends had expressed concerns about my memory over the past few years. They started saying, "John, you just told me that same story five minutes ago." I hoped my memory issues could be a result of old football injuries, including several concussions I sustained in college, or by a more recent accident when an ATV I was riding on at our farm in North Carolina tipped over, landing me in a ditch. When those causes were ruled out, I began a program of intensive mental exercises. But when that protocol didn't help, I went through a series of tests with a cognitive therapist.

The MCI diagnosis was definitely not something I ever envisioned. When the doctor shared the test results, Christy and I responded the same way. Neither of us reacted emotionally; we stayed quite calm. We were actually relieved to have a diagnosis, to understand what had been going on and why. "Thank God we now know what we're deal-ing with," we both said.

I might be like this for many years without further progression. We just don't know. For now, there is no cure, but I have great doctors and I'm following their advice. We're being pragmatic. We're living day to day. Whatever happens, Christy and I, along with our kids, will take this on together.

I've started telling my friends and the board members I serve with about this issue. I'm much more comfortable having the news out in the open. I've always faced things head-on, and I have always dealt with them, relying on my judgment, my instincts, and my pragma-tism. And that's the way I'm facing MCI. Telling people puts *me* in control. It means I'm not giving up that power to other people's inter-pretation. I don't leave people guessing. That's not how I ever operated in business or in my relationships. This new diagnosis is part of my life. I talk about it. My approach to dealing with this and to being open about it is exactly who I am: direct, honest, forceful.

As with anything, not dealing with my condition *is* dealing with it. In other words, I could try to keep it a secret. But at the end of the day, I'm revealing that there's a problem every time I repeat myself. Let's get it out in the open so that people aren't whispering, "Did you notice how John keeps repeating things? What's going on?" Just tell them.

I don't know what the next years will bring, but for now, I'm keep-ing up with the markets, advising entrepreneurs and helping people, playing golf on occasion, enjoying my life with Christy, going out to dinner with friends, pulling pranks (I've still got my sense of humor!), and spending quality time with my kids and granddaughter.

My prognosis is far from perfect, but my life is perfect. If I were to go back to when I arrived in New York City, I wouldn't change any-thing. I have fucking killed it. I knocked the cover off the ball in the financial world. I ran a great company. I stood up to the government, telling them that I wouldn't sell Morgan Stanley. I played every card.

I couldn't write a life story better than my life story. At the center of it all is the incredible woman who walked into my life in 1972 and has been my rock ever since. I hit the jackpot with Christy.

My family and I know there may be hard times ahead. But my fifty years of marriage, my kids, my granddaughter, and my friends are all I could ever really ask for, want, or need.

That is the lesson of my life.